Woutei

C000260580

# STOCKHOLDING, PRICE STABILIZATION AND FUTURES TRADING

## Some Empirical Investigations of the Indian Natural Rubber Market

International Books, 1998

©Wouter Zant

ISBN 90 5727 023 4

Keywords: commodity markets, price risk, risk aversion, risk reduction, stockholding, futures trading, price stabilization

Cover design: Marjo Starink
Cover photograph: Wouter Zant
Printed by Drukkerij Haasbeek

Published by International Books,
Alexander Numankade 17, 3572 KP Utrecht, The Netherlands,
tel. +31302731840, fax +31302733614, email i-books@antenna.nl

# PREFACE

This thesis is a by-product of a joint project with the Rubber Board of India, financed by the Indo-Dutch Programme on Alternatives in Development (IDPAD). I keep very good memories to the implementation of this project and specifically to the cooperation with Hidde Smit, with whom I travelled many times to Kerala, India. Hidde introduced me to the field of commodity modelling, and of natural rubber in particular. From the Indian side, the help of many people at the Rubber Board of India is gratefully acknowledged, in particular I would like to mention R.G.Unny and Mrs. Lalithakumari.

I am indebted to my supervisors Jan Willem Gunning and Kees Burger. They did endless reading of preliminary versions of the chapters, never hesitating to be critical, which substantially improved the quality of the manuscript. Both supervisors motivated me to write Chapter 7 and influenced its direction.

A list of people either provided insights into the specific field of my thesis or gave comments on preliminary version of chapters of this manusscript. Without the intention to be exhaustive I would like to thank: Panos Varangis (World Bank); Lamon Rutten (UNCTAD), Ben Vogelvang (FEW/FUA), Chris Elbers (FEW/FUA), Henk Kox (FEW/FUA), Peter Boswijk (FEW, UvA), Caroline Jongkamp (Center of Environmental Science, University of Leiden), Hinrik Vrieze (L.Wurfbain&Co, BV.), Sree Kumar (Spices Board, Cochin), Menno Pradhan (ESI/VU), Remco Oostendorp (ESI/VU), Jan Ter Wengel (ESI/VU)

Parts of this Chapter 2 are based on K. Burger, V. Haridasan, H.P. Smit, R.G. Unny and W. Zant (1995), *The Indian Rubber Economy: History, Analysis and Policy Perspectives*, Manohar Publishers and Distributors, New Delhi. Chapter 5 is an adjusted version of W. Zant, 1997, 'Stabilizing Prices in Commodity Markets: Price Bounds versus Private Stockholding', *Journal of Policy Modeling*, 19, 3, pp. 253-77. Chapter 7 is an adjusted version of an article that is currently under revision for publication by a professional journal. Permission to use the material in this thesis is gratefully acknowledged. Earlier versions of Chapter 3, 4 and 5 have appeared as discussion paper of the Tinbergen Institute. Some of these papers have been submitted in article form to professional journals. Despite the mixed success of these submissions, my thinking on these subjects benefitted much from the referee reports that I have received. Therefore I would like to thank the anonymous referees of these journals. If you ever make yourselves known I will send you a copy of this thesis!.

Due to an inintended coincidence the Economic and Social Institute guaranteed me oceans of time with relative certainty on the duration of my appointment, to complete my thesis (and to raise my children). Although this appeared, in a later stage, and for both employer as well as employee, to be a mixed blessing, I thank the personnel department of the Free University (great move to change the CAO in 1995!), the managers of the Economic and Social Institute and the IDPAD secretariat, for this privilege.

Finally I would like to thank my partner Ellen for giving me support during the genesis of this thesis. My son Kasper and my daughter Eva, who also were born during this period, guaranteed sufficient distraction, without being aware of it, in often painstaking labour. The three of them, together with some friends, made me clear what life really is about ( ... and how much time it takes!)

# CONTENTS

# 1    PRICE RISKS OF FARMERS AND STOCKHOLDERS

## 1.1    Introduction

Primary commodities are important to developing countries: a large share of income of many developing countries and also, in many cases, a large share of income of individual farmers is earned with primary commodity production. Fluctuations in income earned with primary commodity production are due to fluctuations in costs, but even more so to fluctuations in production and price. Fluctuations in production originate mainly from weather conditions, diseases and other natural causes. To the extent that such fluctuations lead to compensating changes in prices they may have little effect on income. However, price fluctuations originating elsewhere will have a large impact on income. Production of most primary commodities requires the commitment of resources for a considerable period of time. This is particularly apparent in the case of perennial crops, crops that need a number of years to mature and then generate output for several decades. Once resources are committed to the production of such a crop, fluctuations in price directly affect income from these crops. This should not necessarily be a problem if price fluctuations can be evened out over time, by saving and dissaving or loans, or if welfare of producers is not affected by potential fluctuations of income. Saving, however, requires properly functioning capital markets: banks should be prepared to provide loans to farmers in the case of bad harvests, with future income as security. Such credit facilities are, in general, not available and especially not in developing countries. Absence of credit markets makes income risk a serious issue. This is even more relevant, and this refers to the second point, as most primary commodity producers are farmers cultivating only a very small plot of land and have few financial opportunities. Primary commodity producers are, therefore, often averse to fluctuations in income. Risk aversion implies that potential fluctuations in income adversely affect their welfare.

There are a number of economic responses intended to reduce income risk due to price fluctuations. In the review of the theory, presented in the following sections of this chapter, we discuss the major risk reduction options. A few of these options deserve attention at this stage. An important form of risk spreading is private stockholding: by transferring commodities from periods with low prices to periods with high prices, price fluctuations can be evened out by private stockholding. Stockholding in a primary commodity market could also be performed by a specific group of agents in the market. In this thesis we specifically consider a market that consists of producers, stockholders and consumers. Under specific assumptions (stable consumption demand and inelastic production) these stockholders play a crucial role in price formation. Whether arbitrage activities of private stockholders in the end increase income of primary commodity producers is unclear. However, price fluctuations are reduced by stockholders by the transfer of commodities from low price periods to high price periods, hence, mitigating income risk for primary commodity producers.

Another option to deal with income risk is to hedge income risks on futures markets. A hedging operation entails the combination of a physical transaction with a transaction on the futures market that is exactly the reverse of the physical transaction. When the transactions are settled, the loss in the physical market is offset by the profit in the futures market, or vice versa. In this case the risk is transferred from the hedger to the speculator. Futures trading is also believed to promote stockholding, and by that mechanism, to stabilize prices. Hence, in a market with primary commodity producers and stockholders that hedge their risk on a futures exchange, the income risk of primary commodity producers is affected in two ways: directly through the hedging operation and indirectly by reduced price fluctuations due to increased stockholding.

A buffer stock price stabilization scheme constitutes a popular policy response to reduce income risk due to price fluctuations. A price stabilization scheme is a policy where the price of a specific commodity is restricted to fluctuate within a band. If the price decreases below the floor price a buffer stock manager buys the commodity on the market until the market forces push the price above the floor price. If the price increases to the ceiling price, the buffer stock manager sells the commodity from stocks until the market forces move the price below the ceiling price. Newbery and Stiglitz (1981) have argued forcefully that price stabilization based on such schemes are a rather inefficient instrument to deal with income risk of farmers. Also in practice these price band schemes have typically shown a poor record (see Gilbert (1996)).

In the case of the Indian natural rubber market, the domestic market has been unaffected by world market prices for a long time. This offers a good opportunity to study the impact of stockholding on price formation. The operations of a buffer stock mechanism from 1984 to 1989 provide the case to study once more the effectiveness of such a mechanism, and the extent to which stockholding behavior is affected. A futures market for natural rubber did not exist in India. The implications of such a risk reducing facility are studied in the hypothetical case of introducing futures for the period after opening of the domestic market to world market influences.

The risk reduction options studied in this thesis, represent an important, however limited, set of all options open to farmers: alternative risk reduction options - possibly of considerable importance - are not analyzed in detail. For example, we consider in the empirical work a single primary commodity market and implicitly assume that farmers and stockholders are mainly engaged in cultivating and stockholding of a single primary commodity, and derive their entire income from this commodity. Such an approach ignores diversification of income earning activities, another way of dealing with income risk.

Also the choice of a perennial crop requires some additional comments. Supply response to fluctuating prices differs by type of crop, annual or perennial. In the case of perennial crops most investment outlays are made long before harvesting is possible. The remaining decision of perennial crop growers during the year is the input of labor for harvesting and some for maintenance (e.g. fertilizing, weeding, irrigation). In the case of an annual crop the decision to cultivate is to a much larger extent subject to short run expectations. Consequently, and in most cases, such crops have a larger flexibility and will be less vulnerable to price risk. The empirical work in this thesis is based on a perennial crop, implying a limited response to (expected) price fluctuations in the short run as far as new planting or replanting is concerned. Additionally, income risk considered in this thesis is limited to income risk due to price fluctuations: risk due to production uncertainty is assumed to be negligible. Such a characterization fits reasonably well to natural rubber - the perennial crop in the empirical work - although some production uncertainty remains. Obviously, we consider a storable commodity as this allows arbitrage activities. In short, in this thesis we study reduction of income risk due to price fluctuations by perennial crop growers and stockholders of a storable primary commodity.

We make use of monthly time series data of the Indian natural rubber market for the period from 1965 to 1995. Data are available for production, consumption and stocks, import, export and prices. The data on stockholding distinguish between stockholding on the supply side (stockholding by growers and dealers) and stockholding on the manufacturing side (stockholding by manufacturers). The sample period covers a number of regime switches. In some cases these regime switches offer a nice opportunity to test behavioral reactions, as in the case of a domestic price band scheme. In other cases (e.g. foreign trade regime) we need to take account of these regime switches in a proper way. Details on these regime switches are given in the following chapters.

In the remainder of this chapter and before embarking on the empirical work, the theoretical discussion of a number of questions that play a central role in dealing with risk in commodity markets, are reviewed, namely: what is the impact of price stabilization using a buffer stock on welfare; what is the impact of the introduction of futures trade on welfare; and what drives the behavior of stockholders. The analysis of welfare implications of price stabilization by use of a buffer stock has a long history in the literature, part of which will be reviewed in Section 1.2 of this chapter. Attention is given to the interaction of private sector stockholding and price stabilization using a buffer stock. A way to deal with price risks is to hedge these price risks on futures exchanges. The attractiveness of such a strategy is elaborated in a series of theoretical contributions that are reviewed in Section 1.3. In the assessment of the welfare implications of futures trading, the benefits of futures trading relative to price stabilization schemes using buffer stocks are obviously of particular interest. These cases are considered independently as well as in combination. Finally, the literature on the behavior of stockholders and how this behavior affects commodity markets is reviewed in Section 1.4 of this chapter. Two aspects of stockholding feature prominently in this literature, namely positive stocks combined with negative returns and non-negativity of stocks. The property of non-negativity of stocks causes an asymmetry in behavior and is shown to have a pervasive impact on price formation in commodity markets. Finally, in Section 1.5 we give an outline of this thesis. In that section we set out how the theoretical work relates to the problem at hand and summarize the major contributions of this thesis.

## 1.2   Price stabilization

In this section we review the theoretical literature on the desirability of stable prices in commodity markets achieved with buffer stocks[1]. The main issue is whether stabilization of prices, achieved by means of a buffer stock, yields a higher welfare compared to a situation with fluctuating prices. Reading through the literature, and anticipating on the conclusion of this section, it appears that the answer to this question is not particularly favorable to price stabilization. The feasibility of achieving price stabilization by use of a buffer stock turns out to be

---

1       There are a number of instructive survey and review articles available on this subject (e.g. Turnovsky (1979), Schmitz (1984), Kanbur (1984), Herrmann et al. (1993), C Chapter 2).

questionable as well, at least theoretically. We discuss suggestions made in the literature of alternative ways to assist primary producers in their attempts to deal with uncertainty of prices and income. Finally, we comment briefly on the existence in practice of price stabilization schemes, given their (theoretical) undesirability and infeasibility.

Prior to the desirability of price stabilization, we consider the feasibility of achieving complete price stability with a buffer stock. Newbery and Stiglitz (1981) argue that complete price stabilization is impossible. If the buffer stock absorbs the excess supply, arising from the randomness of output, and output fluctuations are uncorrelated over time, the increments to the buffer stock will also be random, and the size of the buffer stock will follow a random walk. Non-negativity of stocks and the limited availability of finance (see Townsend (1977), Ghosh *et al.* (1987)) constitute a lower and upper reflecting barrier to the size of the buffer stock. Although the expectation of the time to hit either the upper or lower reflecting barrier is different depending on the nature of the stochastic process underlying the excess supply, such a date will come with a unit probability. Any positive contribution from theorizing on price stabilization therefore should consider partial price stabilization instead of complete price stabilization[2]. Feasibility of price stabilization schemes is further constrained by the presence of private stockholders and speculators. Attempts by the buffer stock manager to change the fluctuation of prices, diminishes the arbitrage returns from storage and consequently leads to reductions in private storage. The reduction of private storage will increase the costs of the buffer stock manager: Newbery and Stiglitz (1981) show that the buffer stock authority has to store more to achieve a given degree of price stabilization.

A different line of research argues that price stabilization by use of a buffer stock is altogether impossible due to the activities of speculators. Using the Hotelling model of exhaustible resources, modified for agricultural production, Salant (1983) shows that a government which attempts to stabilize prices by use of a buffer stock will inevitably be vulnerable to a speculative attack. The mechanism behind the speculative attack is rational behavior of private stockholders. A threshold size of the buffer stock combined with expected price increase will trigger private speculators to buy the entire buffer stock from the

---

2      The effects of partial price stabilization on export earning instability is studied in Nguyen (1980) and Gemmill (1985). Nguyen shows that price stability and earning stability, which by some authors are claimed to be incompatible, can be achieved for almost all commodities. Gemmill (1985) is reviewed in Section 1.4.

government. Such an attack leads to the failure of the buffer stock scheme. It should be noted that a speculative attack is directed at the upper price of a price band scheme and, hence, at the capacity of the buffer stock to stop price rises by selling stocks[3]. The behavioral explanation contrasts with the mechanical reasoning that exploits the random walk character of the buffer stock combined with upper and lower limits to the size of this buffer stock as well as with the view that speculative attacks are irrational or driven by non-economic motivations.

In general theory on the welfare implications of price stabilization, however, takes the feasibility for granted. Besides, most theoretical contributions select a specific type of price stabilization, namely complete stabilization at the mean[4], achieved without costs. The main argument against the desirability of price stability is fairly simple. With a convex profit function average profits are at least as large as profits with a price stabilized at the mean value due to Jensen's inequality (see e.g. Varian (1992, p. 43)). In many cases, however, production of commodities has a low elasticity, or can be classified as inelastic in the short run. To suppose flexible production is clearly not appropriate in certain cases. Nevertheless, it is also evident that the property of being able to adjust production easily, makes price stabilization undesirable. With risk-averse producers an additional element is introduced in favor of price stabilization: the question whether price stabilization is desirable with risk averse flexible producers cannot be answered on theoretical grounds. Risk neutral flexible producers, on the other hand, clearly make price stabilization unattractive, while the reverse is the case for inflexible risk averse producers.

The starting point of the modern academic literature on the desirability of price stabilization is the Waugh-Oi-Massell framework (Waugh (1944, 1966), Oi (1961), Massell (1969, 1970)). Massell (1969) concludes that: producers gain from price stabilization if price instability is caused by supply shocks; consumers gain from price stabilization if price instability is caused by demand shocks; if both demand and supply are subject to shocks, gains depend on the relative size of these shocks and the slope of the demand and supply curve; overall gains of price stabilization are always positive, i.e. gains more than offset losses. Their conclusions rest on a set of highly restrictive assumptions, the most important of which are linearity of the supply and demand functions, costless buffer stock

---

3       The failure of the buffer stock to maintain the price band rests on the non-negativity of stocks (cf. the competitive storage model, see Section 1.4).
4       It should be noted that stabilization at the mean is impossible with non-linear supply and demand functions.

operations and no private sector storage. Many authors have shown the shortcomings of this framework and the mistakes in its conclusions (Hazell and Scandizzo (1975), Subotnik and Houck (1976), Turnovsky (1976, 1978), Newbery and Stiglitz (1981), Williams and Wright (1991)).

In the Waugh-Oi-Massell framework welfare is measured as the sum of surplus of consumers[5] and expected profit of producers. These so-called Marshallian welfare measures ignore any impact of risk. This is strange as the major direct welfare gain from price stabilization is the reduction in risk borne by producers. A more general micro-economic approach that incorporates a large part of the above criticisms and allows a formalization of attitudes towards risk, is the use of expected utility as a welfare measure. The impact of non-neutral attitudes towards risk can be assessed through the convexity or concavity of utility functions. Measuring welfare by means of expected utility (Hicksian welfare measurement) is therefore considered appropriate in the context of uncertainty. The expected utility approach is extensively utilized in a standard reference work in the field of price stabilization in commodity markets, Newbery and Stiglitz (1981, below abbreviated as NS). The favorable attitude towards price stabilization in commodity markets according to the Waugh-Oi-Massell framework contrasts quite drastically with the analysis by NS[6]. Their view is summarized with the following statement:

*'The major result of our analysis is to question seriously the desirability of price stabilization schemes, both from the point of view of the producer and of the consumer'*

NS model a risk averse producer (producing country), having a von Neumann Morgenstern utility function with income as argument. The benefits of price stabilization are calculated as the change in expected utility from income with and without price stabilization. A first order Taylor series approximation of this expression is constructed and under standard assumptions (risk originates on the supply side, output is lognormally distributed, demand is stable with a constant elasticity), an expression for producer benefits is derived (NS, equation 6.59, 6.61, both under perfect price stabilization):

---

5    Consumer surplus is the difference of what consumers are willing to pay and what they actually pay and is measured diagrammatically as the area enclosed by the demand curve, the market price and the axis.

6    Quantitative estimates of the welfare changes of price stabilization are presented in Newbery and Stiglitz (1981), Chapter 20 and Chapter 9.

B                                 $\frac{1}{2}(\varepsilon-1)\,\sigma^2_p + \frac{1}{2}\,R\,\Delta\,\sigma^2_y$                                        (1)

where

B        = total (per unit) benefit of producers

$\varepsilon$        = own price elasticity of demand

R        = coefficient of relative risk aversion;

$\sigma^2_y$        = squared coefficient of variation of income

$\sigma^2_p$        = squared coefficient of variation of price

From this approximation risk benefits and transfer benefits of price stabilization are identified. Risk benefits ( $\frac{1}{2}\,R\,\Delta\,\sigma^2_y$) are formalized as the change of the coefficient of variation in income with and without price stabilization and weighted with the Arrow-Pratt coefficient of relative risk aversion. Transfer benefits ($\frac{1}{2}(\varepsilon-1)\,\sigma^2_p$) refer to the change in income due to price stabilization, that are purely re-distributive in character, i.e. shifting income from producers to consumers or vice versa. Transfer benefits cannot be considered as net benefits from price stabilization, but could, however, be important if welfare of a specific group (producers) or country (producing country) is concerned. NS show that size and direction of transfer benefits are highly sensitive to the specification of demand and supply.

Empirical estimates of producer benefits for a range of commodities are presented, using a number of assumptions to simplify the calculations (loglinear demand, no supply response, no storage, multiplicative disturbance in supply and demand). Transfer benefits[7] are calculated using demand elasticities by commodity, as opposed to calculations by country in the case of risk benefits. Transfer benefits are calculated to be negative for producers for most commodities. Total benefits of price stabilization, the sum of these two, are shown to be very low and in a number of cases even negative, indicating a transfer of benefits from producing to consuming countries.

In a similar way NS derive expressions for the benefits of price stabilization of consumers. Consumers are assumed to maximize a von Neumann Morgenstern utility function, given prices of goods and income, and subject to a budget constraint. This yields under standard assumptions, demand equations for goods and a (von Neumann Morgenstern) indirect utility function. Again, benefits of price stabilization are calculated as the change in expected (indirect) utility from income with and without price stabilization. This is approximated with a

---

7        The transfer benefit depends critically on the elasticity of demand and the variance of price; estimates of both show large variations.

Taylor series expansion around mean income and mean price of the relevant good. Risk aversion with respect to the price of the relevant good depends on the form of the indirect utility function. With the help of the properties of the indirect utility function (Roy's identity), a general expression is derived for the benefits of price stabilization to consumers. Order of magnitude estimates are obtained by evaluating a special case (constant price and income elasticity). This leads to an expression for the total benefits of price stabilization to consumers (NS, equation 9.19):

$$B^c = \tfrac{1}{2}\,\sigma^2_p - R^c\,\lambda\,\varepsilon\,\sigma^2_p\,/\,\eta \qquad\qquad (2)$$

where

| | |
|---|---|
| $B^c$ | = (per unit) total benefits of consumers |
| $\sigma^2_p$ | = coefficient of variation of price |
| $R^c$ | = coefficient of relative risk aversion of consumers |
| $\lambda$ | = squared correlation coefficient of price and income |
| $\varepsilon$ | = own price elasticity of demand |
| $\eta$ | = income elasticity of demand |

Or (NS, equation 9.17 and 9.18):

$$B^c = [\tfrac{1}{2}\,(1\text{-}\varepsilon)\,\sigma^2_p] + [\tfrac{1}{2}\,\varepsilon\,(1\text{-}\,2\,R^c\,\lambda\,/\,\eta)\,\sigma^2_p] \qquad\qquad (3)$$

Equation (3) allows to identify transfer benefits ($\tfrac{1}{2}\,(1\text{-}\varepsilon)\,\sigma^2_p$) and efficiency or risk benefits ($\tfrac{1}{2}\,\varepsilon\,(1\text{-}\,2\,R^c\,\lambda\,/\,\eta)\,\sigma^2_p$) separately. With unit price elasticity ($\varepsilon=1$) the transfer benefit vanishes. The risk benefit will be negative for plausible values of the parameters, although very small. As in the case of producer benefits, empirical calculations show that all these types of consumer benefits are small, implying that consumers do not have a clear preference for price stability.

A final issue is the cost of price stabilization: point estimates of these costs are extremely difficult to construct as accurate estimates of trend demand, trend supply and past price volatility are difficult to obtain. Costs are calculated to be a small percentage of the annual average revenue, however, with large standard errors. Under reasonable assumptions benefit cost ratios will be less than one for all commodities except one (see NS, Table 20.7).

NS argue that it is highly impractical to implement stabilization of consumption or welfare by stabilizing prices. The main thrust of their point is that the market offers a variety of methods to deal with income risk that are more effective than price stabilization by use of a buffer stock. These alternative ways to deal with price or income uncertainty also affect the effectiveness of achieving consumption stability through buffer stock price stabilization[8]. We discuss a representative set of these risk reduction options.

Missing risk markets and, if futures markets are available, missing or imperfect credit markets are the major cause of income risk in commodity markets. This points at two alternatives for price stabilization. Futures trading is argued to offer better income insurance than perfect price stabilization unless the correlation between price and output is very low. If these correlations are very low neither is very helpful in reducing income risk. However, futures trading has an additional advantage over buffer stocks: a buffer stock is imposed on all farmers equally, while a farmer is free to choose any hedging position following his individual preferences. The welfare analysis of the introduction of futures in commodity markets is discussed in Section 1.3. Another possibility to deal with income risk is saving and borrowing. If income fluctuates over the years around a trend, fluctuations in consumption can be smoothed by borrowing and lending. If such a facility would be available to primary commodity producers their income risk would disappear.

If futures markets are missing and if credit markets are highly imperfect, a number of ways to deal with risk remain: risk spreading, risk transfer, risk reduction, risk sharing. Income risk can be diminished by crop diversification or, more general, by allocating labor time to different income earning activities (e.g. non-farm activities). Income earning activities of farmers comprise, in practice, a broad set of activities ranging from cultivating different crops (both annual and perennial), trading in different commodities, processing of agricultural production, but also activities outside agriculture, like wage labor for private sector enterprises or the government. It is easy to imagine that a well diversified farm household will have a much lower income risk relative to a household that cultivates only one crop, or earns an income from only one activity. There are often a lot of practical constraints to achieve such risk reduction. Another form of risk spreading is storage: price fluctuations can be evened out by private storage. Storage is effective in stopping the decline of prices, but is not capable, or only up to the point where stocks are depleted, to stop price rises. The analysis of storage in commodity markets and its impact on price formation is discussed in Section 1.4. Private storage response to price stabilization will also make price stabilization schemes more costly, as larger quantities are required to generate the same price change. Crop insurance contracts offer a possibility to deal with

---

8       These subjects are treated in Newbery and Stiglitz (1981), Chapter 12, 13 and 14.

production uncertainty. In combination with insurance of price risk, crop insurance is capable of dealing effectively with income risk. Crop insurance contracts, however, are not popular due to adverse selection and moral hazard problems, and this explains why such an alternative will generally not be available. Risk sharing contracts constitute a final possibility to spread income risk. Risk sharing contracts reduce the cost of risk substantially as the cost of risk increases with the square of risk.

We should comment at this stage on the appropriateness of price stabilization as such. Stabilizing prices does not imply stabilizing consumption. Also, price stabilization may very well increase income fluctuations, or price stabilization may be superfluous. For example, with zero supply response and unit elastic demand, income is fully stabilized by the response of consumers. NS conclude that, if the market offers sufficient opportunities to reduce risk (crop diversification, sharecropping, futures trading, saving/borrowing to smooth income, etc.), little welfare improvement will be realized with price stabilization through a buffer stock. Or, quoting Newbery (1990, p.100):

*'The micro-economic benefits of additional public price stabilization are small, and most of them can be achieved as well in other ways'.*

Consequently, price stabilization as an objective of economic policy *per se* is highly questionable from a micro-economic point of view.

If the micro-economic benefits, although theoretically defensible[9], are quantitatively of small importance, why, then, does price stabilization by buffer stocks occur in practice? Part of the reason that price stabilization schemes are operated in practice, is their claimed macro-economic benefits[10]. It is also suggested that price stabilization schemes serve a different goal, i.e. are mainly intended to support income of primary producers. Newbery (1990, p.80) notes in this respect:

*'The Integrated Program for Commodities was always intended to be more than just a solution to the problem of commodity price instability and its prime aim, at least as perceived by the developing countries, was undoubtedly to raise consumer*

---

9     The market does not provide the optimal degree of price stabilization, due to market failure: missing futures and risk markets, and no perfect information prevent efficient allocation of resources; also no perfect wage and price flexibility.

10     Macro economic benefits of price stabilization are not considered in this review (see e.g. Kanbur (1984)).

*commodity prices to levels which were 'remunerative' and just to producers and equitable to consumers'.*[11]

In summary it may be noted that the major micro-economic benefit of price stabilization for primary producers is the reduction in price risk. The expected utility approach allows a formalization of these benefits. Price stabilization by use of buffer stocks has been shown to be a very costly and impractical way to stabilize income. Empirical calculations of the micro-economic benefits of price stabilization show that these benefits most likely will be very small. A number of alternatives to reduce price or income uncertainty are available, that may do the job equally well or even better.

### 1.3    Futures trading

In this section an overview of the literature on how futures trading affects commodity markets is presented. The objective of most of the reviewed literature is to develop insights into the impact of the introduction of futures trading on prices, price volatility, income, income volatility and welfare. A market without futures trading is, obviously, often chosen as point of reference. However, investigating the relative impact of price stabilization by use of a buffer stock and futures trading is a major policy issue. Also the interaction between private stockholding and futures trading is analyzed.

In an early contribution (McKinnon (1967)), optimal forward sales are derived for an individual primary producer, with and without stockholding, based on minimizing the variance of income. With price inelastic random output, the share of production sold forward is the only choice variable of the producer. The futures price is assumed to be an unbiased estimate of the expected price, an assumption that is also made in much of the literature reviewed below. It is shown that a combination of private stockholding with forward sales is superior to private stockholding alone when dealing with income risk. In practice, when one considers institutional imperfections in the capital market, forward selling and individual stocks will be complementary.

A more fundamental approach is chosen by Newbery and Stiglitz (1981). They make use of a framework that is known as the mean-variance model, a

---

11    The Integrated Program for Commodities is a program launched by UNCTAD in 1976 proposed to set up buffer stocks of a number of core commodities in order to stabilize their prices on a world wide scale.

model that has been widely used in the analysis of risk[12]. Essentially the mean-variance model states that, given certain conditions, attitudes of agents under uncertainty can be characterized by the mean and variance of income. A necessary condition to apply the mean-variance model is that the choices made by agents preserve the normality of the distribution of income. Newbery and Stiglitz show that this should be the case for utility functions with constant absolute risk aversion (CARA).

The mean-variance approach is particularly suited for portfolio choices with jointly normally distributed returns of the different assets. An important result of the mean-variance approach is the portfolio separation theorem. This theorem states that portfolio decisions are taken in two stages. First, the combination of crops (assets) is decided, given returns of crops (assets) and their variances. The efficient portfolio locus is found by minimizing the variance of different combinations of crops (assets) with a given income. A reference income is determined by devoting all resources to the one single safe crop (asset). Connecting this with the point of tangency of the efficient portfolio locus gives the efficient combinations of crops (assets). Secondly, the amount of the risky asset or crop is decided as the point of tangency of the indifference curve and efficient combinations of crops derived in the first step. Only the second choice is affected by the attitude towards risk.

It should be noted that the use of CARA utility functions is not without problems. Changes in wealth do not affect the portfolio choice: the income effect of the portfolio choice is zero and attention is concentrated on substitution effects. This is a highly questionable property of this utility function. Assuming normality also seems problematic: production is non-normal because of non-negativity and even if assumed normal, then the product of two normally distributed variables will not be normal. In a later article Newbery (1988) shows that the mean-variance framework does not necessarily break down if the assumption of non-stochastic production is relaxed. Newbery develops a procedure to calculate the error that is made if the mean-variance model is maintained. This error is negligible for the futures price and the welfare gains, though potentially larger for volumes. It should also be noted that covariance of returns is an important determinant of attractiveness of an asset and this result is also valid without the assumptions on which the mean-variance approach is based.

---

12    The relevant chapters in Newbery and Stiglitz (1981) are Chapter 6, Section 5 and Chapter 13; a concise presentation of the mean-variance model can also be found in Varian (1992), Chapter 11.

For the case of futures trading on commodity markets the mean-variance framework gives rise to linear demand schedules for forward sales, which can easily be aggregated and solved for prices. An expression can be derived for optimal forward sales of producers, assuming multiplicative supply risk and joint normality of prices and production. The producer benefits of introduction of futures market trading, compared to the case where there is only a spot market, are specified as (Newbery and Stiglitz (1981), equation 13.20):

$$B_{FM} = \tfrac{1}{2} R \, \bar{y} \, (\sigma_p + r\sigma)^2 \qquad\qquad (4)$$

where

| | |
|---|---|
| R | = coefficient of relative risk aversion |
| y | = income |
| $\sigma_p$ | = coefficient of variation of price |
| r | = correlation coefficient between price and quantity |
| $\sigma$ | = coefficient of variation of quantity |

and, with some manipulation of this expression, it is shown that these benefits are higher compared to the benefits of price stabilization with a buffer stock. After imposing equilibrium it is shown that the ratio of the variance of income with and without futures trading is quite small for plausible values of the parameters. Except when the correlation between price and output is low, the income risk under perfect price stabilization still exceeds the income risk with unbiased futures market. And, in general, unbiased futures markets provide superior income risk insurance to price stabilization using a buffer stock, because farmers are left free to choose the optimal hedge. NS put forward a few issues that might affect these results: futures market may be (or may believed to be) biased; price stabilization will change prices; supply response will be different; transaction costs of futures trading are not incorporated in the analysis; with futures trading there are no arbitrage benefits.

In Turnovsky (1983), Turnovsky and Campbell (1985), and Kawai (1983a,b) the result of behavior under risk using the mean variance approach is integrated in a rational expectation market equilibrium model. Due to non-existence of an analytical solution and the non-linearity of the relationships in the model, a general conclusion is not possible and Turnovsky (1983) analyses a number of specific polar cases (risk-neutral producers and/or inventory holders, pure production or inventory holding, risk-neutral inventory holders or infinitely risk averse inventory holders) which do allow the conclusion that the introduction of futures markets most likely stabilizes (spot) prices and lowers its long run mean. Turnovsky and Campbell (1985) complement and extend Turnovsky (1983) by using simulation methods in the analysis of the effects of introduction of futures market in a market with a storable commodity and risk-averse optimizing producers and speculators. In order to obtain generality a wide range of values is used for the parameters of the model in the simulation exercise. Turnovsky and Campbell (1985) conclude: the variance of the (spot) price is always reduced by the introduction of a futures market; the price stabilizing impact of futures trading is bigger for demand shocks than for equally large supply shocks; with demand shocks the mean (spot) price is always reduced by the introduction of a futures market; effects of introduction of futures market on fluctuation of prices and welfare vary considerably between parameter sets; producers tend to loose with demand shocks, while consumers and speculators always gain, primarily caused by the fall in the (spot) price; with supply shock a comparable pattern arises but producers may also gain depending on the specific parameter set.

Kawai (1983a) considers three special cases, namely risk-neutral producers or risk-neutral dealers; infinitely risk-averse dealers; infinitely large marginal cost of inventory holding. With plausible but arbitrary values of parameters, it is shown that: futures trading tends to stabilize (spot) prices when consumption demand disturbances are the primary random element in the commodity market; futures trading tends to de-stabilize (spot) prices when inventory demand is the primary random element; and futures trading generates an ambiguous outcome in the case of production disturbances. There is some scope for a government policy of stabilizing (spot) prices through futures intervention depending on the relative size and origin of the disturbances: with relatively large shocks in consumption or production (spot) prices will be stabilized in the short run, with unstable inventory demand disturbances such an intervention should be avoided.

Gemmill (1985) also investigates the relative effectiveness of futures trading and buffer stock price stabilization, but reaches conclusions which are less favorable to futures trading. Gemmill argues that only quite risk averse nations are likely to benefit from a buffer stock to a sufficient extent to justify the costs. In forward contracting there is no trade-off between benefits and costs, and each country can choose its own level of stabilization. The effectiveness, however, depends on the degree of bias in forward prices. Empirically, forward contracting comes out slightly more attractive relative to buffer stocks for the majority of investigated commodities. Hughes Hallett and Ramanujam (1990) investigate the same problem, assuming arbitrary distributions for market clearing prices and quantities and certain rules governing stockholding and operations on the futures/options market. They conclude that the best policy depends on the size of elasticities, but a rule of thumb is to use price stabilization with a buffer stock with inelastic demand and a negative correlation between price and quantity, and to use hedging with elastic demand or a positive correlation between price and quantity.

The combination of price stabilization and futures trading is investigated in Gilbert (1985). Gilbert shows, assuming costless trading on futures markets, that the risk benefits to price stabilization become zero or negative if producers and consumers are able to trade costlessly on an unbiased futures market in contracts that correspond to the lead time of their activity. Futures eliminate the effects of price variability on the utility of producers and consumers (provided that they are unable to influence the price) and, hence, are a perfect substitute for price stabilization. Even with large producers, futures markets are superior to international intervention: for these producers futures trading is a substitute for the optimal degree of price stabilization.

The interaction between private storage and futures trading is interesting, given their risk reducing potential. Gilbert (1989) argues that futures trading facilitates storage, and, as storage has a stabilizing impact on prices, futures trading also stabilizes (spot) prices in commodity markets. Slightly different from Newbery and Stiglitz (1981) who claim that futures trading is a substitute to physical storage[13], Gilbert suggests that these activities are complementary (see also McKinnon (1967)). Hedging demand for storable commodities is mainly done through stockholders and the increased storage due to hedging will have a stabilizing impact on prices. The model, containing expectations of future prices, makes use of an algorithm developed by Deaton and Laroque (1992) to characterize a Stationary Rational Expectation Equilibrium (SREE). This SREE is used to simulate a number of different situations (hedging, no-hedging; risk-averse, risk-neutral) and the simulations support the above claim. Gilbert (1989)

---

13    Newbery and Stiglitz (1981, pp. 178-181) investigate the claim that futures markets only offer significant income risk insurance to producers of discontinuously stocked commodities. Data show that continuously stocked commodities show no difference in variability of cash and futures prices, while for discontinuously stocked commodities, the futures price is significantly more stable. It is concluded that for commodities which are not stocked continuously, futures markets can provide a similar kind of reduction in price variability as storage did for other crops. Newbery and Stiglitz (1981) formulate this proposition for a non-storable commodity while Gilbert (1989) considers a storable commodity. Somewhat further Newbery and Stiglitz conclude (p. 188):'Indeed, it is logical to see storage and futures markets as complementary, not competitive, activities, since futures markets both guide stockpiling decisions, and provide hedging facilities to stockholders.'

concludes that futures trading is a complement and not a substitute to physical storage, and risk neutrality will lead to much higher storage and hence more stable prices as compared to risk aversion with hedging.

The review of this literature has shown that the approach to modelling behavior of primary producers, stockholders, speculators and consumers as expected utility maximizing risk-averse agent under price uncertainty, with CARA utility functions and, subsequently applying a mean-variance model, is firmly established. The mean-variance model gives rise to futures demand that is linear in prices and, hence, can be aggregated across agents. The introduction of futures markets most likely stabilizes (spot) prices and reduces their long run mean. Futures trading will probably be superior to price stabilization by use of a buffer stock and will most likely stimulate stockholding and, hence, stabilize prizes.

## 1.4    Stockholding

In the theoretical literature on the behavior of stockholders and other features of stockholding in commodity markets, the central question is what motivates stockholding and how stockholding affects the market. The non-negativity of stocks takes a prominent position in this literature and will be given ample attention here.

The early contributions in this field, however, focus on a different aspect of the behavior of stockholders. Working (1949) studies intertemporal price relations, i.e. the relation between spot and futures prices at one point in time, or futures prices for different periods in the future. Intertemporal price relations are asserted to be affected by supplies in existence at the start and not by future supply: costs of carrying stocks over time explain these intertemporal price relations. Futures markets and the possibilities to hedge on these markets, give stockholders a measure of return to be expected from storage and, through hedging, a means of assuring receipt of that return. Working's empirical observations of the relationship between the return of storage (the difference between spot and futures prices at one point in time, and denoted by Working as the 'price' of storage) and the supply of storage show an exponentially increasing supply of storage at high returns, a low supply at low positive returns and an even lower but nevertheless positive supply at negative returns.

These negative returns are of particular interest: why would one store if the return is negative? Convenience yield, first introduced by Kaldor (1939/40), is suggested as a possible explanation for negative returns on storage. Working elaborates the concept of convenience yield as follows:

*'.. the owners of large storage facilities are mostly engaged either in merchandising or in processing, and maintain storage facilities largely as a necessary adjunct to their merchandising or processing business. And not only are the facilities adjunct; the exercise of the storing function itself is a necessary adjunct to the merchandising and processing business. Consequently the direct costs of storing over some specified period as well as the indirect costs may be charged against the associated business which remains profitable and so also may appear as direct losses on the storage operation itself.'*

Brennan (1958), elaborating further on convenience yield, derives demand for storage by inserting the equilibrium condition in the inverted consumption demand function. He shows that price spread - the difference of (spot) price and expected or futures price - is a decreasing function of stocks and may be positive or negative. The supply of storage is derived from the behavior of firms in an uncertain world. Firms maximize expected income by accumulating stocks up to the point where net marginal costs of storage equal the expected change in price per unit of time. The net marginal cost is defined as the marginal outlay on physical storage plus marginal risk aversion factor minus the marginal convenience yield on stocks. These components are elaborated as follows. Marginal outlay on physical storage is assumed constant. A number of motivations for convenience yield are suggested: a producing firm is able to meet sudden increases in demand and takes advantage of price increases; a processing firm avoids trouble, cost and delays of frequent spot purchases; and a wholesaler can easily vary his sales. At high levels of stocks marginal convenience yield will approach zero. Finally, the marginal risk aversion factor is either constant or an increasing function of stocks and this completes the components of the net marginal cost of storage. Brennan showed that net marginal cost could very well be negative. Data on stocks of several agricultural commodities, both with and without an active futures market, and both durable and (semi-) perishable, corroborate the framework convincingly.

After Working and Brennan, little additional theoretical work on convenience yield has been done. The concept of convenience yield has seen only a few empirical applications (see e.g. Weymar (1968), see also Chapter 3). A few recent theoretical contributions are known, both in favor and against the concept of convenience yield (Newbery and Stiglitz (1981), Chapter 14, Ghosh *et al.* (1987), Viaene (1989) and Wright and Williams (1989), Brennan, Williams and Wright (1997)): however, the issue does not seem to be settled yet. Some authors argue that convenience yield is caused by spatial aggregation and should not be given any behavioral interpretation (Brennan, Williams and Wright (1997)), or by an inaccurate account of location and grades of physical storage (Wright and Williams (1989)). The mainstream of theoretical interest in the explanation of stockholding has shifted to a different line of research, which represents the current leading model of commodity prices, and is outlined below.

Prior to discussing this model of commodity prices, the so-called competitive storage model, a characteristic feature of profit maximizing stockholders is set out. Optimal behavior of stockholders is characterized by the so-called complementary inequality conditions. These conditions state that two regimes can be identified for a profit maximizing stockholder. The first regime refers to one in which stocks are positive and all arbitrage opportunities are fully exploited. This implies that current price (plus costs) equals discounted expected future price (see the upper part of equation (5)). The other regime is one in which there are no arbitrage profits possible because the discounted expected future price is below the current price (plus costs), and stocks are zero (see the lower part of equation (5)). In formula the complementary inequality conditions are specified as (in e.g. Deaton and Laroque (1992)):

$$I_t \geq 0 \text{ if } \beta (1-\delta) E_t P_{t+1} = P_t$$
and $\hspace{6cm}$ (5)
$$I_t = 0 \text{ if } \beta (1-\delta) E_t P_{t+1} < P_t$$

where

t is a time subscript

E is the expectation operator

I $\quad$ = inventory demand

$\beta$ $\quad$ = discounting factor ($\beta=1/(1+r)$)

$\delta$ $\quad$ = deterioration rate of inventory

P $\quad$ = price

Note the implicit asymmetry in the optimal behavior of stockholders: if there are arbitrage opportunities, optimizing stockholders react by accumulating stocks, until discounted expected price adjusted for deterioration equals current price. If no positive income can be earned from arbitrage, optimizing stockholders react by de-cumulating stocks. However, after depletion of initial stocks, no reactions are possible. In short, downward movements of the current price can be cushioned by stockholders, but little can be done against price rises. This behavior is also reflected in typical price developments of primary commodities: long periods of relatively stable prices combined with occasional peaks (see e.g. Deaton and

Laroque (1992)). The non-negativity of stocks accounts for the non-linearity in prices.

Gardner (1979), following the seminal work of Gustafson (1958a,b), considers how commodity storage is optimally carried out in terms of a social welfare criterion[14]. Optimal storage is shown to be zero if supply is less than trend production. If supply is above trend production the marginal propensity to store, represented by the slope of the storage function, is positive. However, optimal carry-over is increasing slightly faster with increasing levels of supply. Optimal storage depends on the uncertainty of future production (+), the welfare function (+/-), storage costs (-) and the discount rate of future welfare (-), with the expected sign of these determinants in brackets. Note that the behavior of stockholders is not specified: optimality in stocks is obtained purely by maximizing expected social welfare, i.e. equating expected marginal welfare in every period. Only the dynamic property of stockholding - stocks at the end of the period contribute to the supply in the next period - is considered. The optimal storage rule - in subsequent work labelled as competitive storage rule - can also be derived directly from competitive arbitrage conditions, and, hence, is equivalent to the storage rule with profit maximizing stockholders (see Gardner (1979), p.62; Newbery and Stiglitz (1981); Gilbert (1988b)). Intuitively this is easy to understand: optimization implies that discounted marginal utility (or value) of the commodity - the price of the commodity - of current and future periods is equalized and arbitrage activities of stockholders are a vehicle for transferring quantities from a low marginal utility (value) to a high marginal utility (value) period, in other words, to establish such an equalization.

Optimal storage is derived with stochastic dynamic programming techniques, a slightly inconvenient technique for practical purposes. Hence, some authors have attempted to derive analytical approximations. Newbery and Stiglitz (1982; also 1981, Chapters 29 and 30) develop an analytically solvable approximation of the competitive storage rule for risk neutral agents. With linear

---

14      Due to the dynamic character of storage - current storage contributes to next period supply - no analytical solutions for optimal storage can be derived: stochastic dynamic programming is used to achieve optimality. This is implemented as follows: from a period in the future, in which dynamics is ignored, all the paths are considered by which that final period could be reached. The path that maximizes the (dynamic) social welfare function, given initial supply, is selected as optimal. The final period is determined by adding periods to the total horizon taken into account and calculate the optimum. The horizon, and hence the final period, is increased until the optimum does not change anymore. Ignoring dynamics in that period only creates a marginal error. Gardner suggest this to be at most 15 years for the US grain market.

demand - or linear approximations of non-linear demand - the approximation to the competitive stock rule is a piece-wise linear function of supply, with the successive slopes becoming steeper and steeper. The approximation is shown to be accurate relative to stochastic dynamic programming results. Optimal storage rules provide a bench-mark to evaluate e.g. price stabilization but also other policies: the approximation to the storage rule is used to measure the degree of stabilization achieved and to measure the loss of efficiency of a bandwidth rule compared to the efficient competitive storage rule. The net gains from competitive storage, though small, are significantly greater than those from e.g. maintaining prices within a bandwidth. Newbery and Stiglitz (1981) also suggest a method to measure the bias in the competitive storage rule with risk averse producers.

Gilbert (1988b) shows, elaborating on the same model, that the market composed of a large number of risk averse speculators may be considered as a market with nearly risk neutral agents. A certainty equivalent linear approximation of the competitive storage rule is developed[15]. In the derivation of this approximation a semi-logarithmic specification of production and consumption is a key element as it allows for the linearity in the market clearing identity combined with loglinearity in the intertemporal price path. Gilbert summarizes the features of the certainty equivalent storage function as follows: storage depends on total supply (carry-over plus inherited stocks); the certainty equivalence storage function is piece-wise linear; the marginal propensity to store is dependent only on total supply, and is independent of both the interest rate and the supply and demand elasticities; the initial storage point is a multiplicative function of the interest rate and the sum of supply and demand elasticities. Comparison of the semi-logarithmic functional form with linear specifications shows that the separability property whereby the interest rate only affected the initial storage point and not the marginal propensity to stock, is lost, leading to a significantly more complicated storage function. Lagged supply response is shown to increase the marginal propensity to store.

Williams and Wright (1991) focus their research on the dynamic behavior of storage, production and prices (a simple consumption function is added to complete the model) from a purely theoretical perspective. Stockholders are

---

15    A certainty equivalent approximation is obtained by substituting certainty equivalent values for expectational values and conditioning current storage on positive certainty equivalent storage one period ahead. Subsequent segments of the piece-wise linear approximation of the storage rule are found by making the same steps starting with the certainty equivalent equation for storage one period forwarded and now also using the outcome of the first segment.

assumed to be risk neutral, in order to concentrate on the dynamic aspects of behavior of stockholders and to avoid mixing up of dynamic and risk aversion effects. Throughout their entire study the complementary inequality conditions that apply to the optimal behavior of stockholders are central to the analysis. The complementary inequality conditions do not allow an analytical solution of prices. Stochastic dynamic programming techniques are used to find optimal storage. With these methods it is shown that these conditions, combined with (standard) maximizing behavior of farmers generate price paths that diverge from what one would expect given the randomness of weather conditions. Williams and Wright (1991) claim that all work on behavior of stockholders that ignores the non-negativity of stocks implied by these conditions - and this is most work in which a structural equation for stockholding is postulated - ignores an essential aspect of this behavior:

*"..ignoring the non-negativity constraint gives the wrong storage rule. (..) from the perspective of understanding commodity markets the system behaves over time in a markedly different manner".*

In the same spirit as Williams and Wright (1991), Gustafson (1958) and Gardner (1979), the analysis of optimal stockholding and the behavior of prices under optimal stockholding has been continued by Deaton and Laroque (1991, 1992, 1994a,b). The purpose of their work is to investigate whether the competitive storage model is capable of explaining the actual behavior of prices. In Deaton and Laroque (1992) stylized facts of a number of real world annual commodity prices (1900-1987) are summarized: these series show high first-order and second-order auto correlation, have a high volatility, little persistence, do not have trends, seem mean-reverting and show substantial skewness and kurtosis (for many of these prices). A variant of the competitive storage model is suggested to explain the properties of these prices. The model distinguishes producers and consumers and stockholders. With respect to production and consumption a number of standard assumptions are used, namely harvests are independently and identically distributed (i.i.d.), consumption is continuous and a strictly decreasing function of price, prices are non-negative and inventories are costly. Optimality implies the complementary inequality conditions in the case of stockholders. Deaton and Laroque (1992) prove the uniqueness of a Stationary Rational Expectations Equilibrium (SREE). As there is no simple analytical solution for the equilibrium price function numerical approximations are required. Prices are simulated to gain a better understanding of the model, using a selection of specifications for examination (linear and iso-elastic demand; low and high variance of the no-storage price distribution).

Deaton and Laroque (1992) show that a number of observed properties of commodity prices can be replicated (skewness, kurtosis, 'spikiness'). However, autocorrelation, both first and second order, is substantially lower than in the actual series. Next, the derived testable relationships with respect to the expected price and the conditional variance of price are estimated using a generalized methods of moments technique (GMM). Deaton and Laroque (1992) conclude that the estimation results of the expected price equation as well as some other estimation results provide some although not convincing support for the competitive storage model. In subsequent work of Deaton and Laroque (1991, 1994a,b), building on the 1992 article, the simulations are repeated after a number of technical improvements: the conclusion is that the simple model cannot account for the evidence: the autocorrelation properties of the data are quite different from those generated by the model. The model is not capable of transforming identical and independently distributed shocks in supply into prices with a high autocorrelation. Deaton and Laroque (1991, 1994a,b) suggest two explanations: on the supply side, harvest shocks will not be i.i.d. in the case of perennial crops and, more likely, on the demand side

*'a demand for stocks even when prices are expected to fall, a demand that might be provided by the activities of processors or manufacturers, for whom the commodity is a factor of production, and who will pay to avoid the possibility that they might run out of stocks'.*

This seems an explanation that comes very near to convenience yield.

In summary we may note that two features of stockholding have received considerable attention in the theory, notably positive stocks with negative (expected) returns and non-negativity of stocks. Combining arbitrage behavior and the non-negativity of stocks results in the complementary inequality conditions that characterize optimal behavior of stockholders. There is no analytical solution for optimal storage in these so-called competitive storage models: optimal storage rules have to be found with stochastic dynamic programming techniques. It should be noted that the competitive storage literature ignores negative returns on stockholding or convenience yield, an explanation for these negative returns. Empirical observations, however, do confirm negative returns on stockholding. It should also be noted that competitive storage models assume risk neutral stockholders: a few attempts at incorporating risk aversion into the competitive storage model are known (notably Gilbert (1989)). The competitive storage model, however, is not capable of adequately describing price developments of commodities, in particular the high autocorrelation of prices, and this main result is qualified by some proponents themselves as disappointing (see Deaton and

Laroque (1994)). A possible explanation of this failure is that the model does not incorporate convenience yield.


## 1.5    Theory and thesis

As mentioned in the introduction of this chapter the central issue in this thesis is how perennial crop growers and stockholders of a storable primary commodity have dealt with income risk due to price fluctuations. In the empirical work we make use of data of the Indian natural rubber market for the period from 1965 to 1995. From the start of this period to the beginning of the 1990s prices in this market are determined by domestic supply and demand and independent of the world market. This allows the identification of the contribution of different groups in the market to the formation of prices. Such a price formation characterizes the regime of the empirical work presented in Chapter 3, 4 and 5. The specification of the behavior of groups in the market, and in particular of stockholders is the main objective of Chapter 3. Stockholding is considered an important device to reduce income risk due to price fluctuations. For a number of years during the period under consideration, a price band scheme has been effective. Such schemes are popular policy reactions to overcome income risk. The impact of this scheme on price formation and behavior of stockholders, and the assessment of its effectiveness are the subjects of Chapter 4 and 5. From the beginning of the 1990s onwards we assume that domestic prices are entirely determined by world market price. Such price formation characterizes the regime of the empirical work presented in Chapter 7. A hypothetical introduction of futures, another device to deal with income risk, is analyzed with the data of this period. Chapters 3, 4, 5 and 7 represent the major empirical work of this thesis.

Two chapters, namely Chapter 2 and Chapter 6, have a more descriptive character. An extensive description of the data of the Indian natural rubber market is given in Chapter 2. We present data and developments on a broad range of subjects, whatever information was available to us and is relevant for our subject. The chapter considers the functioning of the market, the players in the market, size and structure of production, consumption and trade, distribution of risks, possibilities to deal with income risk, domestic and world market prices and the regulatory and institutional organization of the market. In Chapter 6 we investigate if and how financial risk management instruments can play a role in the Indian natural rubber market. In the 1990s both UNCTAD and the World Bank have promoted the use of these instruments by developing countries in order to deal with their income risk. The liberalized trade regime in India which has started in the 1990s suggests more support from the government to use financial risk management instruments. In that chapter the main financial risk management instruments are explained and we consider to what extent they could play a role in the Indian natural rubber market. We review a number of exploratory studies on the use of these instruments. We discuss in some detail the requirements for implementing hedging strategies and possible problems that might arise. In the final section we reflect on the prospects of using these instruments in the current Indian situation.

In Chapter 3 we set out the basic model. We explain the behavior of producers and stockholders with the help of the expected utility approach. As we expect little production flexibility with the perennial crop, we give extensive attention to the formalization of the behavior of stockholders, one of the major options of risk reduction in this market. For reasons highlighted in the chapter itself we have chosen to discard the competitive storage framework. We do, however, allow convenience yield in the specifications used for estimation of behavior of stockholders. In particular we attempt to identify different types of behavior of stockholders by direct estimation. In these chapters we assume that producers, consumers and stockholders are all risk neutral. This assumption is made purely on practical grounds: the combination of risk aversion and rational expectations - an appropriate assumption of the process of expectation formation in the case of short run arbitrage behavior - would create insurmountable problems to solve the model for prices. The outcome of this chapter clearly emphasizes the crucial role that stockholding play in this market in the short term price formation. The larger part of responses to short run fluctuations in prices is due to stockholding and much less to consumption (or production). This underscores the effectiveness of stockholding as a way of dealing with income risk.

During part of the sample period a domestic price band scheme was in operation, the so-called Buffer Stocking Scheme. Chapters 4 and 5 analyze in detail the impact of this price band scheme on behavior of stockholders and on prices. In Chapter 4 we incorporate the price band scheme into the model, leading to the estimation of truncated expected prices. Implicitly we assume in this chapter that the behavior of agents remains the same: only the truncation of (expected) prices, an explanatory variable, affects the outcome. The result of this exercise is not impressive: with the applied technique we were unable to detect a large impact of the price band scheme. In Chapter 5 we investigate if stockholders behave differently under a price band scheme: in other words, we investigate if the parameters of the behavioral equations change due to this scheme. Although the interaction between a price band scheme and private stockholding has been discussed in the literature (see Newbery and Stiglitz (1981), Chapter 14), little attention is given to the possibility of a change in behavior of private stockholders due to such a price band scheme. The empirical analysis shows that the extent to which stockholders react on identical arbitrage opportunities is lower during a price band scheme. Additionally a simulation is implemented to assess the effectiveness of stabilizing prices by using a buffer stock or by relying on the arbitrage activities of private stockholders. The simulation exercise makes use of the result from Newbery and Stiglitz that the welfare gains from price stabilization are proportional with the square of the coefficient of variation (CV) of prices. It is shown in this chapter that private stockholders are more effective in stabilizing prices.

The assumption of risk neutrality is relaxed in Chapter 7. In this chapter we specifically consider the most recent part of the sample period: price formation during this period, and hence also expectation formation, is dominated by the world market. This allows us to set aside the rational expectation framework and adopt a simpler specification of expectation formation. With the help of the mean-variance approach optimal production. stockholding and forward sales are derived. These expressions reflect the portfolio separation theorem implied by the mean-variance approach. Welfare gains of hedging price risks of domestic producers and local traders on an international futures exchange are quantified. The risk and cost parameters of the model used in simulations are obtained by estimations and compared with the ones used in similar experiments reported in the literature. The exercise shows that producers and stockholders can realize considerable welfare gains by hedging. Costs for a commodity board that intermediates between domestic producers and stockholders and the international futures exchange, are shown to be small. With a surcharge on the price offered in the domestic market, welfare gains are calculated at the break even strategy of the board.

In a final chapter, Chapter 8 the major conclusions are summarized and the issues raised in the theoretical review of this chapter are considered again.

## 2    THE INDIAN RUBBER MARKET:
##      DEVELOPMENT, STRUCTURE AND INSTITUTIONS[1]

### 2.1    Introduction

In this chapter we present a quantitative description of the Indian natural rubber market for the period 1965-1995.[2] The purpose of this chapter is to obtain a better view on how the market functions: Who are the players in this market? What is the size and structure of production, consumption and trade? Who bears the price risk? Are there opportunities to diversify these risks? What is the influence of the world market on domestic price formation? Are there regulations that affect price formation? How and to what extent does the government intervene in this market? Can regime shifts be identified? Answers to these questions are believed to provide an indispensable background for doing empirical analysis.

The supply side of the market consists of production and import of natural, synthetic and reclaimed rubber.[3] In Section 2.2 production of rubber, and in particular natural rubber, is discussed in detail, focusing on the economic environment of the individual natural rubber grower. Both the input side (prices and quantities of production factors) and output side (prices and quantities of marketed output) are considered. Additionally, attention is given to the structure of production, determinants of production, production capacity, technical progress and substitution possibilities on the production side. Some developments in supply of synthetic rubber and reclaimed rubber are presented in view of the substitution possibilities on the demand side (and despite their small share in total rubber production).

The demand side of the rubber market consists of the demand by rubber products manufacturing industry, both domestically and abroad. Domestic demand, however, is most important and is treated in detail in Section 2.3. Again, the individual manufacturer is taken as the unit of study. Attention is given to the

---

1       Parts of this Chapter are based on Burger *et al.* (1995).

2       Data are shown in the first place for the period 1965 to 1995. However, in a number of instances data for a longer period will be presented, and in a number of instances, mainly due to a lack of data, data for a shorter period are shown.

3       Natural, synthetic and reclaimed rubber are in some instances denoted with the acronyms NR, SR and RR.

structure of rubber products manufacturing industry, substitution between different types of rubber and prices of end-products.

Last but not least, trade and stockholding is treated in Section 2.4. As in the case of growers and manufacturers, an effort is made to characterize the individual stockholder and its economic environment. Institutional organization of the marketing of natural rubber as well as regulations and agreements on stockholding - as far as documented - are described. A number of regime shifts can be identified during the period under consideration. Some of these shifts are obvious from the data and can easily be demonstrated: such identification will be attempted. However, some shifts have an impact that is more difficult to trace. One example of a shift in regime, the change in behaviour of stockholders as a result of a price band scheme, is studied in Chapter 5.

After the treatment of the major economic groups in the market - growers and traders of natural rubber and manufacturers of rubber products - the development of prices, both nominal and real, and both domestic and international, is discussed in Section 2.5. Attention is given to the fluctuation of domestic prices, and to the relationship between the domestic market and the world market. In the section 2.6 developments in the regulation of import of natural rubber and the policy of the government with respect to domestic prices is discussed.


## 2.2    Production

Favourably environmental conditions to grow rubber trees, especially in the southern states (Kerala, and to a lesser extent Tamil Nadu and Karnataka), have contributed to a long tradition of producing natural rubber in India. During the last 30 to 40 years area under rubber has seen a continuous and at times rapid growth (see Figure 2.1).[4] In the period 1965-66 to 1994-95, the average annual rate of growth of the area was 3.6%. From 1978-79 to 1994-95 the average annual growth was even 4.5%. Growing of rubber trees is heavily concentrated in the south of India, in particular in the state of Kerala where, averaged over this period, 91.1% of the total area is located. Tamil Nadu and Karnataka have small percentages of area with natural rubber plantations (average 4.8% and 2.4%). The regional distribution is slightly changing over time in the direction of so-called non-traditional areas, reducing the share of (traditional) Kerala in total area. In the

---

4      Most data are taken from various issues of the Indian Rubber Statistics. In appendix 2.1 to this chapter a complete account is presented of the sources, consistency checks, errors and corrections of the data used in this study.

beginning of the 1990s around 8% of total area under rubber is located in these non-traditional areas.[5]

**Figure 2.1**    Aggregate area under rubber (at the end of each fiscal year)

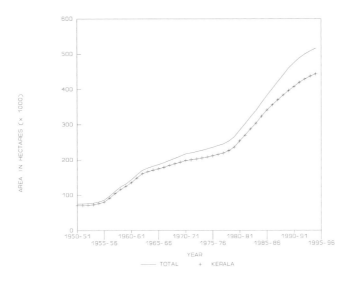

Source:        Indian Rubber Statistics, various issues.

Two specific groups can be identified among growers of natural rubber, namely smallholders and estates. This distinction has substantial bearing on the type of business: estates are, on average, large sized mono-crop plantations, usually owned and professionally managed by companies; smallholders, on the other hand, are, mostly small-scale agricultural households that have earnings from various agricultural as well as non-agricultural activities. Both in terms of aggregate area and aggregate production, the smallholder sector is by far the largest. The share of smallholdings in total area has increased from 60-65% in the beginning of the 1960s to 80-85% in the beginning of the 1990s. Sizes of plantations in the smallholder sector are, however, tiny. Table 2.1 summarizes information on the size distribution of holdings and estates. The table shows that around 90% of the holdings is smaller than 2 ha. From survey data it is estimated that the average holding size is around 0.5 ha. Around 10% of the largest estates

---

5        Non-traditional areas are Tripura, Assam, Meghalaya, Nagaland, Mizoram, Manipur, Andaman and Nicobar Islands, Goa, Maharashtra, Orissa and Andra Pradesh.

control 30-40% of the total area of estates. Over time the number of smallholders increased steadily, while the number of estates decreased. In the estate sector a clear process of increasing concentration is taking place, with the total number of companies decreasing and the average size of the area increasing during the period 1965-1995. Within the estate sector an increasing share is due to public sector corporations and government departments which are active in non-traditional areas (see Tharian George and Thomas (1997)).

**Table 2.1**     Size distribution of smallholdings and estates

|  | in % of total smallholdings | | | | | |
|---|---|---|---|---|---|---|
|  | 0-2 ha. | | 2-4 ha. | | >4 ha. | |
|  | Units | Area | Units | Area | Units | Area |
| 1965-66 | 90.6 | 58.9 | 5.8 | 14.7 | 3.6 | 26.4 |
| 1975-76 | 88.2 | 54.8 | 7.6 | 17.3 | 4.2 | 27.9 |
| 1985-86 | 95.7 | 76.4 | 2.8 | 9.1 | 1.5 | 14.5 |
| 1994-95 | 97.9 | 83.6 | 1.6 | 8.7 | 0.5 | 7.8 |

|  | in % of total estates | | | | | | | | | | | |
|---|---|---|---|---|---|---|---|---|---|---|---|---|
|  | 0-40ha | | 40-200ha | | 200-400ha | | 400-600ha | | 600-800ha | | >800 ha. | |
|  | Unts | Area | Unts | Area | Unts | Area | Unts | Area | Unts | Area | Unts | Area |
| 1965-66 | 51.1 | 15.0 | 39.0 | 32.1 | 4.7 | 13.4 | 3.0 | 14.8 | 0.6 | 4.2 | 1.6 | 20.4 |
| 1975-76 | 48.3 | 12.3 | 40.5 | 28.8 | 4.5 | 11.0 | 2.8 | 12.1 | 1.5 | 9.1 | 2.3 | 26.8 |
| 1985-86 | 35.7 | 5.9 | 44.5 | 19.8 | 6.3 | 10.1 | 4.7 | 12.5 | 3.6 | 12.8 | 5.2 | 38.9 |
| 1994-95 | 37.9 | 4.7 | 38.5 | 14.6 | 6.4 | 8.0 | 6.1 | 13.6 | 5.0 | 14.4 | 6.1 | 44.7 |

Source:         Indian Rubber Statistics, various issues.

Aggregate production of natural rubber has experienced a tremendous growth in 1980s and the 1990s (see Figure 2.2). Average annual growth rate from 1985-86 to 1994-95 approaches 10% per annum. Such high growth rates should partly be ascribed to the developments in area as set out above and partly to higher yields. The share of production of smallholders in total production increases substantially: in 1965-66 smallholders had a share of 40.4%, increasing to 61.4% in 1975-76, 74.4% in 1985-86 and 86.0% in 1994-95. Apparently the smallholders sector has grown faster than the estate sector. Both production and area growth in natural rubber are relatively high compared to other crops cultivated in India (see Tharian George and Thomas (1997)).

**Figure 2.2**     Production of natural rubber

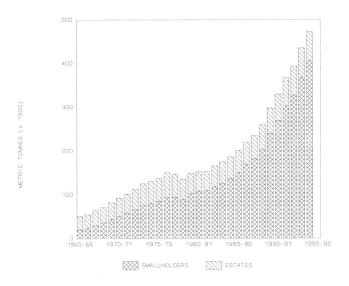

Source:        Indian Rubber Statistics, various issues.

The development of yield, the other component of production, also has contributed substantially to the high growth rates of production. Yield, measured as
production per hectare of tappable area, shows a continuous increase. In the
period 1965-1995 average yield grew from 448 kg. per (tappable) hectare in 1965-
66 to 1363 kg. per hectare in 1994-95, implying an average annual growth rate of
3.9%. There are some regional differences: average yield is highest in Tamil
Nadu, somewhat lower in Kerala, and again lower in Karnataka and the non-
traditional areas. It should be noted, however, that the production in Kerala has by
far the biggest weight in the country-wide average. The continuous increase in
yield is obviously due to the increase in the use of high-yielding varieties.
Especially in the 1980s the use of RRII-105 has been heavily promoted by the
Rubber Research Institute of India.[6] The area under high yielding varieties
increased from 59.6% in 1965-66, 73.0% in 1975-76, 90.7% in 1985-86 to 95.2%
in 1994-95. Estates have been somewhat faster in adopting high yielding varieties
on a large scale: by the late 1970s almost 100% of estate area was covered with
high yielding varieties. In the smallholder sector around 90% of the area was
under high yielding varieties in the beginning of the 1990s.

---

6      RRII-105 refers to a clone developed by the Rubber Research Institute of India.

Production of a perennial crop like natural rubber shows a specific long run dynamic pattern. Rubber trees only start to produce after a relatively long gestation period of five to  seven years. After this immaturity period the annual yield of trees depends on the age of the tree, the particular variety of the tree, the tapping intensity, the availability of labor and the seasonal conditions (to the extent that these conditions are different over the years). After some 25 to 35 years a decision about replanting or uprooting is made. The life cycle of a rubber tree combined with the differences in plots and plantations (age of the trees, variety of the trees, grower, region) generate a specific long run dynamics, typical to many perennial crops (see e.g. Burger *et al.* (1995)).

The decision to uproot and to replant obviously is made on the basis of expected net earnings to be generated by the cultivation of natural rubber trees, compared to earnings from alternative crops. With an immaturity period of five to seven years and a life of a tree of 25 to 35 years it is clear that the decision to newplant or replant is a major investment decision for a farmer or agricultural household. In Figure 2.3 the development of new planting and replanting is presented. From the figure it is seen that replanting shows a gradual and slowly increasing development over time. Newplanting shows a peculiar development: after a shock it stays more or less at the same level for a number of years, and then another shift occurs. Two periods of relatively high levels of newplanting stand out, namely from 1955-1962 and 1978-1990.

Explanations of this pattern should be sought, as noted above, in the development of expected earnings, or of components of these expected earnings (prices of natural rubber, subsidies on newplanting, availability of land, technical progress, costs of production, etc.). Expectations on future prices is of course an important component of expected future earnings. Procurement prices for natural rubber, an income guarantee for rubber producers, and in general support policies to stabilize prices of natural rubber or intentions to do so, will therefore most likely affect investments in rubber trees. Also government subsidies, especially to overcome the 'no-income' immaturity period will influence the decision to discard/replant or newplant through the expected net future income to be earned.

Under the Rubber Plantation Development Scheme during the VI Five Year Plan from 1980-81 to 1984-85 (see Burger *et al.* (1995), pp.22-24),[7] the subsidy and additional assistance then covered about 50% of the cost of planting

---

7      The Five-Year Plans cover the following periods: I 1951-52 to 1955-56; II 1956-57 to 1960-61; III 1961-62 to 1965-66; IV 1969-70 to 1973-74; V 1974-75 to 1978-79; VI 1980-81 to 1984-85; VII 1985-86 to 1989-90.

and maintenance. Loans were given an interest subsidy of 3% of the loan by the Rubber Board. During the VII Plan period both cash and interest subsidy was restricted to smallholders owning up to 5 ha. in traditional areas and to all growers in non-traditional areas. The financial assistance then granted by the Board covered only 35% of the planting and maintenance. The spurt in planting activities due to the improvement of rubber prices and the introduction of cash subsidy for new planting in the 1980s support a number of the above mentioned determinants empirically (see Figure 2.3). The step-wise development of new-planting corresponding to the changes in subsidy schemes under the different five-year plans suggest a large impact of these subsidies on newplanting.

**Figure 2.3**    Newplanted and replanted area

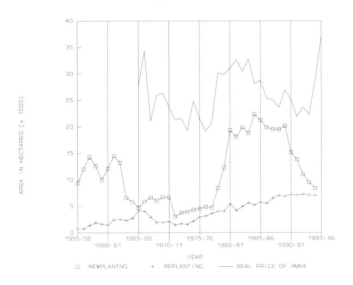

Source:        Indian Rubber Statistics, various issues.

Weather has a profound impact on the monthly pattern of production and yield of natural rubber. Rainfall has a direct negative impact on production: tapping of rubber trees is not possible during rain showers, unless the gird of the trees is protected (rainguarding), in which case tapping is not hindered. Rainguarding, however, is not widely practised among smallholders. Rainfall will also have, with some delay, an impact on the capacity of trees to generate field coagulum. Rainfall stimulates field coagulum per tree and, on the other hand, a lack of rainfall has a negative impact on field coagulum per tree. Finally, production in the months February and March is negatively influenced by the wintering season. For this reason, labourers in the estate sector are sent on leave or take leave for a number of weeks during these months, which makes the fall in production in these months even more extreme. The seasonal pattern[8] is summarized in Figure 2.4. The figure shows large negative deviations during the months June, July and August, confirming the negative impact of the monsoon on production. Also the wintering season during February and March is clear. From September to January weather conditions seem on average optimal for high production levels. A peak season that follows the monsoon[9] corroborates the above mentioned positive influence of rainfall on production.

**Figure 2.4**     Seasonal fluctuation in production

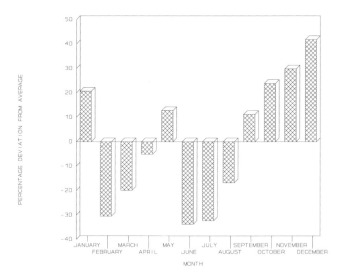

Source:        Indian Rubber Statistics, various issues.

Unlike the pronounced seasonal fluctuations, production uncertainty of natural rubber cultivation relative to other crops is very low. This has a number of

---

8      The seasonal pattern is constructed by taking the percentage deviation of monthly production from average monthly production. Average monthly production is calculated for each individual year. Calculated deviations are averaged over a number of years (1980.011-993.12).

9      The monsoon in the south of India starts in June and lasts until the first weeks of August.

explanations. Natural rubber is harvested all year round: above or below seasonal production can easily be compensated in the next period, smoothing out all within-season shocks. Natural rubber is not a 'fruit crop', like coffee, cocoa or pepper, the growth of which is particularly sensitive to the timing of sunshine, rainfall, humidity, wind, etc. Diseases that destroy the entire crop, like for example foot rot in case of pepper, hardly play a role in natural rubber. Due to storm damage or diseases, the density of rubber plantations declines on average with only around 1% per year (see Burger *et al.* (1995), p. 87). There is no real danger of crop failure due to frost as, for example, is the case in (Brazilian) coffee. Despite the certainty of production of natural rubber relative to other crops, the shocks in production, i.e. divergences of a expected seasonal pattern, are of a much larger size than shocks in consumption (see Gemmill (1985) for an application of this stylized fact).

Rubber production requires on average 160 working days per hectare (Burger *et al.* (1995), p. 53). With the average plot of a smallholder around 0.5 hectare this implies a workload of 80 working days per year. The bulk of the workload consists of tapping. Only a marginal number of working days is spent on other activities. Almost three quarter of the work is carried out by hired labour (Burger *et al.* (1995), p. 54). A tree crop like natural rubber has rather poor substitution possibilities for the individual grower. With low marginal costs, shifting to other crops when at the beginning of the season the expected price at harvest time is low, hardly occurs. Expectations on future prices do play a role in the decision to uproot trees and to replant or set up newplanting, as pointed out above. Indian rubber growers grow rubber almost exclusively. Survey data reveal that on average around 55% of total income is from rubber cultivation; 65% of total cultivated area is cultivated with rubber trees; major other crops are paddy (12%) and coconut (15%, see Burger *et al.* (1995), p.48). The bigger part of the smallholders have other sources of income. For almost 50% of all smallholders the income from rubber growing is supplementary to income from some kind of non-agricultural occupation (government servant, self-employment, private companies). It seems that smallholders have diversified the price risk of cultivating natural rubber to some extent.

Total domestic production of rubber also includes synthetic rubber and reclaimed rubber. Synthetic rubber plays a minor role in the Indian rubber market. Both production and consumption are relatively small compared to natural rubber (see Figures 2.5 and 6), being between 10 to 20% over the whole period. Production of synthetic rubber started only in 1963 with a factory in Uttar Pradesh (Synthetics and Chemicals Ltd., Bareilly) using an alcohol based technology, widely described as obsolete, to produce styrene butadiene (SBR).[10] A second factory (Indian Petro Chemicals Corporation Ltd., Baroda) started commercial production in 1978, producing poly butadiene (PB). Initial installed capacity of both general purpose[11] synthetic rubber factories is around 52,000 tonnes. Three substantially smaller factories (M/s APAR Ltd., M/s Asian Paints (India) Ltd., M/s Gujarath Apar Ltd.), producing mainly special purpose synthetic rubber, with a combined initial capacity of 11,000 tonnes, started operating at the end of the 1980s and the beginning of the 1990s. Domestic factories mainly produce general purpose synthetic rubber: nearly 100% of synthetic rubber production is general purpose synthetic rubber, although this share is decreasing somewhat in the beginning of the 1990s. On the consumption side some 70% consists of general purpose synthetic rubber, and the remaining 30% for special purpose synthetic rubber. With little domestic production of special purpose synthetic rubber this is almost entirely imported. Especially butyl, required to make tubes, is a major category in these special purpose synthetic rubber imports. Prices of synthetic rubber in general move above natural rubber prices (see  below). Prices of synthetic rubber are, however, administrative prices that protect local producers.

Reclaimed rubber, a type of rubber that is peculiar to India and a few other Asian countries, completes the domestic supply of rubber in India. Reclaimed rubber is obtained from scrap rubber from tires, other wastes of rubber products, or wastes of manufacturing of rubber products. Quality is considered low compared to synthetic and natural rubber, but so is the price. Annual production has varied between 7.2% (1960-61) and 14.3% (1978-79) of total domestic production and annual consumption between 8.9% (1960-61) and 11.4% (1978-79) of total consumption. In Figures 2.5 and 2.6 the development of production and consumption of reclaimed rubber absolute and relative to natural and synthetic is shown.

The dominant position of natural rubber relative to synthetic rubber, both in production and in consumption, is typical to India, and contrary to the situation on the world-market. While on the world market synthetic rubber covers 60 to 70% of the market with the remaining share for natural rubber, in India natural rubber covers 60 to 70% of the domestic market with the remaining share for

---

10    Synthetic rubber is usually produced with nafta as basic input.
11    General purpose synthetic rubber contain styrene butadiene (SBR) and poly butadiene (PB). Special purpose synthetic rubber contain butyl, nitrile, EPDM, polychloroprene and some quantitatively less important types. The economic significance of this distinction is that general purpose rubber is a close substitute to most grades of natural rubber, while special purpose synthetic rubber is not.

**Figure 2.5**    Production of rubber: natural (NR), synthetic (SR), reclaimed (RR)

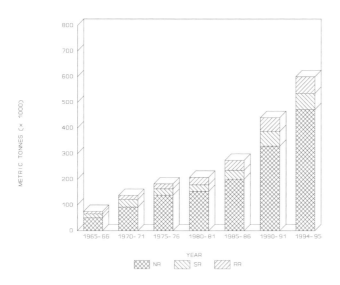

Source:    Indian Rubber Statistics, various issues.

**Figure 2.6**    Consumption of rubber: natural(NR), synthetic(SR), reclaimed(RR)

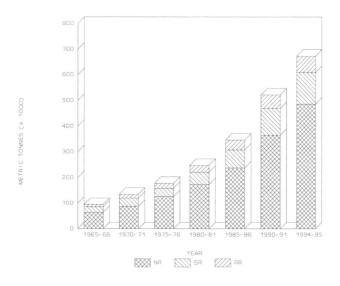

Source:    Indian Rubber Statistics, various issues

synthetic and reclaimed rubber. This is partly due to a deliberate policy of the government to increase the production capacity of natural rubber with only a marginal role for synthetic rubber. The low capital requirements of natural rubber production, its low production costs and large employment opportunities are just a few arguments brought forward to defend this policy. The differences in relative shares are also an indication of the extent that the Indian natural rubber market can be considered as a closed market (see also Section 2.5 and 2.6): with free trade the shares in India would be closer to the ones on the world market. This also suggests a direction of development with increasing trade liberalization.

India has a modest but increasing world market share of natural rubber production,[12] gradually increasing from 2.1% in 1965, 4.0% in 1975, 4.5% in 1985 to 8.5% in 1995. These figures, however, should not be seen as an indication of India's position in natural rubber on the world market: until the beginning of the 1990s the Indian natural rubber market was completely oriented towards the domestic economy. This reflects a longstanding policy of the Indian government to promote domestic production of natural rubber to meet domestic rubber demand completely. This policy was supplemented by restrictions with respect to foreign trade. Foreign transactions required a license and, especially in times of scarcity of foreign exchange, this created a barrier to imports. As in almost all international commodity markets, India's position in natural rubber on the world market until the beginning of the 1990s was negligible, largely because of the deliberate isolation from the world market (see also Section 2.5 and 2.6).

## 2.3    Consumption

The policy to become self supporting in the total requirements of rubber by promoting domestic production of natural rubber has resulted in a situation in which domestic supply is almost balanced with domestic demand. With negligible exports during the period 1965-1995, it is observed from Figure 2.7 that by far the bigger part of domestic consumption of natural rubber is supplied by domestic producers.[13] Average consumption of natural rubber is around 10% higher than production. Consumption of natural rubber exceeds production at most by around 20% (annual basis).

---

12     Source: Statistical Bulletin, International Rubber Study Group, various issues.
13     Small amounts of natural rubber have been exported in the period 1973-1978 and 1991-1996, in particular in 1973-74 2700 metric tonnes (mt), 74-75 350 mt, 76-77 12296 mt, 78-79 11078 mt, 91-92 5834 mt, 92-93 5999 mt, 93-94 186 mt, 94-95 1961 mt.

**Figure 2.7**     Aggregate production, consumption and import of natural rubber

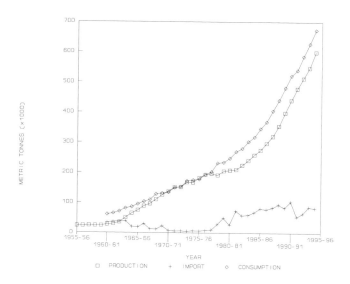

Source:     Indian Rubber Statistics, various issues.

Natural rubber is 'consumed' by manufacturers of rubber products. This manufacturing industry contains in more than one respect a wide range of production units. The distribution of consumption of rubber by end-product averaged over a number of years is shown in Table 2.2. The left-hand side of the table shows consumption of natural (NR), synthetic (SR) and reclaimed rubber (RR) by end-product, as a percentage of total consumption of these types of rubber. By far the largest share of natural rubber is consumed by tire and tube manufacturers. Tire and tube manufacturers, classified by the first three end-products (automobile tires and tubes (ATT), cycle tires and tubes (CTT) and camel back[14] (CB)), account for 65% of total consumption. The remaining share of consumption is due to manufacturers of a wide range of rubber products, including footwear, belts and hoses, latex foam and dipped goods,[15] battery boxes and cables and wires. For most of these categories the shares remain more or less the same over time, indicating a growth alongside the growth of aggregate consumption. An exception to this is latex foam and dipped goods that experience an increasing share. The right-hand side of Table 2.2 shows the share of the different types of rubber (NR,

---

14     Camel back is the material used in retreading old tires.
15     Dipped goods are, for example, condoms and surgical gloves.

SR and RR) in total rubber used in manufacturing the end-product. From the table it is observed that natural, synthetic and reclaimed rubber is used in end-products, on average, in the proportions 70/20/10. Over time there are only marginal shifts in these shares. In specific cases end-products are manufactured using rather diverging proportions of rubber input: latex foam and dipped goods are made entirely of natural rubber; battery boxes have a high content of reclaimed rubber. Manufacturers can shift to synthetic rubber to the extent that the technical requirements of the product allow such a shift. In the manufacturing of tires such a shift is easily implemented. However, the price of domestic synthetic rubber relative to domestic natural rubber usually do not make this a serious option (see Figure 2.8). The use of reclaimed rubber seems economically attractive. Prices of reclaimed rubber are only a fraction of natural rubber prices (between 23% and 31%). However, in a large number of applications use of reclaimed rubber deteriorates the quality of the product, and reclaimed rubber is for this reason only a marginal component of supply. Also irregular and low supply of uncertain quality add to this situation.

**Table 2.2**    Consumption of rubber by end-product
(averages over 1975/76-1994/95)

| | (in % of total NR, SR and RR) | | | | (in % of total rubber by end-product) | | | |
|---|---|---|---|---|---|---|---|---|
| | NR | SR | RR | Total | NR | SR | RR | Total |
| ATT | 46.3 | 53.2 | 18.6 | 44.6 | 73.3 | 22.5 | 4.2 | 100 |
| CTT | 12.4 | 11.1 | 29.4 | 13.8 | 63.4 | 15.2 | 21.3 | 100 |
| CB | 5.8 | 5.4 | 6.9 | 5.8 | 70.4 | 17.7 | 11.9 | 100 |
| FW | 12.9 | 15.3 | 12.5 | 13.6 | 65.1 | 24.2 | 10.7 | 100 |
| BH | 6.7 | 6.0 | 7.1 | 6.5 | 71.9 | 17.2 | 10.9 | 100 |
| LF | 4.4 | - | - | 3.1 | 100 | - | - | 100 |
| CW | 0.4 | 1.0 | 0.9 | 0.5 | 47.5 | 36.0 | 16.5 | 100 |
| BB | 0.3 | 1.7 | 14.5 | 2.0 | 11.1 | 16.4 | 72.4 | 100 |
| DG | 3.7 | - | - | 2.6 | 100 | - | - | 100 |
| Oth | 7.2 | 6.3 | 10.1 | 7.3 | 69.6 | 16.3 | 14.1 | 100 |
| Total | 100 | 100 | 100 | 100 | 71.0 | 18.9 | 10.1 | 100 |

ATT = automobile tires and tubes; CTT = cycle tires and tubes; CB = camel back; FW = footwear; BH = belts and hoses; LF = Latex Foam; CW = cables and wires; BB = battery boxes; DG = dipped goods; Oth = other;
Source:        Indian Rubber Statistics, various issues

The total number of manufacturers of rubber products has grown from 1844 in 1975/76, to 3769 in 1985/86 and to 5408 in 1994-95. In Table 2.3 the size distribution of the rubber products manufacturing industry is summarized. From the table a highly skewed distribution is apparent: 80 to 90% of the smallest manufacturing units consume 10-15% of total natural rubber, while less than one percent of the largest manufacturing units consume 60-65% of total natural rubber. The 80-90% smallest units in the manufacturers each use less than 50 tonnes annually. The largest firms use more than 1000 tonnes annually. Apart from a few big tire companies, the rubber products manufacturing sector consists mainly of small-scale firms.

**Figure 2.8**    Domestic price of synthetic rubber (SBR,PB) relative to natural rubber (RMA4)

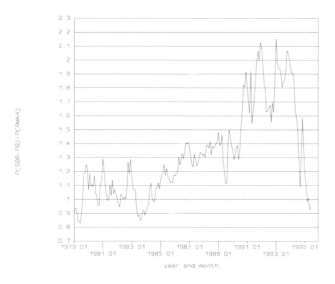

Source:        Indian Rubber Statistics, various issues;

Price development of a number of rubber products are known: for the period 1970-71 to 1994-95 average annual price increase was 7.7% for tires an tubes, 6.7% for camel back, 5.1% for rubber and plastic products (shoes), 9.0% for rubber belting and 9.1% for hoses. It should be noted  that natural rubber prices increased 9.4% during that period, and the general consumer price index 5.1%. Fluctuations of prices of rubber products over time (not shown) suggest that increases in natural rubber price are passed on to consumers of rubber products.

Growth rates of prices of rubber products are non-negative and, not surprisingly, much less volatile than prices of natural rubber itself.

**Table 2.3**    Distribution of manufacturers according to their total consumption of rubber

| $cns_i$ in metric tonnes | 1975-76 | | | 1985-86 | | | 1994-95 | | |
|---|---|---|---|---|---|---|---|---|---|
| | No's | NR | T | No's | NR | T | No's | NR | T |
| 0-10 | 59.5 | 4.1 | 3.5 | 51.9 | 3.3 | 2.9 | 41.8 | 2.2 | 2.1 |
| 10-50 | 27.3 | 9.6 | 8.4 | 35.0 | 10.9 | 9.8 | 39.8 | 9.4 | 9.0 |
| 50-100 | 7.3 | 7.3 | 6.4 | 6.4 | 6.0 | 6.5 | 8.9 | 6.2 | 6.2 |
| 100-500 | 4.6 | 10.7 | 10.8 | 5.3 | 13.8 | 14.8 | 7.7 | 12.8 | 15.4 |
| 500-1000 | 0.5 | 3.8 | 4.0 | 0.6 | 3.5 | 4.5 | 0.9 | 5.7 | 5.3 |
| >1000 | 0.8 | 64.4 | 66.8 | 0.9 | 62.4 | 61.5 | 0.9 | 63.7 | 61.9 |

$cns_i$ = average consumption of rubber per manufacturer of rubber products; no's = number of manufacturers as a percentage of total number of manufacturers; NR = consumption of natural rubber as a percentage of total natural rubber consumption; T = consumption of all types of rubber (including synthetic and reclaimed rubber) as a percentage of total of all types of rubber.
Source:        Indian Rubber Statistics, various issues

## 2.4    Domestic trade and stockholding

Next to production and consumption, another economic activity in this market is worth mentioning, and, in fact, of particular interest to price formation in specific commodity markets. This activity is trading and stockholding. In the Indian economic policy debate these activities do not always get the credit that they deserve. Promoting trade or stockholding, in some way or another, is seldom considered as a target of official policy. This is partly because arbitrage (both inter-temporal and intra-regional), one of the means of existence of traders and dealers, has a rather negative connotation in the Indian economy. Arbitrage, somewhat less neutrally referred to as speculation, is regarded as non-productive and profiteering. Nevertheless, by transferring supply from low demand periods to high demand periods, inter-temporal arbitrage mitigates price fluctuations, and, under some conditions, income fluctuations. For this reason arbitrage activities of traders and stockholders in commodity markets can be highly attractive to both producers and consumers. In Chapter 5 it will be shown that the arbitrage activities of private dealers are especially effective in stabilizing prices, and most likely much more effective than interventions.

Stockholding activities are performed on either side of the market: both growers of natural rubber and manufacturers of rubber goods have stocks and are engaged in arbitrage activities, as a supplementary activity next to their main business. Of course, there is also a group of genuine dealers, that earns an income from arbitrage. In the Indian natural rubber market a dealer is specified as a person who has taken out a license from the Rubber Board of India for dealing in natural rubber or holding stocks of natural rubber. Under the Rubber Act all dealers of natural rubber and all manufacturers of rubber goods (the consumers of natural rubber) should acquire a license from the Rubber Board. Dealers can be classified in three categories (see Krishnan Kutty (1985)): village level primary dealers, intermediary dealers and wholesale dealers. Village level primary dealers purchase a major share of small holders' natural rubber and sell it mostly to intermediary dealers. Intermediary dealers operate in bigger trading centres and purchase both from smallholders as well as from village level primary dealers. They sell to wholesale dealers and manufacturers of rubber products. Wholesale dealers purchase from dealers, but also from large estates, and sell to manufacturers or their agents. Some large growers sell their natural rubber directly to manufacturers. In 1971 the Kerala State Co-operative Rubber Marketing Federation Ltd. was registered as an apex institution of the primary Rubber Marketing Co-operative Societies and has become the largest single dealer in India, with a share of 14% of all sales in 1994-95 (see Tharian George and Thomas (1997)). Through its members natural rubber is purchased from smallholders. The number of societies has grown from 11 in 1965-66, to 37 in the late 1970s and has stabilized to a level of 33 at the start of the 1990s. The coverage of the societies has grown from 706 rubber growers in 1965-66 to more than 100,000 at present (approximately 23% of all smallholdings). The Federation also runs a number of processing factories, that aim at value addition through higher quality grades. It has also been acting as a procurement agency for the Government of India through the State Trading Corporation (STC, see Section 2.6). All efforts of co-operative societies aim at realizing a larger share of the value of natural rubber production for small rubber growers: the reduction in trade margins of dealers and the acceptance of smallholders' rubber sheets as graded sheets are argued to contribute to this aim (see Tharian George and Thomas (1997), see also below).

The number of licensed dealers increased from 608 in 1965-66 to 8295 in

1994-95, an almost fourteen-fold increase. The total purchased quantities by licensed dealers increased from 87,518 tonnes in 1965-66 to 879,159 tonnes in 1994-95, a ten-fold increase. Due to the structure of the trading business it is impossible to relate these figures to aggregate consumption or production. In Table 2.4 the distribution of licensed dealers according to their purchase is summarized. It is observed that around 50% of the smallest licensed dealers account for less than 5% of the purchases, and 5% of the largest licensed dealers account for around 50% of the purchases. Like the structure of the manufacturers side, the structure of (genuine) trade is also highly skewed.

**Table 2.4**      Distribution of numbers of licensed dealers (left) and of total
            purchased quantities by size of annual purchase (right)
            period[*]: 65/66-94/95

| purchases in tonnes | numbers in % of total | purchased quantities in % of total |
|---|---|---|
| 0-10 | 44.0 | 2.1 |
| 10-25 | 13.7 | 2.2 |
| 25-50 | 12.1 | 4.0 |
| 50-100 | 9.5 | 6.4 |
| 100-250 | 10.2 | 15.8 |
| 250-500 | 4.8 | 15.8 |
| 500-1000 | 3.2 | 20.9 |
| >1000 | 2.6 | 32.8 |

*      To calculate averages over 10 year periods only a limited number of annual observations are available (see Indian Rubber Statistics, Vol.21, 1996, T40), namely 65/66 and 70/71 for the period 65/66-74/75; 75/76 to 78/79, 81/82 and 83/84 for the period 75/76-84/85; and 85/86, 87/88, 91/92 and 94/95 for the period 85/86-94/95.
Source:      Indian Rubber Statistics, various issues.

Costs for traders are storage costs, interest costs (either opportunity costs or credit costs), and deterioration costs. Little is known about storage costs: around Rs 2000 (1989 prices) per metric tonne per annum is mentioned by representatives of trade organizations: elsewhere a figure of Rs 2500 is mentioned (cf. 'News and Notes', Rubber Chemical Review, May 1989). Such storage costs correspond to around 1% of average price on a monthly basis. Real interest cost, calculated by deflating the commercial lending rate (source: IMF/IFS) with the consumer price index, moved from 0.1% to 1.0% on a monthly basis with an average of 0.5%. No information is available on deterioration of natural rubber stocks: deterioration seems to be of negligible importance in case of natural rubber, at least for periods shorter than 6 months.

If dealers are assumed to have natural rubber, on average, three months in stock,[16] and if dealers are assumed to be successful in purchasing low and selling high, the average premium of arbitrage can be calculated. This premium is, in real terms and after subtraction of costs, around 3% per three months and fluctuates from practically zero to above 10%. Next to offering processing services (smoking of rubber sheets, a treatment for the conservation of natural rubber), dealers also earn income from grading of natural rubber, especially because the grading standards are not particularly clear and large quantities are purchased as ungraded.[17] In Figure 2.19 (Section 2.5) premiums in constant prices on different grades of natural rubber are shown.[18] From the figure it is observed that the highest quality grade (RMA1), has a grading premium of between 4% and 7%. The decrease in these premiums over time is explained by the marketing activities of the cooperative societies: a study conducted by the Rubber Board of India (see Sree Kumar *et al.* (1990)) showed that premiums of good quality sheets of natural rubber all contributed to the income of dealers (see also Krishnan Kutty (1985)). Competitiveness among dealers was considered insufficient to guarantee that growers would reap the benefits of producing higher quality grades. To overcome this problem and to promote quality awareness of farmers, direct trade between manufacturers of rubber products and the growers, through the intermediation of the Rubber Marketing Co-operative Societies has been arranged. This turned out to have created lasting trade relationships. However, next to this explanation, also the increasing number of dealers, assuming increased competitiveness among dealers for trade income, could explain the declining margins.

---

16    Communications with local dealers and their representative organisations (eg. the Kerala State Cooperative Rubber Marketing Federation Ltd.) confirm such a timing of arbitrage activities.

17    Dealers have an incentive to downgrade smallholders' natural rubber in order to make their purchases cheaper and to increase their margins. This is supported by survey data on the grade-wise distribution of sales and purchases of dealers (see Krishnan Kutty (1985)).

18    Premiums are calculated by relating prices of different grades (RMA1 to RMA5) to prices of ungraded natural rubber, deflating these with a consumer price index, and compute twelve months moving averages.

Data that are only related to dealers give a partial impression of stockholding in the market, as noted already at the start of this section. A large part of arbitrage activities is performed by producers and consumers themselves. In the available data on stockholding, a distinction is made between stockholding by growers and dealers on the one hand, and stockholding by manufacturers on the other hand. Additionally there are also data on stocks at the State Trading Corporation (STC). In Figures 2.9 and 2.10 the development of private sector stocks over time is shown. From the data it is calculated that stocks at growers and dealers are, averaged over the whole period, one and a half times as high as stocks at manufacturers, with the exception of the period 1975 to 1978 when stocks at growers and dealers were almost two and a half times as high. Stocks at growers and dealers seem to grow trend-wise over time, with a structural break in 1978. Stocks at manufacturers show a comparable trend-wise development, but with a slower pace and with structural breaks in 1974-75 and 1978-79.

In Figures 2.11 and 2.12 stocks, measured at the end of each month, are related to annual consumption, in order to control for trend-wise developments. It is calculated that stocks at growers and dealers never fall below 5.2% of annual consumption and are, averaged over the whole period, 13.3 % of annual consumption. The period from 1978 onward shows regular fluctuations and seems to be without structural changes. Erratic fluctuations are observed in the period before 1978. Comparable observations can be made with respect to stocks at manufacturers: stocks never fall below 3.3% of annual consumption and, averaged over the whole period, these stocks are 10.7% of annual consumption. Until 1974-75 the developments are slightly erratic, but from 1975 onwards a more stationary pattern arises that shows a marginal trend-wise decrease over the years: apparently there was less reason to keep stocks in a constant share to consumption. Total private stocks, the sum of stocks at growers and dealers and stocks at manufacturers, never fall below 9.5% of annual consumption and are on average 24.1% of annual consumption.

Regime shifts can have a substantial impact on the underlying behaviour of economic agents. Such shifts should be identified in order to incorporate them into the formal analysis, or to adjust the period considered in the empirical analysis. A number of regime shifts and their possible causes can be observed directly from data.

A first development that might have caused a structural break is the shift of being self-supporting in natural rubber to becoming a net importer/exporter. The intuition of such a shift runs as follows: private stockholders will argue that the uncertainty of and delays in filling the gap between domestic supply and

**Figure 2.9** Stockholding by growers and dealers

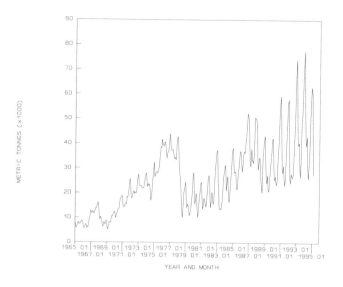

Source: Indian Rubber Statistics, various issues

**Figure 2.10** Stockholding by manufacturers

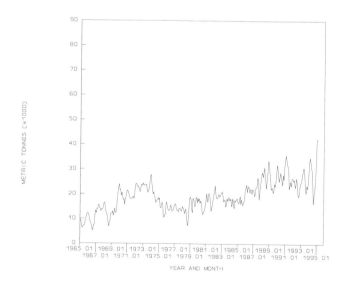

Source: Indian Rubber Statistics, various issues

**Figure 2.11**   Stockholding by growers and dealers relative to consumption

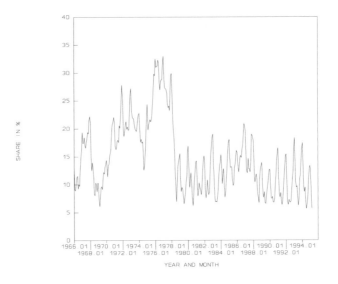

Source:            Indian Rubber Statistics, various issues

**Figure 2.12**   Stockholding by manufacturers in % of annual consumption

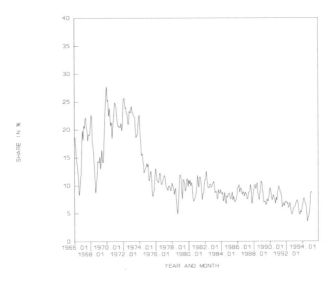

Source:            Indian Rubber Statistics, various issues

demand by imports by the government agency that is in charge of imports (see Section 2.6), creates an effective shortage in the domestic market and this will push up prices. Genuine traders will become hesitant to tie up funds in stocks with more uncertainty on price formation. On the demand side the same uncertainty might induce higher stocks to secure input. From Figures 2.13, 2.14 and 2.15 it is observed that stocks and, not surprisingly, also prices react heavily to the net external position. From 1978 onwards, when India has become a net importer, stockholding by growers and dealers falls to a structurally lower level, while the opposite occurs on the manufacturing side of the market, where stockholding experiences a, somewhat smaller, upward jump to a structurally higher level.

If world market prices rise above or fall below domestic prices, a similar type of shift might be identified. The reasoning is as follows: the STC might be reluctant to import natural rubber if this activity is at a loss. Private stockholders might anticipate to such a change in behaviour: their reaction could be either way depending on the type of stockholder. Although there are a few periods in which world market prices are above domestic prices (1974 (due to the first oil crisis), 1976-77, 1980 (due to the second oil crises), 1993-94; see Figure 2.21) this does not correspond clearly with shifts in stocks. A similar type of exogenous impact on behaviour of domestic private stockholders might be due to the foreign reserve position of India. Import of natural rubber could be restricted in periods of severe shortages of foreign reserves. Such shortages are only known to have occurred at the end of the 1980s and the beginning of the 1990s (see Section 2.6) with a real crisis in 1991. It seems most likely that the foreign reserve position and the priorities of the central government in allocating these reserves for imports, must have an impact on import that goes beyond these crises. However, purely on the basis of visual inspection of the time series available it is difficult to detect any impact of this crisis on the behaviour of private stockholders.

Finally, changes in agreements with respect to desired stockholding by different groups might have caused breaks. Operational stocks are held in India according to norms that are agreed upon between consumers, producers, dealers and the STC (see National Council of Applied Economic Research (1980)). Until 1974 operational stocks held by growers and dealers were equivalent to six weeks of total Indian consumption (three weeks held by growers and three weeks held by dealers), and by manufacturers eight weeks of total Indian consumption. Following the acceptance of the Tandon Committee Report on Bank Credit in 1975 the total stock norm was reduced to 12 weeks (from 16 weeks), to be distributed in such a way that four weeks of stocks should be held by growers and

**Figure 2.13**    Stocks at growers and dealers (upper line) and import (lower line)

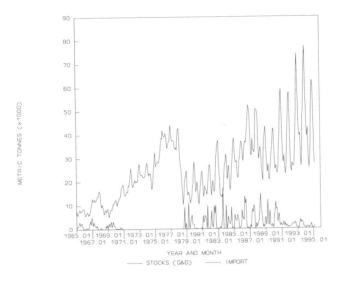

Source:               Indian Rubber Statistics, various issues

**Figure 2.14**    Stocks at manufacturers (upper line) and import (lower line)

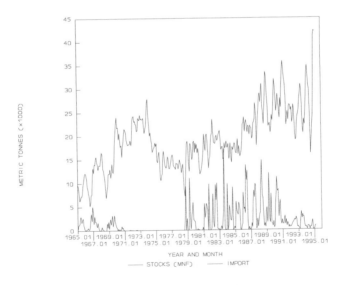

Source:               Indian Rubber Statistics, various issues

**Figure 2.15**

Domestic price of natural rubber (RMA4, upper line) and stocks at growers and dealers (lower line); scales for the two lines are different.

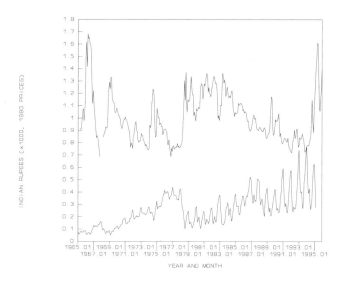

Source:         Indian Rubber Statistics, various issues

dealers. The major rubber consumers agreed to bring down stocks held by manufacturers to six weeks.[19] It should be noted that these agreements are not binding: it is by no means an official policy that is enforced by the government and stockholders can be assumed to be free in making there inter-temporal choices in buying and selling stocks.

In Figures 2.16 and 2.17 the level of stocks implied by the above agreements is plotted with symbols together with actual stocks. Stocks at growers and dealers seem to follow a rather independent path and do not seem to be affected by these agreements. However, the downward jump in stocks at manufacturers in 1974-75 does coincide with the change in desired stocks. It should be noted that stocks at manufacturers diverge dramatically from desired stocks from the end of

---

19    The All India Rubber Industries Association, an organisation representing small manufacturers, did not agree with this norm. In its turn it recommended a total stock norm of 18 weeks, with a 10 weeks stock held by growers and dealers (five weeks held by growers and five weeks held by dealers), and a 4 weeks stock held by manufacturers of rubber products.

**Figure 2.16** Stocks at growers & dealers and agreements on desired stockholding

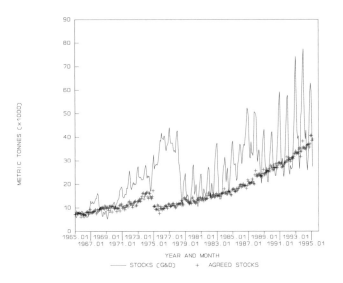

Source:          Indian Rubber Statistics, various issues

**Figure 2.17**   Stocks at manufacturers and agreements on desired stockholding

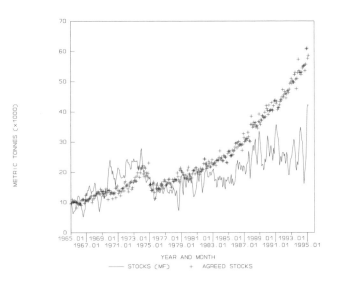

Source:          Indian Rubber Statistics, various issues

the 1980s onwards, while stocks at growers an dealers more or less follow the trend. In summary, it seems sensible in view of the identified breaks to use both time series in the empirical work only from 1979 onwards. It seems also sensible to regard the period from 1990-91 onwards separately, as from then onwards a more liberalized trade policy has been set in.

## 2.5    Prices

Natural rubber in India is sold on the market in a number of grades. Until 1995-96 quality grades of natural rubber were specified as RMA1 to RMA5, with quality becoming less the higher the grade number. RMA grades are only used in India. From 1995-96 onwards by instruction of the Ministry of Commerce domestic grades were renamed in line with international standards: RMA1 became RSS1, RMA2 became RSS2 etc. RSS (Ribbed Smoked Sheets) grades and are a common quality denominator on the world market. Higher grades carry higher premiums as has been shown in Figure 2.18: the highest grade is around 4% more expensive compared to ungraded natural rubber. On average the prices of different grades gradually move towards each other over time.

**Figure 2.18**   Price differences of grades of natural rubber (RMA1-RMA5) relative to ungraded natural rubber in constant prices (RMA1 is the highest line; RMA2 the second highest, etc.)

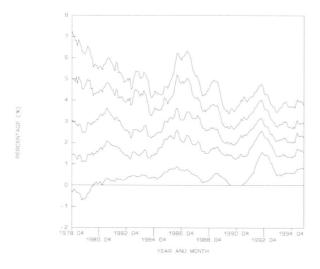

Source:         Indian Rubber Statistics and International Financial Statistics

**Figure 2.19**  Domestic price of natural rubber (RMA4/RSS4)

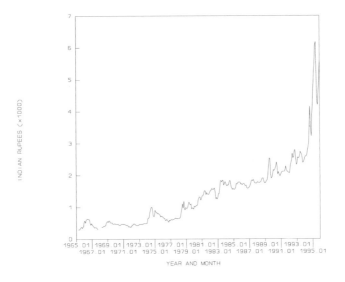

Source:    Indian Rubber Statistics, various issues

**Figure 2.20**  Domestic price of natural rubber (RMA4/RSS4; constant prices)

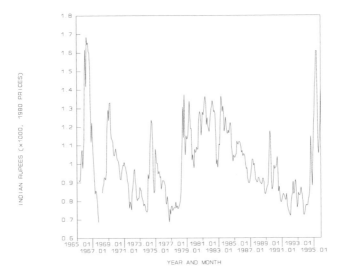

Source:    Indian Rubber Statistics, various issues;
           International Financial Statistics

By far the most common grade in terms of the volume of domestic production is RMA4/RSS4. Prices of RMA4, both nominal and real (1980 constant prices) are shown in Figures 2.19 and 2.20. Nominal prices show a slowly upward trend. Prices increase tremendously in the years 1994 and 1995. After deflating it is apparent to what extent this trend-wise increase in nominal prices holds out: during the 1980s and the beginning of the 1990s there is a trend-wise decrease in prices. The attractiveness of growing natural rubber is presumably not due to the development in real price, but much more to increases in yield (see also Section 2.2). The peak in price development in 1994 and 1995 still shows in terms of real prices.

From the perspective of price stabilization it is interesting to obtain insight into the variation in natural rubber prices, compared to those of other commodities, and between different sub-periods. To this end coefficients of variation of domestic price of natural rubber for a number of periods have been calculated, and of world market prices of a number of commodities. The outcome is presented in Table 2.5. From the table it is observed that volatility of domestic natural rubber prices compares reasonably well with volatility of international commodity prices: in nominal terms it is between the highest coefficient of variation (CV) of sugar and the lowest of rubber. Over time there is considerable fluctuation in the volatility. In Chapter 5 a more detailed analysis of the volatility of domestic prices is presented in view of a price band scheme (Buffer Stocking Scheme) that has been in operation during a part of the period under consideration.

**Table 2.5a**    Coefficient of variation[*] of Indian natural rubber prices

| period | nominal | real |
|---|---|---|
| 1979.01-1994.12 | 29.3 | 16.9 |
| 1965.01-1970.12 | 18.9 | 21.7 |
| 1971.01-1978.08 | 27.2 | 14.4 |
| 1978.09-1984.03 | 20.2 | 8.8 |
| 1984.04-1988.03 | 5.0 | 8.7 |
| 1988.04-1990.12 | 10.7 | 9.5 |
| 1990.12-1995.12 | 36.5 | 24.1 |

Source:        Indian Rubber statistics, various issues;
               International Financial Statistics, IMF;

**Table 2.5b**   Coefficient of variation of nominal international commodity prices,
                 79.01-94.12

| commodity | CV | commodity | CV |
|---|---|---|---|
| coffee | 39.8 | sugar | 53.9 |
| cocoa | 41.1 | natural rubber | 20.6 |
| tea | 33.5 | palm oil | 31.3 |

* the coefficient of variation CV(x) is computed as: $CV(x)=\sqrt{[VAR(x)/(AVG(x))^2]}$

Source: UNCTAD, Monthly Commodity Price Bulletin, various issues

In Figure 2.21 the development of the Indian natural rubber price (RMA4) is presented relative to the world market price of natural rubber (RSS1, Singapore) and in Figure 2.22 relative to synthetic rubber (SBR export unit values, Japan). From these figures it is observed that during large parts of the period under consideration, the world market price of both natural rubber and synthetic rubber are below prices of domestically produced natural rubber. Inspection of the Figure 2.22 suggests that world market prices of RSS3 and SBR move rather independently from prices of domestically produced RMA4. Granger causality tests on the relationship between nominal domestic (RMA4) and world-market prices (RSS3, Singapore and SBR export values, respectively) over the period 1965-1990, in differences and with a lag varying from one to thirty six months, indicate that the null-hypothesis of non-causality can never be rejected.

As domestic prices of natural rubber will follow world market prices without government intervention, the relatively independent price development in the Indian natural rubber market until the beginning of the 1990s requires an explanation. There is some scope for independent price formation[20] with supply and demand of comparable size for a large number of years. However, there is a much more pervasive factor that causes independent price formation. India has a long tradition of insulating its domestic market from the world market through administrative barriers (eg. licensing, foreign currency requirements) and effectively implemented this policy until the beginning of the 1990s (see Joshi and Little (1994)).[21] Import licensing, foreign exchange shortages, and the monopolization of imports through the STC, have effectively insulated the Indian rubber economy from the world market. Substantially different NR/SR shares in con-

---

20    If domestic supply continuously straddles the point at which domestic supply is equal to demand, domestic prices should not necessarily follow world market prices.
21    A detailed assessment of the organisation of imports is given in Section 2.6.

**Figure 2.21** Domestic price of natural rubber (RMA4/RSS4) relative to the world market price of natural rubber (RSS1)

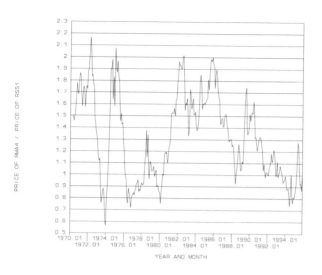

Source:       IRS, various issues; Statistical Bulletin, IRSG, various issues;

**Figure 2.22** Domestic price of natural rubber (RMA4/RSS4) relative to the world market price of synthetic rubber (Export Unit Values, Japan)

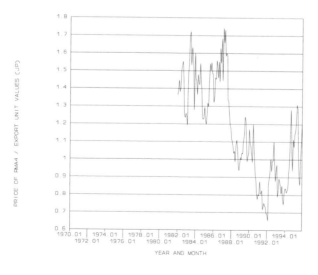

Source:       IRS, various issues; Statistical Bulletin, IRSG, various issues;

sumption between domestic and world market are just another piece of evidence that the Indian rubber market is insulated from the world market. For the above reasons we regard natural rubber in India until the beginning of the 1990s to be close to a non-traded commodity, with a price formation that is completely separated from the world market. In the beginning of the 1990s serious steps were undertaken to liberalize foreign trade. For natural rubber this has resulted in prices that move much closer to world market prices.


### 2.6    Import and price policies

The development of total import of natural rubber and the part of import bought directly by manufacturers is shown in Figure 2.23. Small amounts of rubber have been imported, except for the period 1972-77. At the end of 1968 the State Trading Corporation (STC), a public agency engaged in foreign trade transactions of a number of agricultural commodities, was brought into the natural rubber field to import natural rubber and to regulate supplies so that the gap between indigenous supply and demand could be bridged without damaging the interest of domestic producers. Initially, the STC functioned more or less as an advisory body for monitoring and regulating imports. During the period from 1970-71 to 1977-78 STC entered the domestic market and carried out price support operations including export of very small quantities as domestic supply during the period was in excess of the demand, mainly as a result of the slack in demand caused by the energy crises and strikes that adversely affected the production of natural rubber. However, from 1978-79 the country became a net importer and the STC has been authorized to import and distribute natural rubber to actual users. From the end of 1968 to 1982 the STC had a monopoly on import of natural rubber. Since 1982 a separate scheme, which is restricted to large tire and tube manufacturers, is operated for exporters of rubber goods so that these exporters are allowed to import natural rubber duty-free for manufacturing export goods, enabling them to compete in the international market. Direct imports by manufacturers only gradually gained importance and from October 1991 onwards STC stopped importing altogether (see also Figure 2.24). Licensing and import duties, however, remained even after the withdrawal of the STC from imports. Regulation of imports is treated more extensively below.

Imports of natural rubber by the STC - mainly from Malaysia, but also from Singapore, Thailand and Sri Lanka - are not directly sold on the domestic market: at times larger amounts are imported than released in the domestic market, or there is a delay of one or two months in releasing. This is observed in

**Figure 2.23**     Imports of natural rubber

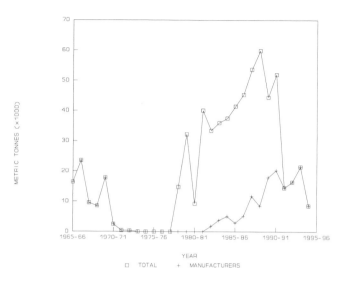

Source:              Indian Rubber Statistics, various issues.

**Figure 2.24**     Imports and releases of natural rubber by the STC

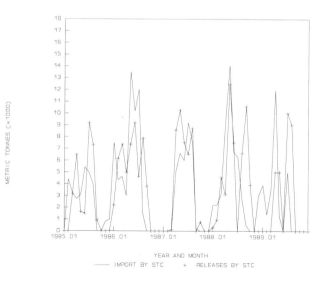

Source:              Indian Rubber Statistics, various issues.

**Figure 2.25**

Domestic price of natural rubber (RMA4, upper line) and imports (lower line)

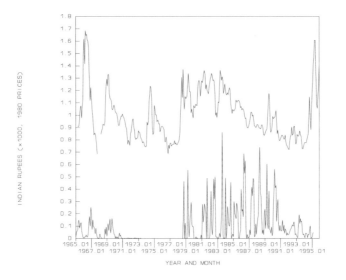

Source:          Indian Rubber Statistics, various issues

Figure 2.24. In the figure both imports and releases by the STC are plotted on a monthly basis and for a limited period (1985-86 to 1989-90). Apart from unavoidable delays, misjudgments in the required imports and statistical inaccuracies, these differences also point at possible commercial motives in timing the releases of natural rubber. In the Section 2.4 we already noted the impact of the balance of domestic supply and demand on stocks and prices. In Figure 2.25 it is shown how domestic prices of natural rubber react on imports of natural rubber. From the figure it is seen that prices move to a structurally higher level after becoming a net importer in 1978/79.

Imports are heavily regulated almost continuously during the thirty years prior to the beginning of the 1990s, with periods of severe tightening and moderate relaxation of these controls depending on, amongst other things, the foreign exchange reserves. Central to the import regulation is the import licensing system. All imports require a license. Final consumer goods are completely banned with a few minor exceptions. Intermediate goods and capital goods are divided into three categories: 'banned', 'restricted' and 'Open General License' (OGL). Even import of OGL goods is restricted to the actual user of the good. Goods are also required not to be available in the domestic market. Import regulation, in general, is supported by the actual user policy which forbids imports by intermediaries, the import monopoly for a number of goods (so-called canal-ized items) by of a number public sector agencies (so-called canalizing agencies) and, if capital goods or technology is involved, the industrial license system. Clearance for these licenses may be denied if the foreign exchanges requirements are too high (Joshi and Little (1994)).

With domestic demand continuously exceeding domestic supply it is interesting to understand how decisions on imports of natural rubber are organ-ized. From official documents (see appendix 2.2 to this chapter) it is apparent that natural rubber is a canalized item, meaning that import is entirely in the hands of a public sector agency. Activities of this public sector agency controlled by two committees, that are composed of government officials. These committees determine the actual quantity imported, (and, implicitly, the timing of these imports) and the selling price of imported natural rubber to domestic consumers. Formally, the quantity of imports may be adjusted on the basis of consultations with the domestic consumers (the Actual Users). Imports of natural rubber are also subject to the release of foreign exchange. From 1988 to 1992 the foreign exchange position of India (total reserves minus gold, source: IMF/IFS) has experienced a gradual and continuous deterioration, to reach critical levels in 1991. With a government that has extensive powers over foreign trade, the impact of the foreign reserve position on imports of natural rubber has been large, also during periods other than periods of foreign reserve crises.

In the official documents (see appendix 2.2 to this chapter) vague refer-ences are made with respect to the grounds on which decisions are, or have to be based: making use of the possibilities of bulking imports, meeting the essential requirements of some items of mass consumption and servicing the requirements of small Actual Users. It is far from clear if the suggested economies of scale are realized (Joshi and Little (1994)). These notions are also not specific enough to understand fully who supplies information for the determination of the gap between supply and demand, how this gap is calculated, at what time the imports are released and what is the basis of the selling price of these releases? It does confirm that the government has the administrative power to decide on the quantity and timing of imports and releases and on the selling prices of releases.

Observers argue that imports by the STC are highly dependent on the world market price relative to the domestic price: in the case of natural rubber the public agency will only be prepared to import whenever the world market price is below the domestic market price. Natural rubber is mainly used for tires which is considered a luxury good. Due to the type of product it is considered not necessary in view of the Central Government to keep the price low domestically at the cost of running a loss or not making a profit in the importing activity. Some simple calculations yield insight into the development of the revenues derived from the activities of the STC in the field of natural rubber (importing, releasing and procuring). Total net revenues consist of revenue from selling imported rubber in the domestic market, minus purchasing costs from imported rubber, minus costs of procuring rubber domestically and minus costs of stockholding (interest, storage and waste). Formalized we have:

total net revenue of the STC = $rls_t \cdot p_{d,t} - m_{stc,t} \cdot p_{w,t} - proc_t \cdot p_{d,t} - \gamma \cdot s_{stc,t}$

where

| | | |
|---|---|---|
| $rls_t$ | = | releases by the STC to the domestic market; |
| $p_{d,t}$ | = | price of NR on domestic market; |
| $m_{stc,t}$ | = | imports by STC; |
| $p_{w,t}$ | = | price of NR on world market in Indian Rupees; |
| $proc_t$ | = | procurement by STC; |
| $s_{stc,t}$ | = | stocks held by STC |
| $\gamma$ | = | costs of stockholding per metric ton[22] |

From Table 2.6 we observe that on the whole the natural rubber activities of the STC are relatively profitable. However, profitability dropped at the end of the 1980s: the calculations indicate losses in 1988 and 1991. Causes for this decline in profitability are the decrease in the difference between domestic and world market prices (see Figure 2.21): in June 1988 and October 1991 world market prices are even higher than the domestic price; But also the size of the stocks have contributed to this development: before 1986 stocks at the STC have been moderate, but since the inception of the Buffer Stocking Scheme (BSS) these stocks were growing steadily, reaching quite substantial sizes between 1988 and 1991 (see Figure 2.29). However, in general the costs of holding these stocks are moderate and can easily be offset when domestic prices are higher than international prices. The development of net revenue and the withdrawal from import activities (1988/89) indeed suggest that potential profitability of importing plays a role in the steps taken by the STC. The establishment of the STC, import licensing, and foreign exchange shortages have effectively isolated the Indian

---

22      In the calculations we have assumed a Rs 2000 costs of stockholding per metric tonne per annum in 1989, which is a rather conservative estimate: elsewhere a figure of Rs 2500 is mentioned (cf. 'News and Notes', Rubber Chemical Review, May 1989).

rubber economy from the world market and this has ensured that domestic pricing and distribution is subject to government discretion.

**Table 2.6**     Total net revenue of the STC on an annual basis
(as a percentage of the value of annual imports)

| 81 | 82 | 83 | 84 | 85 | 86 | 87 | 88 | 89 | 90 | 91 |
|------|------|------|------|------|------|------|------|------|------|------|
| 27.2 | 37.7 | 43.5 | 22.4 | 38.5 | 27.0 | 33.0 | -4.2 | 18.6 | 8.1 | -47.0 |

Source:          own calculations

The central government attempts to control prices of a range of commodities (some 55 major commodities of the wholesale price index comprising 350 commodities, with a weight of 30.85%, see Joshi and Little (1994)). Fully administered items include petroleum products, coal, electricity, fertilizers, iron and steel, nonferrous metals, drugs and medicines, paper and newsprint. Partially administered explicitly under a dual pricing scheme in which the existence of a free market is officially and equally recognized include rice, wheat, sugar, vanaspati and cement. Objectives of these administered price policies are to provide poor groups with basic necessities, to provide key inputs for the development process at low prices, to encourage the use of certain commodities such as fertilizers, and to control inflation. The basic objective of price and distribution controls in agriculture is not to even out price fluctuations but to provide food cheaply to low income consumers and to provide incentives to farmers. This last objective has apparently played a major role in the natural rubber market.

The domestic price of natural rubber in India was statutorily controlled by the government from May 1942 to September 1981 with a short break of about 15 months from October 1946. Minimum and maximum prices were calculated on the basis of studies on costs of production and are revised regularly.[23] Officially the policy is intended to serve two goals. Prices should provide:

'*..incentives to the producers to expand and modernize cultivation and production of natural rubber and be fair to manufacturers of rubber products*'.

From September 1981 to February 1986 there was no effective control on the domestic price of natural rubber. STC operations were thought to be sufficient to regulate the prices, but the market price fluctuated sharply during 1981-83 due to (at times) inadequate imports and (at times) excess imports, and unexpected

---

23     In some issues of the Indian Rubber Statistics summary statistics are presented on the 'Structure of Notified Price of RMA1 Grade Rubber' in the past.

variations in production due to climatic changes. There was a conflict of opinions among the rubber growers and the rubber users with respect to the demand-supply gap and the reasonable price of natural rubber. It was felt that it would no longer be possible to ensure stability in natural rubber prices based on releases of imported natural rubber during the lean season alone. Accordingly in February 1986 a Buffer Stocking Scheme was introduced on a pilot basis to ensure the stability of the market price of natural rubber so that rubber producers could be assured of a reasonable return on their investment and rubber goods manufacturers of an adequate supply at a reasonable price. Features of the scheme are:

*fixation of the bench mark price for natural rubber on the basis of the cost of production (and this bench mark price is revised every now and then);*

*lower and upper trigger price level fixed at Rs. 30 per 100 kg. below and above the bench mark price;*

*the STC enters the market when the market indicator price of natural rubber (=15 days moving average daily price) falls below the lower trigger price level and releases natural rubber when the market indicator price is above the upper trigger price level;*

*the market intervention by the STC should ensure that the price of natural rubber does not fall below the floor price or exceeds the ceiling price. These prices are fixed at Rs. 50 per 100 kg. above and below the bench mark price;*

*the buffer stock should at least contain 2500 tonnes at any time; This minimum requirement should be drawn down at the beginning of peak season.*

The STC carried out procurement practices of natural rubber to support prices during peak production periods in 1986, 1988, 1991 and 1992 and released natural rubber to the user industry in all the years in the lean season to arrest the upward price trend. In Figure 2.26 the development of the minimum and maximum price when operational and the market price is shown.

Although no participant in the Indian natural rubber market would deny the existence of the Buffer Stocking Scheme (BSS) from 1986 onwards, we were unable to get hold of an official document, issued by the Central Government with details on the operating rules of this scheme other than the statistical publication of the Rubber Board of India, the Indian Rubber Statistics (IRS). The Rubber Board of India, Ministry of Commerce, Government of India has a range of formal responsibilities and objectives.[24] In practice the Rubber Board provides

---

24    The following text appears in one of the first pages of each volume of Indian Rubber Statistics:

**Figure 2.26**   Domestic price, maximum and minimum prices (BSS)

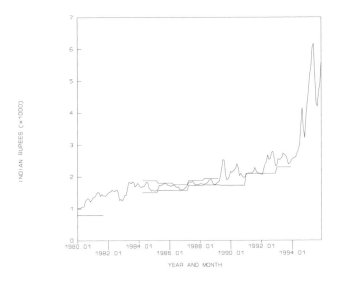

Source:          Indian Rubber Statistics, various issues; State Trading Corporation.

facilities to producers in the field of research, it mediates between supply and demand, settles their conflicting interests, and maintains a statistical record of the rubber market.[25] It should be noted that the Rubber Board of India is not em-

---

The Rubber Board is a statutory body constituted under the Rubber Act, 1947.

    The functions of the Board under the Act are: [1] to promote by such measures as it thinks fit the development of the rubber industry; [2] without prejudice to the generality of the foregoing provision the measures referred to therein may provide for: [a] undertaking, assisting or encouraging scientific, technological or economic research; [b] training students in improved methods of planting, cultivation, manuring and spraying; [c] the supply of technical advice to rubber growers; [d] improving the marketing of rubber; [e] the collection of statistics from owners of estates, dealers and manufacturers; [f] securing better working conditions and [g] carrying out any other duties which may be vested in the Board under the rules made under this Act.

    It shall also be the duty of the Board: [a] to advise the Central Government on all matters relating to the development of the rubber industry, including the import and export of rubber; [b] to advise the Central Government with regard to the participation in any international conference or scheme relating to rubber; [c] to submit to the Central Government and such other authorities as may be prescribed, half yearly reports on its activities and the working of this Act; and [d] to prepare and furnish such other reports relating to the rubber industry as may be required by the Central Government from time to time.

25    See Tharian George and Thomas (1997) for a description of the functions and an evaluation of the achievements of the Rubber Board and the Rubber Research Institute.

powered to carry out duties that commodity boards in other countries often do: all foreign trade activities in natural rubber as well as matters concerning the implementation of domestic price policy, are dealt with through the STC. Objective, formal functioning and actual choices made with respect to the level and timing of the bench mark price and the size of the interventions of the BSS are described in the introduction of a number of issues of the Indian Rubber Statistics (see appendix 2.3 to this chapter).

The Buffer Stocking Scheme is a standard price band scheme: a bench - mark price is determined by the central government. The bench mark price and its revisions are based on a study on the cost of production of natural rubber conducted by the Cost Account Branch of the Ministry of Finance.[26] The bench mark price is not connected to the world market price in one way or another, or to some kind of long run market equilibrium between supply and demand. Revisions of the bench mark price are taking place with some frequency, often every one or two years. A ceiling and floor price are determined at 50 rupees per 100 kg. on either side of the bench mark price. Next to ceiling and floor price, an upper trigger price and a lower trigger price is determined at 30 rupees per 100 kg. on either side of the bench mark price.

To implement the price policy, market operations are undertaken by the STC, the public sector agency in case of natural rubber. According to the operating rules of the BSS, the STC is expected to act as follows. As long as the market price of RMA4 moves within a band of 30 rupees per 100 kg. of the bench mark price the STC will take no action. If the price decreases below the lower trigger price, or even below the floor the STC buys (procures) natural rubber on the market at the floor price, until the market forces the price above the lower trigger price. In the same way, if the price increases above the upper trigger price, or even above the ceiling price, the STC sells natural rubber from stocks, or releases imports on the market at the ceiling price, until the market forces the price below the lower trigger price. Intervention points of other grades of natural rubber are determined simultaneously with more or less fixed price differentials between grades.

The probability of speculation against a ceiling price seems small: the STC has monopsony power in the foreign trade activities and the probability of running out of stock with such an import monopoly is considerably smaller. Additionally, individual dealers lack the required information that tells them if stocks at the

---

26    These cost studies, unfortunately, are not available publicly. See also Kapoor (1988).

STC are at a critical level. Lack of financial power and credit constraints further limit the capabilities of dealers to step up their investment in stocks. Last but not least there are some doubts whether the STC is prepared to defend a ceiling at all.

This brings us to the actual functioning of the BSS. Data on minimum and maximum prices are provided by the STC. According to these data the market price stays nicely within the upper and lower bounds with the exception of December 1991 and January 1992. On the other hand if we look at the actual price development of RMA4 and plot the bench mark price, as well as the ceiling and floor for the period January 1984 to December 1993 on the basis of the information from IRS 1991 and 1993 (not shown), it is immediately obvious that during a large number of periods the STC has not been able to keep the market price within these ceiling and floor prices (not shown). During a few months in 1987 and in 1992 the floor price could not be maintained,[27] while there has been virtually no year in which the ceiling price has been maintained.[28] Releases as such cannot be interpreted as proofs of the efforts to maintain the ceiling price. These releases are not necessarily intended to stop prices from rising as a part of an announced price policy, and even if so, it is difficult to separate these releases from 'regular' releases (see Figure 2.28). On the other hand, the record of procurement (see Figure 2.27) is an obvious confirmation of the efforts to maintain the floor price.

The asymmetry in defending the floor and ceiling price is also corroborated by the comments of representatives of supply and demand. In the periodicals on natural rubber one can find a lively debate on the price policy of the central government, implemented by the STC; especially the divergences from announced operations lead to fierce reactions, of course heavily influenced by the particular interest of the group the author represents. Going through these periodicals it is clear that the exact determination of the cost of production of natural rubber, and, hence, the determination of the bench mark price is a heavily debated subject. Discussions are intensified by the lack of background information on the final decisions of the Central Government. The above mentioned studies on the cost of production of natural rubber conducted by the Cost Account Branch of the Ministry of Finance are not publicly available. Experts in the field argue that the

---

27    It is altogether unclear if the Government still felt responsible to implement a price policy in 1992.

28    Note that the ceiling price has not been fixed from September 1988 to the 15th of January 1991 for reasons that are unclear: with peak prices realised during this period it is difficult to understand the meaning of the phrase *fair to the rubber user industry* - the stated objective of the Buffer Stocking Scheme.

**Figure 2.27**   Procurement by STC

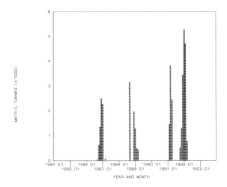

**Figure 2.28**   Releases by STC

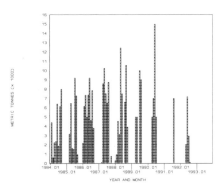

**Figure 2.29**   Stocks at the STC

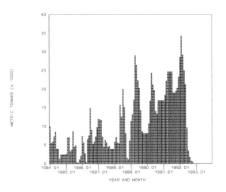

Source (Figure 2.28, 2.29 and 2.30): State Trading Corporation

interventions of the central Government/STC with respect to the ceiling price are limited to undertake imports whenever the domestic price rises above the ceiling price: the ceiling price is used as a trigger price for imports. Effective defense of a ceiling price, and running losses on importing activities only takes place under special circumstances. For some goods - mainly food items - the central government wishes to keep down the prices for consumers and the public agency is prepared to run a loss. The case of vegetable oils is an example in this respect. Above it is made clear that natural rubber is not such a good.

## 2.7 Summary and conclusion

From the quantitative description of the Indian natural rubber market in this chapter, a number of observations can be made. Production of natural rubber experienced a tremendous growth during this period, largely due to promotion of cultivation of rubber trees by the government. Large increases in yield from 1970 to 1990, combined with low production uncertainty and reasonable demand prospects, has made natural rubber an attractive crop in the South of India. Natural rubber is grown on estates and on smallholdings. Smallholders account for the largest share in aggregate production and area. However, a great majority of smallholders of natural rubber have very tiny plots. Price risks of cultivating natural rubber are to some extent diversified, by cultivating other crops and having non-agricultural sources of income. The combination of extensive promotion of natural rubber growing combined with restricted imports, obviously aimed at becoming self-supporting in natural rubber. As a result natural rubber accounts for 70% of the domestic rubber market (synthetic only 20%), as opposed to 30-40% natural rubber and 60-70% synthetic rubber on the world market. Natural rubber production is also almost exclusively consumed domestically, mainly for tire manufacturing. On the demand side there are a large number of small consumers, with a small share of aggregate consumption and a limited number of large tire companies consuming the largest share. Substitution of natural rubber by synthetic rubber is technically possible but economically unattractive due to high (administrative) prices of synthetic rubber. Both growers of natural rubber, manufacturers of rubber products, as well as specialized dealers are engaged in arbitrage activities. From the data no stock-outs can be observed from 1965 to 1995. Price policies have a mixed record in the natural rubber market: floor prices seem to have been defended fairly well. Government commitment to maintaining ceiling prices seems to be dependent on the returns to importing and on the foreign exchange reserves. Until the beginning of the 1990s the establishment of the STC, import licensing, and foreign exchange shortages have effectively isolated the Indian rubber economy from the world market and this has ensured that domestic pricing and distribution is subject to domestic supply and demand conditions and government discretion. From the beginning of the 1990s onwards prices are much closer linked to world market prices.

**Appendix 2.1**

**Data on the Indian rubber market:**

**sources, consistency checks, errors and corrections**

The purpose of this appendix is to report the data sources and to document how consistency of the data-set is obtained. The bigger part of all the data used in this study is published in the Indian Rubber Statistics. This publication appears every two years and is published by the Rubber Board of India. Most data in this publication are primary source data. Series on releases and procurement by the State Trading Corporation (STC), required to calculate the market clearing identity, are not published. These series are supplied on request by the State Trade Corporation by intermediation of the Rubber Board of India. Weather variables are provided by the Rubber Research Institute of India (RRII). Data on the world market of rubber are taken from the Statistical Bulletin of the International Rubber Study Group. General economic variables are taken either from Economic Survey, Central Statistical Organization, Government of India, or from the International Financial Statistics of the International Monetary Fund (IFS/IMF). Data of the Tokyo Commodity Exchange (TOCOM) were, initially, kindly provided by Albert van Feggelen and Hinrik Vrieze of L.WURFBAIN & Co B.V., Zaandam, The Netherlands. In a later stage of the study original daily quotations of futures prices and turnover of TOCOM in natural rubber were made available through Ryoichi Seki, Planning Department of The Tokyo Commodity Exchange. These data have been used in Chapter 7. Most data are available on a monthly basis, and the empirical analysis, of Chapters 3, 4, 5, and 7 is done either on a monthly or a quarterly basis. For descriptive purposes in the current chapter annual data are used to a large extent. Indian statistics report most annual data in fiscal years: a fiscal year is from April to March. Fiscal years, as opposed to calendar years, are indicated with two dates e.g. 1985-86.

In the empirical work we make use of a data-set with monthly observations for the period from January 1965 (65.01) to December 1995 (95.12), thus covering 30 years, and containing 360 observations per variable. Variables on natural rubber in the data-set are:

production $(q)$,

imports $(m)$,

imports by the STC $(m_{stc})$,

imports by manufacturers $(m_{mf})$,

consumption $(c)$,

stocks at growers and dealers $(s_{gd})$,

stocks at manufacturers $(s_{mf})$,

stocks at the STC ($s_{stc}$),

exports ($x$),

exports by the STC ($x_{stc}$),

exports by growers and dealers ($x_{gd}$),

releases by the STC (rls),

procurement by the STC (proc),

prices of RMA4 grade of natural rubber ($p$).

A number of series are available on synthetic rubber (production, imports, consumption, stocks and prices) and reclaimed rubber (production, consumption, stocks and prices). The following general economic variables are used:

gross industrial product in constant 1980.01 prices (gip),

general consumer price index (cpi (IFS/CSO))

interest rates (IFS)

Finally some weather variables are used:

rainfall per month in mm (rfmm),

number of days per month with rainfall (rfnd).

The following identities apply to the data of the natural rubber market. Total imports ($m$) is given by the sum of imports by the STC ($m_{stc}$) and imports by the manufacturers of rubber products ($m_{mf}$). A similar identity applies to exports. Stock formation (by growers and dealers ($\Delta s_{gd}$) and by manufacturers($\Delta s_{mf}$)) is the difference of current and one period lagged stocks. Stock formation by the STC ($\Delta s_{stc}$) is equal to the imports by the STC ($m_{stc}$) plus procurement (proc) minus releases (rls) minus STC exports. Formally this yields:

$$m_t = m_{stc,t} + m_{mf,t}$$

$$x_t = x_{stc,t} + x_{mf,t}$$

$$\Delta s_{gd,t} = s_{gd,t} - s_{gd,t-1}$$

$$\Delta s_{mf,t} = s_{mf,t} - s_{mf,t-1}$$

$$\Delta s_{stc,t} = m_{stc,t} - rls_t + proc_t - x_{stc,t}$$

Quality of data on stockholding is usually very poor: these data are often incomplete or do not satisfy the market clearing identity. The monthly data-set is checked for consistency with the help of the market clearing identity. This identity says that supply equals demand. The demand for natural rubber consists of consumption (c), exports by manufacturers ($x_{mf}$), stock formation by manufacturers ($\Delta s_{mf}$), stock formation by growers and dealers ($\Delta s_{gd}$) and procurement by the STC. Supply of natural rubber consists of the production (q), the imports by manufacturers of rubber products ($m_{mf}$) and releases by the STC. In formula this is:

$$c_t + x_{gd,t} + \Delta s_{mf,t} + \Delta s_{gd,t} + proc_t = q_t + m_{mf,t} + rls_t$$

Implicit in the above market clearing identity is that all foreign trade of the STC (import and export) is outside the rubber market.[29] Consistency errors in the data set are corrected, following a procedure set out below. The procedure outlined is reported to account for corrections on the original data and to arrive at consistency of the data-set: it is not intended to be particularly 'scientific'. Next to questioning the quality of the series on stocks, both at growers and dealers, and at manufacturers, we are particularly suspicious about errors in the constituent parts of stock formation at the STC, cq. imports, releases, procurement and exports by the STC: releases and procurement are not published, but supplied on request by the STC through intermediation of the Rubber Board of India; besides, the observations on imports, imports by the STC, and stocks at the STC have been revised by the STC frequently in the course of time. Revised figures of imports were adjusted in stock figures at the end of the (fiscal) year. Both two matters do not make us confident about the quality of these series. Thus, in case of an imbalance in the market clearing identity we are inclined to adjust these series in the first place.

If both sides of the market clearing identity balance the data are assumed to be consistent with respect to the market clearing identity;[30] alternatively, imbalance is assumed to indicate an error. In the original data-set the data satisfy

---

29    An identical market clearing identity that incorporates the stock identity of the STC runs as follows: $c_t + x_t + \Delta s_{mf,t} + \Delta s_{gd,t} + \Delta s_{stc,t} = q_t + m_t$
30    Indeed, once the researcher starts to question the quality of data, even the quality of data that do not fail the market clearing identity becomes questionable: Is it not by coincidence that the market clearing identity is satisfied? However, as stated above we do not dwell upon this point any further (for example, by investigating the way the various variables are observed statistically), but assume that consistency with respect to the market clearing identity is satisfied in this case.

the market clearing identity in 47.2% of the observations.[31] The identity on stocks at the STC together with the market clearing identity allowed to identify the error directly in a considerable number of months. If imbalances appear only in two subsequent months of, more or less, the same size but with opposite sign, it is assumed that such an imbalance can be attributed to stock formation at the STC and stocks at the STC are corrected accordingly. More in general such imbalances are assumed to indicate spill-overs from one month to subsequent months or errors in the timing of registration. If the imbalance cannot be removed in this way, they are corrected through adjusting releases. In the years 1989, 1990 and 1991 values of the original series of releases indicate, for whatever reason, a some what decreased degree of accurateness: all figures are rounded to multiples of thousand, quite contrary to the figures reported for earlier years. Adjustments for these years have been made by distributing releases over months in such a way that the annual aggregate of the corrected series equals this aggregate of the original series: such a reshuffling turned out to be possible within the limits of the balance equation. All corrections have been applied to a limited number of variables, namely the variables of the STC and imports. A complete record of corrections is available on request.

---

31    With an imbalance relative to consumption of natural rubber of less than 1%, we postulate that the market clearing identity is satisfied.

## Appendix 2.2

### Import regulations applicable to natural rubber

(from: Import and Export Policy, Ministry of Commerce, Government of India (1985-88))

(Chapter IV, CANALISATION OF IMPORTS)

67. Whenever a shortage arises or is apprehended in respect of any item the import of which is not permitted, its import may be arranged by the Chief Controller of Imports and Exports,[32] New Delhi, through a public sector agency. In such a situation the following provisions in this Chapter as well as those in Chapter IV of Handbook of Import-Export Procedures 1985-88 will be as applicable thereto as if it were an item canalized for import.

*Pricing Committee*

71. There will be a Pricing Committee under the Chairmanship of the Chief Controller of Imports and Exports, New Delhi, and consisting of the representatives of the Department of Commerce, the Ministry of Finance (Department of Economic Affairs), the Department of Steel, the Economic Adviser in the Ministry of Industry, the Director General of Technical Development, the Development Commissioner (Small Scale Industries) and the other administrative Ministry concerned with the item for determining/prescribing the selling prices of items appearing in Appendix 5 Part-A from time to time.

*Monitoring Committee*

72. In order to oversee the working of the scheme of canalization, there will be a Monitoring Committee under the Chairmanship of the Chief Controller of Imports and Exports, and consisting of the members as mentioned in para 71 above. The actual quantum of items appearing in Appendix 5, Part-A to be imported by the canalizing agency will be decided by the administrative Ministry concerned in consultation with the Ministry of Commerce, the Department of Economic Affairs, the Ministry of Industry, other Ministries/Departments concerned and the canalizing agency. However, this Committee will continue to review the arrangements made for meeting the registered demands of the Actual Users from time to time. In cases or circumstances where the Committee considers it necessary or desirable to expedite supplies, it may recommend to the Chief Controller of Imports and Exports the issue of import license(s) directly in the name(s) of the concerned Actual User(s).

---

32    The Chief Controller of Imports and Exports is currently known as the Directorate General of Foreign Trade and is a government department under the jurisdiction of the Ministry of Commerce.

**Appendix 2.3**

**The Rubber Board on the Buffer Stocking Scheme**

*(from: Indian Rubber Statistics 19, 1991)*

"In February 1986 Government of India introduced a Buffer Stocking Scheme with a view to stabilize the price of natural rubber at a reasonable level so as to make it remunerative to the rubber growers and fair to the rubber user industry. Under the Scheme, the fair price (bench mark price) of RMA4 grade rubber was initially fixed at Rs. 1650 per quintal within an upper and lower price band of Rs. 1600 and 1700 per quintal respectively. The State Trading Corporation of India Ltd. is operating the Buffer Stocking Scheme and the market price is regulated by releasing the imported rubber, or by procuring the domestic rubber. In May 1987. the fair price was revised to Rs. 1700, with Rs 1750 as upper and Rs. 1650 as lower level of the price band. In September 1988 the fair price was revised to Rs. 1780 with the lower price band at Rs. 1730 while the upper price band was not fixed. On the 15th of January 1991 the bench mark price was revised to Rs. 2145, the upper and lower price bands were changed to Rs. 2195 and 2095 respectively. The revisions are carried out based on the Study into the cost of production conducted by the Cost Account Branch of the Ministry of Finance. (..)"

*(from: Indian Rubber Statistics 20, 1993)*

"On the 5th of January 1993, government revised the bench mark price for RMA4 grade rubber to Rs. 2345 per quintal. The price prior to the revision was Rs. 2145 which was introduced on the 15th of January 1991. The slow down in demand and steady increase in production of NR necessitated price support operations during the period from February 1991 to April 1991 and again from October 1991 to March 1992. The State Trading Corporation (STC) of India procured 7,700 tonnes of RMA4 grade rubber during the first period and 7,165 tonnes of RMA5 grade and 8,816 tonnes of RMA4 grade during the second period. The continued sluggish demand and heavy accumulation of stocks necessitated the Government to allow export of rubber. From the surplus stock from 1991-92, STC exported 5,834 tonnes in March 1992 and 5,988 tonnes during April to June 1992 The entire export was RMA5 grade sheets, which the industry was not able to absorb. In addition, a small quantity of centrifuged latex of 11 tonnes (dry rubber content) was exported by one rubber growing company."

The Indian Rubber Statistics 18, 1987-88, contains identical information on the BSS as IRS 1991.

# 3     PRICES AND STOCKHOLDING WITH RATIONAL EXPECTATIONS

## 3.1     Introduction

From the survey of the literature in Chapter 1 we have learned that there are two lines of research in stockholding. The first one is concerned with explaining the negative returns on stockholding and suggests convenience yield as an explanation. Attempts to provide a solid theoretical basis for the concept of convenience yield have not been successful, and there appears to be scepticism on the mere existence of convenience yield. The second line of research, on the other hand, has established itself firmly in theory. This line of research, represented by the so-called competitive storage model, has the incidence of stock-outs as its basic feature. Non-negativity of stocks in the competitive storage model is shown to have a pervasive effect on expectation formation, and, through expectation formation, on supply and demand relationships, even if the non-negativity does not become effective. The dynamic character of stockholding combined with the non-negativity of stocks prevents the estimation of behavioral relationships with standard techniques. Proper estimation of this model involves disequilibrium maximum-likelihood techniques in combination with stochastic dynamic programming. Attempts in this direction on a simulation basis have shown moderate success (Williams and Wright (1991), Deaton and Laroque (1992)). Very few efforts are known that apply this framework empirically (Miranda and Glauber (1993)).

  The purpose of this chapter is to identify different types of behaviour of stockholders empirically by direct estimation of stock equations. It should be noted that the competitive storage model, despite its rigorous formalization of speculative behaviour of stockholders, ignores any other motives to hold stocks. The non-linearity of the stock equation, due to the non-negativity of stocks, makes direct estimation of stock demand relationships impossible and erroneous from the perspective of the competitive storage model (see Williams and Wright (1991)). For that reason and prior to formalizing the behaviour of stockholders, it is set out why we consider the competitive storage model not suitable to our problem and we give the reasons for adopting an alternative approach. Empirical results of the approach used in this study are reasonably good: estimations support speculative behaviour of stockholders, as well as convenience yield; elasticities with respect to price are estimated to be two to three times higher for stock demand than for consumption. The derivations provide a framework for further analysis in Chapters 4 and 5, where the impact of a price stabilization scheme is evaluated.

The chapter is organized as follows. In Section 3.2 the formalisation of the behaviour of stockholders is explained. Although the behaviour of stockholders is the primary focus of our analysis, producers and consumers are also modelled in order to be able to run system estimations. Producers' and consumers' behaviour is formalized in Section 3.3. Relationships that complete the model are presented in Section 3.4. In Section 3.5 the price equation is derived. In Section 3.6 estimation results of behaviourial equations are presented. A summary and conclusion is formulated in Section 3.7.


### 3.2    Deriving a stock demand specification

In the derivation of stock demand and the subsequent empirical work we ignore the possibility of zero stocks. We have assumed that a stock-out in the Indian natural rubber market can be considered an improbable event because of the sufficiently high convenience yield on carrying inventories. Support for this proposition is obtained from inspection of the data. Newbery and Stiglitz (1982, see Chapter 1) propose a piece-wise linear approximation of the non-linear competitive storage rule. The piece-wise linear function is an approximation of the non-linear relationship between stocks and supply, where supply is defined as beginning of period stocks plus production. From this approximation of the competitive storage model it is inferred that it is optimal to have zero stocks, for levels of supply stretching from no supply to a particular (positive) level of supply. In Figure 1 the relationship between aggregate stocks and supply is plotted with the data of the Indian natural rubber market. From the figure the linearity of the relationship is corroborated. However, it is also clear that there is no positive level of supply where stocks are zero. Apparently the behaviour of stockholding is not adequately described with the competitive storage model.

Additional support for ignoring stock-outs is obtained by looking at the data from a different perspective: aggregate monthly data show that stocks with producers and dealers and stocks with manufacturers of rubber products never have been lower than 20% of consumption (monthly data). If minimum values of stocks are related to the highest maximum values in the recent past it appears that stocks at growers and dealers never fall below around 25% of a peak in the recent past and stocks at manufacturers never fall below around 50% of a peak in the recent past (monthly data, see Chapter 2 for more details). Of course, this does

**Figure 3.1**   Aggregate stocks versus aggregate supply
(in thousand tonnes; 1965.01-1995.03)

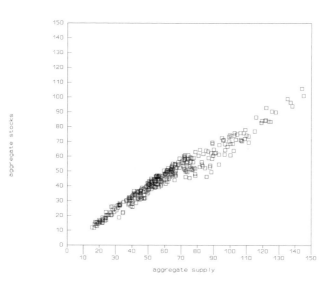

Source:      Indian Rubber Statistics, various issues

not imply that stock-outs did not occur at individual stockholders.[1]
Indeed,aggregation could easily disguise stock-outs at the micro level. However, -
substantial minimum levels of stocks are difficult to reconcile with the
competitive storage model. Positive stocks with a negative return on stockholding
or, if a futures market exists, backwardation of futures prices, cannot be explained
with the competitive storage model. This issue is recognized by the adherents of
the competitive storage model. Williams and Wright (1991, pp.139-140) observe
in this respect:

*'.. empirically it does seem that storage takes place when the spot spread is in
backwardation, if for no other evidence than the disquieting fact that stock-outs
are never observed'.*

And in a footnote:

*'For example, wheat stocks have never been down to zero in 120 years of
warehouse statistics'*

---

1      Stock-outs in aggregate series allow the conclusion of stock-outs at the micro
level; however, no stock-outs at the aggregate level do not rule out stock-outs at the micro
level.

We conclude that substantial minimum levels of stocks can hardly be expected to be consistent with the competitive storage model: the occurrence of substantial stock levels at all time needs further explanation. It should be noted that the strict occurrence of stock-outs is not required for the competitive storage model to be applicable. Through expectations of future prices the incidence of stock-outs is felt long before a stock-out becomes relevant. This also makes clear that no conclusion is possible by simple inspection of the data: confronting empirical data with the model is the only way to find out if it has some power. This brings us to other reservations.

Another reason to ignore the non-negativity of stocks is the explanatory power of competitive storage model. The empirical record of the competitive storage model is not particularly strong. Deaton and Laroque (1992, 1994a,b) claim to confront the theory with the evidence: indeed, the optimal or competitive storage rule is shown by simulation to be able to replicate more or less developments in real commodity markets. However, the competitive storage model did not succeed (yet) in replicating price series with considerable auto-correlation, a characteristic property of commodity prices. Some additional support is obtained from estimating implications of the model with respect to expected price and the variance of price (see Chapter 1), but Deaton and Laroque note that the estimated relationship could also be generated with other models.

There is also a practical reason to model behaviour of stockholders differently from the optimal or competitive storage approach. Replication of empirical data by simulation and testing of implied relationships is rather different from estimating a complete empirical model of a commodity market with full information techniques. The models developed in the competitive storage tradition are simple in the sense that only a few parameters are used (only four in most models), yet the computational burden to solve such a model with dynamic stochastic programming methods is substantial. A fully fledged empirical model of a commodity market built in this tradition requires the estimation of a multiple of these parameters (e.g. around 85 in our, still moderately sized, empirical model). It is questionable if such a model is identifiable. Even if it is, it seems currently far beyond the technical capability and computational capacity available to policy makers and policy researchers. It seems that the complexities of obtaining optimal storage rules in empirical commodity market models are not fully appreciated by their proponents.

To summarize, the approach to model (optimal) behaviour of stockholders with stochastic dynamic programming methods, recommended by Williams and Wright (1991), and Deaton and Laroque (1992), is not implemented. Difficulties to incorporate other motives for stockholding, the poor empirical record and computational problems in implementing estimations are the main reasons to put aside the competitive storage model. Instead we derive optimal behaviour of stockholders by maximizing expected utility with quadratic costs, and without imposing non-negativity on stocks.

Next we come to the formal derivation of the behaviour of stockholders. We assume that stockholders are risk neutral[2]: with risk neutral stockholders, maximization of discounted (discounted) expected utility is equal to maximization of (discounted) expected profit:

$$\sum_{t=1}^{T} E_{t-1} (\pi_{s,t}) \cdot \delta^t \tag{1}$$

where

$E_{t-1}()$ is the expectation conditional on the information at time t-1;

$\pi_{s,t}$   =   profit of stockholders at time t;

$\delta$   =   discounting factor,

subject to a quadratic cost function. Profit of stockholders is characterized as:

$$\pi_{s,t} = s_{t-1} \cdot (p_t - \rho \cdot p_{t-1}) - Z_s(s_{t-1}) \tag{2}$$

where

$s_{t-1}$   =   purchases of stockholders at time t-1;

$p_t$   =   (spot) price at time t;

$\rho$   =   1+interest rate;

$Z_i(.)$   =   cost function of agent i.

Costs of stockholding take the following quadratic form:

$$Z_s(s_{t-1}) = \tfrac{1}{2} z_s \cdot (s_{t-1} - \bar{s}_{t-1} - \varepsilon_{s,t-1})^2 \tag{3}$$

where

$z_s > 0$;

$\bar{s}_{t-1}$   =   a target stockholding level at time t-1;

$\varepsilon_{s,t-1}$   =   a disturbance term affecting costs at time t-1.

---

2    The reason for assuming risk neutral behavior is to keep the derivation of rational expectations tractable. In Chapter 7 we allow the possibility of non-zero risk aversion. Note, however, that Gilbert (1988) has shown that a market composed of a large number of speculators may be considered as a market with a risk neutral speculator (see also Chapter 1).

Costs of stockholding are postulated to be the difference between direct carrying costs (warehouse costs, insurance fees, physical losses), assumed to be related to the size of stocks, and (other) benefits from holding stocks.

At this stage some remarks should be made about other than speculative motives to have stocks. In terms of the competitive storage model, the assumption made in the current study implies that one of the complementary inequality conditions[3], namely that stocks are zero when there are no arbitrage opportunities, will never be binding due to the convenience yield of stockholding. The return to individual stockholders of having stocks on other grounds than speculative ones, is in the literature often denoted with convenience yield (Kaldor (1939), Working (1949), Brennan (1958), see Chapter 1 for a survey of these contributions). The concept of convenience yield needs further clarification. Motives to keep stocks of commodities can be elaborated along the same lines as in monetary theory (see Ghosh *et al.* (1987)): precautionary and transaction motives to hold stocks are distinguished, next to speculative motives to hold stocks. Transaction demand refers to stocks kept as source of input to a production process. In particular this motive refers to the costs associated with leaving other inputs (labour) idle, because of a shortage of material inputs. It might be caused by delays in supply due to transport. Also uncertainty of supply of input or (lack of) information on current and future supply might affect the size of stocks due to transaction motives. Precautionary demand refers to stocks kept to reduce the costs of stock-out and the associated loss of sales and loss of consumers. Further motives that come fairly close to speculative motivates have been suggested: Newbery and Stiglitz point at keeping stocks to reduce risk by exploiting the variation of prices over time (see Newbery and Stiglitz (1981), p.196). It should be noted that having stocks on these grounds is not restricted to particular agents: all groups in the market can perform these tasks.

Formalization of convenience yield has been attempted in Weymar (1968) and Ghosh *et al.* (1987). From these contributions we learn that the following properties of convenience yield should be identified: marginal convenience yield is a declining function of the level of stocks, tends to zero for high levels of stock and becomes substantial with low levels of stocks. Additionally, and separate from considerations concerning convenience yield, we claim that in the short run costs will increase sharply when the capacity limits of stockholding are approached. We have formalized these relations, approximately, by taking up a

---

3      The complementary inequality conditions characterize optimal behavior of stockholders and is a key feature of the competitive storage model (see Chapter 1).

target-level of stockholding in the quadratic cost-function (see equation (3)): positive deviations from target stockholding $(s_{t-1}-\bar{s}_{t-1}>0)$ contribute to costs in a standard way, negative deviations from target stockholding $(s_{t-1}-\bar{s}_{t-1}<0)$ are explained by the opportunity costs of convenience yield. Obviously the quadratic cost function is also chosen as it yields easy-to-handle linear outcomes in the optimization procedure. Expected profit is now written as:

$$E_{t-1}(\pi_{s,t}) = s_{t-1} \cdot (E_{t-1}(p_t) - \rho \cdot p_{t-1}) - Z_s(s_{t-1}) \tag{4}$$

For an optimum we require

$$\partial E_{t-1}(\pi_{s,t})/\partial s_{t-1} = 0 \tag{5}$$

From equations (3), (4) and (5) we derive the following optimal stock demand:

$$s_{t-1} = 1/z_s \cdot (E_{t-1}(p_t) - \rho p_{t-1}) + \bar{s}_{t-1} + \varepsilon_{s,t-1} \tag{6}$$

Equation (6) indicates that stockholding is positively related to the difference of expected spot price $(E_{t-1}(p_t))$ and discounted spot price in the base period $(\rho p_{t-1})$, the target-level of stockholding $(\bar{s}_{t-1})$ and the disturbance term in costs $(\varepsilon_{s,t-1})$, and inversely to the cost parameter $(z_s)$. With expected price equal to base period price plus interest $(E_{t-1}(p_t)=\rho p_{t-1})$ stockholding equals target-level of stockholding plus a disturbance term $(s_{t-1}=\bar{s}_{t-1}+\varepsilon_{s,t-1})$. Recall that by assumption stock-outs do not occur, or $s_t>0$ for all t: this implies that target stockholding is always sufficient to offset sales of stocks on speculative grounds. Forwarding equation (6) one period and redefining the coefficients yields:

$$s_t = g_0 + g_1(E_t(p_{t+1}) - \rho p_t) + g_2\bar{s}_t + \varepsilon_{s,t} , \quad g_1 > 0 \ g_2 > 0 \tag{7}$$
where
$$g_1 = 1/z_s; \qquad g_2 = 1$$

For notational convenience we write $_t p^e_{t+1} = E_t(p_{t+1})$ and, hence,

$$s_t = g_0 + g_1 (_t p^e_{t+1} - \rho p_t) + g_2\bar{s}_t + \varepsilon_{s,t} , \qquad g_1 > 0 \ g_2 > 0 \tag{8}$$

Data on stockholding are available for growers and dealers (taken together) and for manufacturers of rubber products (see Chapter 2 for descriptive statistics). In the empirical model stockholding is formalized for these two groups. Although the

data of the stockholding by growers and dealers are taken together, they do allow
production activities of growers to be assessed separately from stockholding
activities. For growers and dealers we postulate that the target-level of
stockholding is a linear function of production ($\bar{s}_{gd,t} = \phi_{gd} \cdot q_t$, $\phi_{gd} > 0$ where $q =$
production) and for manufacturers the target-level of stockholding is assumed to
be a linear function of consumption ($\bar{s}_{mf,t} = \phi_{mf} \cdot c_t$, $\phi_{mf} > 0$ where $c =$ consumption).[4] Equation (8) together with the specification of target-level of
stockholding, and using the (co)integration tests (see appendix 3.1 to this chapter)
to simplify the specification, yields the following error correction presentation for
the behaviour of stockholders:

$$\Delta s_{gd,t} = \xi_0 + \xi_1 (\Delta_t p^e_{t+1} - \rho \Delta p_t) + \xi_2 \Delta q_t + \xi_3 s_{gd,t-1} + \xi_4 q_{t-1} + \varepsilon_{gd,t}$$
$$\xi_1 > 0; \ \xi_2 > 0; \ \xi_3 < 0; \ \xi_4 > 0; \tag{9}$$

and

$$\Delta s_{mf,t} = \zeta_0 + \zeta_1 (\Delta_t p^e_{t+1} - \rho \Delta p_t) + \zeta_2 \Delta c_t + \zeta_3 s_{mf,t-1} + \zeta_4 c_{t-1} + \varepsilon_{mf,t}$$
$$\zeta_1 > 0; \ \zeta_2 > 0; \ \zeta_3 < 0; \ \zeta_4 > 0 \tag{10}$$

where

| | | |
|---|---|---|
| $s_{gd}$ | $=$ | stocks of natural rubber with growers and dealers; |
| $s_{mf}$ | $=$ | stocks of natural rubber with manufacturers of rubber products. |
| $\xi_1$ | $=$ | $1/z_{gd}$; $\xi_4 = \xi_3 \cdot \phi_{gd}$; $\zeta_1 = 1/z_{mf}$; $\zeta_4 = \zeta_3 \cdot \phi_{mf}$; |

Equations (10) and (11) are estimated: estimation results are presented in
Section 3.6.


## 3.3    Specifying production and consumption

Although the behaviour of stockholders is the primary focus of our analysis, other
groups, or, perhaps better, other activities, are also modelled. Shocks in
production and consumption will influence the behaviour of stockholders as well,
not in the least because the data do not identify stockholders as a separate group,
but only as a separate activity. For this reason an attempt has been made to model
the entire market, that is, to formalize production and consumption, on top of
stockholding. With the help of system estimations it is subsequently explored if
the estimation outcome is affected if we allow for these influences. Econometri-

---

4       It should be noted that this is also an outcome of (co)integration tests (see
appendix 1).

cally it is summarized as follows: with a model containing four behavioral equations (producers, stockholders (2x) and consumers), it is likely that the disturbances from these behavioral equations are correlated; If so, then the technique of system estimation gives more efficient estimates than single equation estimation.

With endogenous prices, system estimations also make the estimation of a separate price equation, required to construct expected prices, superfluous. All the parameters of the price equation, including the cross equation restrictions, are known once the parameters of the underlying behavioral equations are known. This problem provides an additional argument to estimate the behavioral relationships with Full Information Maximum Likelihood (FIML). In the single equation estimations the formation of price expectations has to be modelled separately by deriving and estimating a price equation. It should be noted that exogenous expectational variables, required for the calculation of expected prices, are constructed on the basis of separate estimations. These equations are not added to the system of estimated equations. Using such constructed regressors will give rise to consistent but inefficient coefficient estimates which suffer from biased standard errors (Pagan (1984)). Alternatives are the McCallum Instrumental Variables (IV) and Maximum Likelihood (see Pesaran (1987)). To avoid unnecessary complications we ignore this issue.

### 3.3.1 Production

In the derivation of the behaviour of growers we make the assumption that stockholders use the (same) expected price to base their stockholding decisions on, as is used by growers to base their short run production decision on. Growers use these short term expectations to decide on how much labour input will be used for tapping, how many tappers are going to be hired or to what extent tapping intensity should be changed for output to be produced the coming month(s). These matters can be decided upon on relatively short notice. To put it differently: expected price for growers is related to short term decisions on the level of production with a given capacity, i.e. on the degree of capacity utilization. Decisions on the production capacity itself, that is, the number of rubber trees available for tapping, are not necessarily governed by this expected price. Decisions concerning discarding, new planting and uprooting, are assumed to react to a long term discounted expected price or income, and will not be considered here. The derivation of the behaviour of producers develops along the same lines as in the case of stockholders. In the current chapter producers are assumed to be risk neutral and to maximize discounted expected profit subject to quadratic costs. Discounted expected profit is written as:

$$\sum_{t=1}^{T} E_{t-1}(\pi_{p,t}).\delta^t \tag{11}$$

Profit of producers is characterized as

$$\pi_{p,t} = q_t.p_t - \rho.Z_p(q_t) \tag{12}$$

where $q_t$ = production at time t;

Maximization of expected utility of risky profit is calculated assuming production certainty. Production costs are assumed to have the following specification

$$Z_p(q_t) = \tfrac{1}{2}z_p.(q_t + \varepsilon_{p,t-1})^2 \tag{13}$$

where

$z_p > 0$

$\varepsilon_{p,t-1}$ a disturbance term affecting production costs at t-1.

Expected profit is written as:

$$E_{t-1}(\pi_{p,t}) = q_t.E_{t-1}(p_t) - \tfrac{1}{2}\rho z_p.(q_t + \varepsilon_{t-1})^2 \tag{14}$$

For an optimum it is required

$$\partial E_{t-1}(U_p)/\partial q_t = 0 \tag{15}$$

With risk neutrality maximization of discounted expected utility is equal to maximization of expected profit. From equations (14), (15) and (16) we derive optimal production as:

$$q_t = 1/(\rho.z_p).E_{t-1}(p_t) - \varepsilon_{p,t-1} \tag{16}$$

Equation (16) says that production is positively related to the expected spot price ($E_{t-1}(p_t)$), negatively to the disturbance term in production costs ($\varepsilon_{p,t-1}$) and inversely to the discount factor ($\rho$) and the cost parameter ($z_p$). Equation (16) is rewritten as:

$$q_t = a_0 + a_1 E_{t-1}(p_t) - \varepsilon_{p,t-1}, \ a_1 > 0 \tag{17}$$
$$\text{where} \ a_1 = 1/(\rho.z_p)$$

Changing the notation of price expectations yields:

$$q_t = a_0 + a_1 \ _{t-1}p^e_t - \varepsilon_{p,t-1}, \quad a_1 > 0 \tag{18}$$

To arrive at an equation that can be estimated, corrections are imposed for seasonal influences and the vintage composition of the trees. Rubber trees only start to produce rubber after a relatively long gestation period of 5 to 7 years. After this immaturity period the annual yield of rubber trees depends on the age of the tree, the particular variety of the tree, the tapping intensity, the tapping system, the availability of labour and weather conditions. After some 25 to 35 years a decision about replanting or uprooting is made (see also Chapter 2 for more descriptive information). The focus in this study is on short run price and stock formation. Hence, we will not elaborate on the long run dynamics of production. A method to quantify the specific long-run dynamics of the production of perennial crops is presented elsewhere (Burger *et al.* (1995)). Combined with the long-run dynamics of production due to the vintage composition of tree plots and plantations, equation (18) yields:

$$q_t = a_0 + a_1 \ _{t-1}p^e_t + a_2 \ q_{lr,t} - \varepsilon_{p,t-1}, \ a_1 > 0 \quad a_2 > 0 \tag{19}$$
$$\text{where}$$

$q_{lr}$ = long run production, i.e. production controlled for vintage composition.

An error-correction representation is identified with the help of (co)integration tests. On the basis of the tests (see appendix 3.1 to this chapter) the following specification is selected:

$$\Delta q_t = \alpha_0 + \alpha_1 \ \Delta_{t-1}p^e_t + \alpha_3 \ q_{t-1} + \alpha_4 \ q_{lr,t-1} - \varepsilon_{p,t-1} \tag{20}$$

Some specific seasonal influences can be identified. Rainfall has, with some delay, an impact on the capacity of trees to generate rubber: it stimulates rubber output per tree and a lack of rainfall has a negative impact on output per tree. Obviously this influence of rainfall on production of natural rubber is only felt after some time. The instantaneous impact of rainfall, however, is negative. Tapping of rubber trees is not possible during or shortly after rain showers. And, unless trees are protected against rain (rainguarding), the fluid latex that is dripping down the cut made in the bark of the tree will be washed away. With a small number of rainfall days, or more specific, a small number of days with rainfall during tapping hours, the loss in output may be offset by increased output during the days directly after the rainfall. Production in February and March is negatively influenced by adverse weather conditions: especially these months show a substantially lower production due to the wintering season. These considerations modify the above equation into the following relationship:

$$\Delta q_t = \alpha_0 + \alpha_1 \Delta_{t-1} p^e_t + \alpha_3 q_{t-1} + \alpha_4 q_{lr,t-1} + \Sigma \alpha_{5,i} \, rfmm_{t-i} + \alpha_6 \, rfnd_t - \varepsilon_{p,t-1}$$
$$\alpha_1 > 0; \quad \alpha_3 < 0; \quad \alpha_4 > 0; \, \alpha_{5,i} > 0; \quad \alpha_6 < 0 \tag{21}$$

where

rfmm  =      rainfall in mm.;

rfnd  =      number of days with rainfall.

Systematic monthly influences are controlled for by adding a complete set of monthly dummies in the estimations. Estimation results are presented in Section 3.6.

### 3.3.2  Consumption

Natural rubber is 'consumed' by manufacturers of rubber products. By far the largest share of natural rubber - around 65% (Burger *et al.* (1995)) is consumed by tyre and tube manufacturers. The remaining share of consumption is due to manufacturers of a wide range of rubber products, including footwear, belts and hoses, latex foam and dipped goods, battery boxes and cables and wires (see Chapter 2). Both production of tires and tubes and production of the above mentioned miscellaneous rubber products are either directly or indirectly determined by income, defined in some way. Manufacturers of rubber products will maximize profits or minimize costs. Factor demand equations can be derived on the basis of first order conditions, implying consumption of natural rubber to depend negatively on current prices of natural rubber and positively on the price (possibly current, possibly lagged) of synthetic rubber.

Throughout this study consumers are assumed to be risk neutral and are assumed to maximize quadratic utility subject to a budget constraint, resulting in a linear demand function with income, prices and prices of competing commodities as arguments:

$$c_t = b_0 + b_1 inc_t + b_2 p_t + b_3 p_{sr,t} + \varepsilon_{c,t} \qquad (22)$$

where

$c_t$  =  consumption at time t

$inc_t$  =  income at time t

$p_{sr,t}$  =  price of synthetic rubber at time t.

An error correction representation, using the (co)integration tests (see appendix 3.1 to this chapter) to simplify the specification, runs as follows:

$$\Delta c_t =$$

$$\beta_0 + \beta_1 \Delta inc_t + \beta_2 \Delta p_t + \beta_3 \Delta p_{sr,t} + \beta_5 c_{t-1} + \beta_6 inc_{t-1} + \beta_7 p_{t-1} + \beta_8 p_{sr,t-1} + \varepsilon_{c,t}$$
$$\beta_1 > 0; \quad \beta_2 < 0; \quad \beta_3 > 0; \quad \beta_5 < 0; \quad \beta_6 > 0; \quad \beta_7 < 0; \quad \beta_8 > 0; \qquad (23)$$

Again, estimation results are presented in Section 3.6.

## 3.4   Closing the model

In the formal model of the Indian rubber market we focus on natural rubber: commodity substitution on the production side e.g. the cultivation of alternative (tree) crops, or off-farm labour, is assumed to be negligible in the short term. Commodity substitution on the consumption side i.e. the substitution of natural for synthetic rubber and vice versa by rubber goods producing manufacturers, is possible, but synthetic rubber prices are determined outside the model. Central to the model is the market clearing equation:

$$c_t + x_t + \Delta s_{mf,t} + \Delta s_{gd,t} = q_t + m_{mf,t} + rls_t \qquad (24)$$

where

$x$  =  export;

$m_{mf}$  =  import by manufacturers of rubber products;

$rls$  =  releases by the STC.

The left hand side of equation (24) presents the demand for natural rubber: consumption (c), exports (x), and stock formation by manufacturers ($\Delta s_{mf}$), and stock formation by growers and dealers ($\Delta s_{gd}$). The right hand side of equation (24) represents supply of natural rubber and consists of the production (q), the imports by manufacturers of rubber products ($m_{mf}$) and the releases by the STC (rls). Imports by the State Trading Corporation (STC) are added to stocks held by the STC and do not contribute directly to supply in the domestic market. Imports by the STC are contributing to domestic supply only if these imports are released in the domestic market. As set out in Chapter 2, direct imports by the private sector - imports by manufacturers of rubber products - only came into being in 1982 and are heavily regulated. The market for natural rubber is cleared through the price mechanism. Quantities consumed and placed in stock are negatively related to the fluctuations of (current) rubber prices while production is positively related to these fluctuations. The process of price and quantity adjustment, affecting both supply and demand, continues until equilibrium is realized. The model contains five equations and five unknowns (p, q, $s_{gd}$, $s_{mf}$, c). The following identities are implicit in the discussion above.

$$m_t \quad = \quad m_{stc,t} + m_{mf,t} \tag{25}$$

$$\Delta s_{gd,t} = \quad s_{gd,t} - s_{gd,t-1} \tag{26}$$

$$\Delta s_{mf,t} = \quad s_{mf,t} - s_{mf,t-1} \tag{27}$$

$$\Delta s_{stc,t} = \quad m_{stc,t} - rls_t + proc_t \tag{28}$$

Total imports (m) is given by the sum of imports by the State Trading Corporation ($m_{stc}$) and imports by the manufacturers of rubber products ($m_{mf}$). Stock formation is the difference of current and one period lagged stocks. Stock formation by the STC ($\Delta s_{stc}$) is equal to the imports by the STC ($m_{stc}$) plus the procurement (proc) minus the releases (rls).

For a number of years during the period under consideration there has been a bandwidth price policy effective, the so-called Buffer Stocking scheme. The Buffer Stocking scheme has been operational from 1984 to 1988. In Chapter 2 an extensive description of this price policy, the activities of the State Trading Corporation (STC) and the development of actual, maximum and minimum prices, is presented. In order to formalize such a scheme into our model the following adjustments are required:

$$c_t + x_t + \Delta s_{mf,t} + \Delta s_{gd,t} + proc_t = q_t + m_{mf,t} + rls^{norm}_t + rls^{mx}_t \tag{24'}$$

where

| | | |
|---|---|---|
| proc | = | procurement by the STC; |
| $rls^{norm}$ | = | 'normal' releases by the STC; |
| $rls^{mx}$ | = | releases by the STC due to the bandwidth price policy. |

$$p_t \leq p_{max,t} \qquad \perp rls^{mx}_t \geq 0 \tag{29}$$

$$p_t \geq p_{min,t} \qquad \perp proc_t \geq 0 \tag{30}$$

where

$p_{max}$ = maximum notified price of RMA4;

$p_{min}$ = minimum notified price of RMA4;

$\perp$ indicates that at least one of the two expressions must hold as an equality.

Pure quantity adjustment takes place if the price hits an exogenous maximum or minimum level. At the maximum price the STC increases its market releases to keep the price below or equal to the maximum level (see equation (29)). From equation (29) it follows that the releases by the STC are partly related to maintaining maximum prices ($rls^{mx}$). The other part of releases follows a more standard practise of the STC to release whenever there is a shortage in the market ($rls^{norm}$) and is not related to the maintenance of a price policy. It should be noted that both types of releases cannot be distinguished empirically, only their aggregate can be observed ($rls=rls^{mx}+rls^{norm}$). Likewise the STC intervenes in the market by means of its procurement, if the minimum price is reached (see equation (30)). Procurement enters the market clearing identity (equation (26')) as an additional demand component.

In the empirical work of the current chapter we will ignore the impact of the bandwidth price policy entirely. We claim that ignoring this price policy, as a first step, will not be an obstacle to gaining insight into the functioning of this market. During the major part of the period under consideration, prices in this market were free to move and hence, behaviour of agents reflects to a large extent a situation without price policy. One can hardly imagine that, for example, signs of parameters in the model are affected. This is even more so because there are serious doubts if and to what extent the Buffer Stocking Scheme, when operational, has been effective (see Chapter 2 for descriptive evidence). Finally, developing a model without price policy appears to be a logical first step to obtain a reference for constructing and comparing more complex models in which policies are formalized. For these reasons we will proceed as if the price policy has not been effective. Practically this implies that equations (26'), (31) and (32) are omitted in the remaining part of this chapter. Releases that are related to the defense of a maximum price are treated like other releases, i.e. as an exogenous supply shock known in advance with certainty, and procurement is treated likewise as an exogenous demand shock known in advance with certainty.

Although we ignore price policies in the current chapter, we are in fact interested to study its impact. Extensions to the analysis to allow for price policies are therefore implemented in Chapter 4 and 5. Agents in the market, faced with a bandwidth price policy will adjust their expectations of future prices. To calculate these adjusted expectations, an estimation procedure is needed that incorporates the truncation of prices, and, subsequently, applies these adjusted expectations to the behaviour of these agents. This has been implemented in Chapter 4. A number of authors have emphasized the interaction between private and public stockholding (Salant (1983), Newbery and Stiglitz (1981), Gilbert (1993)). In particular it is claimed that standard interventionist type of price policies are ineffective, or even counter-effective, and extremely costly due to the reactions of the private sector. In Chapter 5 it is investigated if and to what extent the behaviour of stockholders has changed due to the Buffer Stocking Scheme.

The elaboration of the behavioral equations has shown that behaviour of both producers and stockholders depends on expected future prices and a number of other variables. The derivation of forward looking model-consistent expected future prices is presented in the next section, Section 3.5.

### 3.5    Deriving rational expectations of prices of natural rubber

Direct estimation of the behaviour of stockholders and in particular speculative behaviour, requires information about expected prices or, if a futures exchange exists, futures prices. However, there exists no futures exchange in India where natural rubber futures are traded, so the option to use futures prices as approximations for expected prices is not avalable. What remains is to construct expected prices. Expected prices are assumed to be rational in the sense that they are model-consistent and reflect knowledge available in the market $({}_tp^e_{t+1}=E_t(p_{t+1})$; Muth (1961)). As the Indian natural rubber market is effectively insulated from the world market for the period under consideration (see Chapter 2), we consider prices to be the outcome of supply and demand in the domestic market. Model-consistent expected prices are derived in a standard way: estimated behavioral equations of stockholders are combined into a model with producers and consumers in which equilibrium determines market prices. The resulting price equation is used to calculate expected prices.

The rational expectations of prices are calculated following the procedure suggested in Wallis (1980). According to this procedure all behavioral equations (equations 9, 10, 21 and 23) should be substituted into the market clearing identity (equation (24)), and then solved for prices. This generates a second order difference equation in (expected) prices, the solution of which can be shown to be unique under certain assumptions (see Pesaran (1987)). We shall, however, follow a slightly different route. Instead of using all the behavioral equations we only use equations for stockholding (equations 10 and 11) and consumption (equation (23)), insert these into the market clearing identity, (equation (24)), and solve these for prices. Implicitly we make the simplifying assumption that the price elasticity of production is sufficiently small relative to the price elasticities in stockholding and consumption, so that we can ignore this price elasticity. In short: in the price formation production is assumed to be (approximately) exogenous. This seems appropriate for most commodity markets, in particular markets with perennial crops. Solving for prices yields:

$$\Delta p_t = 1/(\rho\zeta_1 + \rho\xi_1 - \beta_2).$$
$$[(\beta_0 + \zeta_0 + \xi_0) + (\zeta_1 + \xi_1)\Delta_t p^e_{t+1} + x_t - (q_t + m_{mf,t} + rls_t) + \beta_1\Delta inc_t + \beta_3\Delta p_{sr,t} +$$
$$(1 + \beta_5 + \zeta_4)c_{t-1} + \beta_6 inc_{t-1} + \beta_7 p_{t-1} + \beta_8 p_{sr,t-1} + \zeta_3 s_{mf,t-1} + \xi_2\Delta q_t + \xi_3 s_{gd,t-1} + \xi_4 q_{t-1}] \quad (31)$$

Collecting terms in a convenient way yields:

$$\Delta p_t = \theta_0 + \lambda \Delta_t p^e_{t+1} + \theta_1 blc_t + \theta_2\Delta inc_t + \theta_3\Delta p_{sr,t} + \theta_4 c_{t-1} + \theta_5\ inc_{t-1} +$$
$$\theta_6\ p_{t-1} + \theta_7\ p_{sr,t-1} + \theta_8 s_{mf,t-1} + \theta_9\Delta q_t + \theta_{10} s_{gd,t-1} + \theta_{11} q_{t-1} \quad (32)$$

$0 < \lambda < 1; \quad \theta_1 > 0; \quad \theta_2 > 0; \quad \theta_3 > 0; \quad \theta_4 <> 0; \quad \theta_5 > 0;$
$\theta_6 < 0; \quad \theta_7 > 0; \quad \theta_8 < 0; \quad \theta_9 > 0; \quad \theta_{10} < 0; \quad \theta_{11} > 0;$
where

$blc_t \quad = -q_t - m_{mf,t} - rls_t + x_t;$
$\lambda \quad = (\zeta_1 + \xi_1)/(\rho\zeta_1 + \rho\xi_1 - \beta_2); \quad \theta_0 = (\beta_0 + \zeta_0 + \xi_0)/(\rho\zeta_1 + \rho\xi_1 - \beta_2);$
$\theta^1 \quad = 1/(\rho\zeta_1 + \rho\xi_1 - \beta_2); \quad \theta_2 = \theta_1.\beta_1; \quad \theta_3 = \theta_1.\beta_3; \quad \theta_4 = \theta_1.(1 + \beta_5 + \zeta_4);$
$\theta_5 \quad = \theta_1.\beta_6; \quad \theta_6 = \theta_1.\beta_7; \quad \theta_7 = \theta_1.\beta_8; \quad \theta_8 = \theta_1.\zeta_3;$
$\theta_9 \quad = \theta_1.\xi_2; \quad \theta_{10} = \theta_1.\xi_3; \quad \theta_{11} = \theta_1.\xi_4;$

The usual way to proceed is to take expectation of both sides, forward all variables of the equation and substitute the result in the original equation. Repeated substitution of expected future prices yields the familiar expression in which expected price is function of an infinite chain of expected current and future demand and supply factors (cf. Gilbert (1990)).

We proceed along these lines, but encounter severe problems in finding a suitable reduced form price equation, due to the error correction specification used in the original behavioral equations. The derivation of an approximate reduced form price equation is set out below. For expositional reasons some drastic simplifications are made: future, current exogenous and lagged endogenous explanatory variables are taken together and the constant term is omitted. This yields:

$$\Delta p_t = \lambda \, \Delta \, {}_t p^e_{t+1} + Z' \Delta X_t + V' Y_{t-1} \tag{33}$$

where

$$Z' \Delta X_t = \theta_1 blc_t + \theta_2 \Delta inc_t + \theta_9 \Delta q_t + \theta_3 \Delta p_{sr,t}$$

$$V' Y_{t-1} = \theta_4 c_{t-1} + \theta_5 inc_{t-1} + \theta_6 \, p_{t-1} + \theta_7 \, p_{sr,t-1} + \theta_8 s_{mf,t-1} + \theta_{10} s_{gd,t-1} + \theta_{11} q_{t-1}$$

Taking expectations from both sides, yields:

$$E_t \Delta p_t = \lambda \, E_t \Delta p_{t+1} + Z' E_t \Delta X_t + V' E_t Y_{t-1} \tag{34}$$

The next step is to forward equation (34) and insert the resulting expression in the original equation, equation (33). This process can be repeated by forwarding equation (34) two periods and inserting the result in the outcome of the earlier step. Repeated substitution of forwarded equations yields the following general expression:

$$E_t \Delta p_t = \lambda^{k+1} E_t \Delta p_{t+k+1} + \sum_{n=0}^{k} \lambda^n \, [\, Z' E_t \Delta X_{t+n} + V' E_t Y_{t+n-1} ] \tag{35}$$

Provided that $\lambda$ lies between zero and one, the impact of expectations in a more distant future will become smaller and smaller. With an infinite number of higher order expected prices substituted, the impact of the last expected price will approximately be zero (or $\lambda^n \rightarrow 0$ for $n \rightarrow \infty$). The number of times this process should be repeated in the price equation will be determined empirically. Hence, for a large value of k, $\lambda^{k+1} \rightarrow 0$, and we may write:

$$E_t \Delta p_t = \sum_{n=0}^{k} \lambda^n \, [\, Z' E_t \Delta X_{t+n} + V' E_t Y_{t+n-1} ] \tag{36}$$

Equation (36) cannot be estimated due to the endogeneity of the term $\Sigma \lambda^n V' E_t Y_{t+n-1}$. To overcome this problem all endogenous variables should be substituted out. This is to some extent implemented in appendix 3.2. Few substitutions make clear that this is a rather troublesome and tedious procedure leading to a highly complex specification that hardly permits a sensible economic interpretation. For that reason we propose to estimate the following equation that contains a limited part of equation (36):

$$\triangle_t p^e_t = \quad \Sigma \ \lambda^n \ Z' \triangle_t X^e_{t+n} \ + V' Y_{t-1} \tag{37}$$

This equation can be estimated as all the right hand side variables are either exogenous or predetermined. With this equation some steps are made on the way to the general formulation of equation (36).


## 3.6    Estimation results of behavioral equations

### 3.6.1    Estimation of expectational variables

Before we are able to estimate equation (37) we need to calculate expectational values of exogenous expectational variables ($blc^e, \triangle inc^e, \triangle q^e$). Expectational values of production and income, both in first differences, are constructed with an auto-regressive process including trend(s) and monthly dummies. Such a presentation is assumed to be stationary over time, which allows the use of the estimated parameters for calculation of expectational variables. An alternative procedure would be to estimate the above relationship recursively, with the obvious drawback of large standard errors for small samples. The auto-regressive terms are 12 months lagged or more: provided that the lead in expected prices is less than 12 months, such a specification also overcomes problems with the information-set that is available at the period of expectation formation. Additional to this specification we controlled for a number of outliers by adding dummies for specific months. One might be suspicious about using these dummies: however, in forming expected values of exogenous variables, one cannot imagine that agents are able to forecast future outliers. Nevertheless, arbitrariness in choosing the dummies remains.

It should be noted that the treatment of production is hybrid: in the current section we treat production as an exogenous variable, while later on we estimate a relationship relating production to expected price. If price elasticities are low, the two procedures are approximately equivalent. The selected equations are presented in Table 3.1.

The estimation results are fairly good (acceptable R2 and no higher order serial correlation). Trend and trend squared did not turn out to be significant in either equation, which is not surprising, given the outcome of integration tests (see appendix 3.1). These explanatory variables are, however, maintained. Both first order and higher order autocorrelation is rejected. It should be noted that a large part of the explanation of the dependent variable is due to the dummies included for outliers. This is especially obvious if the goodness of fit of these

**Table 3.1**     Estimation results

| estimation method: | OLS | |
| --- | --- | --- |
| sample period: | 1978.12-1991.12; | |
| no. of observations: | 157 | |
| dependent variable | $\Delta q$ | $\Delta inc$ |
| CT | 3480.4 (1.1) | 0.933 (0.1) |
| dm1 | -4327.7 (5.7) | -7.695 (4.9) |
| dm2 | -10398.0 (9.3) | -10.65 (5.8) |
| dm3 | 799.3 (0.7) | -1.052 (0.7) |
| dm4 | 1712.7 (2.5) | -19.73 (7.9) |
| dm5 | 1807.7 (2.5) | -7.103 (3.3) |
| dm6 | -8015.6 (9.1) | -6.818 (4.3) |
| dm7 | 474.0 (0.6) | -6.796 (4.1) |
| dm8 | 1190.8 (1.8) | -8.086 (4.1) |
| dm9 | 4219.2 (5.8) | -6.615 (4.1) |
| dm10 | -494.5 (0.6) | -7.187 (4.4) |
| dm11 | -1282.2 (1.8) | -4.526 (2.9) |
| trend | -21.2 (0.7) | 0.0643 (1.0) |
| trend(sq) | 0.051 (0.7) | -.0001 (1.0) |
| $\Delta q_{t-12}$ | 0.2908 (4.9) | |
| $\Delta q_{t-13}$ | 0.0693 (1.1) | |
| $\Delta inc_{t-12}$ | | 0.376 (5.0) |
| $\Delta inc_{t-13}$ | | -0.013 (0.3) |
| log(L) | -1378.9 | -404.3 |
| R2adj | 0.9143 | 0.9308 |
| Dh | -0.947 | -1.245 |

OLS = Ordinary Least Squares; CT = Constant Term; dmX = dummy for month X; absolute t-values are reported in brackets next to the coefficients; log(L) = Log of Likelihood function; R2adj = coefficient of correlation adjusted for degrees of freedom; Dh = Durbin's h alternative;

NB: Not reported in the table are the coefficients of a number of dummy variables included in the estimation to control for outliers (see the text for further details).

equations is compared to the goodness of fit of the behavioral equations of the sections below.

Levels of expected production ($q^e$) are calculated on the basis of the first difference estimation outcome, using realisations of twelve months back. It should be noted that we assumed perfect foresight with respect to releases (rls), import by manufacturers ($m_{mf}$), procurement (proc) and export(x). This completes the calculation of all exogenous expectational variables, including the expected balance of supply and demand, which is defined as export minus the sum of production, import by manufacturers and releases by the STC ($blc^e$ = x - ($q^e$ + $m_{mf}$ + rls) ; see equation (32)).

### 3.6.2 Estimation of expected prices

Calculation of expected prices is based on estimation of equation (37). It should be noted that the non-linearity of the coefficient of expected future price is due to the repeated substitution of lead terms of expected prices. The number of lead terms of expected price (k) included in the estimation, is determined empirically by assessing the impact of adding additional lead terms on the total estimation outcome. Also the value of $\lambda^{k+1}$ is considered as this value should be small, preferably close to zero. In the actual estimations repeated substitution of additional lead terms has been implemented 6 times. This implies that expectational variables of one up to six months ahead, with appropriate restrictions on the coefficients, are included in the estimated price equation. The coefficient of expected price seven periods ahead has a value of $\lambda^7$ = 0.0407217. If expected prices of a more distant future are ignored, an error is made which is considered small enough to skip these expected prices. The selected estimation of the price equations, estimated with non-linear least squares (NLS), is:

$$\Delta_t p^e_t =$$

$$3.982 + \sum_{k=0}^{6} 0.633^k [+0.343E\text{-}4 \ _t blc^e_{t+k} -0.845E\text{-}4 \ \Delta \ _t q^e_{t+k} -0.019 \ \Delta \ _t inc^e_{t+k}]$$

(2.7)       (6.7)        (1.6)              (2.2)                    (0.9)

$$-0.115E\text{-}3 \ s_{mf,t-1} +0.163E\text{-}3 \ c_{t-1} -0.624E\text{-}4 \ s_{gd,t-1} -0.715E\text{-}4 \ q_{t-1}$$

       (2.7)              (1.6)              (2.9)              (1.9)

$-0.518E-2 \ inc_{t-1} \ -0.318 \ p_{t-1} \ +0.077 \ p_{sr,t-1}$
        $(0.3)$          $(5.4)$                $(1.4)$

Sample period:            1980.01-1989.12; number of observations:   120;
R2adj.=0.270;             log(L)=-168.6;

Dependent variable: price of natural rubber (RMA4) deflated by the general
consumer price index; $\Delta$ indicates a first difference of a variable; the superscript e
indicates expectation of a particular variable; t-statistics are presented in brackets
below the coefficient.

In the We maintained the general specification although a few coefficients do not
have the proper sign and are insignificant (see equation (36)).

### 3.6.3   Estimation of behavioral equations: stocks at growers and dealers

Empirical work on stockholding is often obstructed by poor data. The quality of
the stock data is usually low, that is, data are failing the market clearing identity,
and are often incomplete, unreliable or lacking altogether. This problem is of no
relevance for the current empirical study. The data-set of the Indian rubber market
includes data on stockholding, is complete and meets the market clearing identity.
For further details on the quality of the data set we refer to appendix 2.1 to
Chapter 2.

In the Next we come to the estimation of the behavioral equations. The
estimation results are reported in five tables, four of which are on single equation
estimations (Tables 3.2 to 3.5) and one on system estimations (Table 3.6). Prior to
reporting the estimation results a number of decisions with respect to empirical
specification and estimation method are set out. The error correction framework
(Davidson *et al.* (1978), Engle and Granger (1987), Charemza and Deadman
(1992)) proves to be a helpful device in the identification of the different types of
behaviour of stockholders: (co)integration tests allow to include or exclude
explanatory variables in either level or difference form, with reference to the
outcome of these tests. Tests on the order of integration of variables are reported
in appendix 3.1 to this chapter. Short- and long-run relationships are estimated
simultaneously: this estimation method is efficient and allows direct tests on the
cointegrating variables (Boswijk (1992, 1994)). Behavioral equations are estimated
with Ordinary Least Squares (OLS) and Two Stage Least Squares (2SLS), in case
of single equation estimations, and Full Information Maximum Likelihood (FIML)
in case of system estimations. With endogenous regressors (in our case current
and expected future prices) we cannot use OLS, and we need to instrument the

endogenous variable. With 2SLS estimations the following variables are used as instruments in addition to all non-price explanatory variables of the specific equation: production (q), lagged stocks with growers and dealers ($s_{gd,t-1}$) and manufacturers ($s_{mf,t-1}$) and lagged consumption ($c_{t-1}$). Parameters from the single equation estimations are used as starting values in FIML estimations. In all behavioral equations except the consumption equation an additive monthly pattern is imposed in order to capture seasonal fluctuations that are not covered by other explanatory variables. It should be noted that these monthly dummies are not reported in the tables with estimation results.

In Table 3.2 selected estimations of stock demand by growers and dealers are reported. Estimations are based on equation (9). In the first column, estimation (1), a general specification is used with expected prices of six periods ahead included. The other columns show the estimation results of equations with an expected price variable of one particular period in the future. From equation (9) and (10) it is observed that prices of one month ahead determine stock demand: through the chaining of the expected prices, expected prices of months further will matter. For this reason we have experimented in the estimation with including a number of leads of expected future prices. Assuming a negligible rate of interest (or $\rho \approx 1$) it follows from equation (9) and (10), that the coefficient of current price and expected price (for a specific period ahead) should be equal but with opposite sign. The likelihood ratio test statistic ($\chi^2_{restriction}$) is reported in the table to evaluate this restriction.

Estimated equations of stock demand by growers and dealers ($s_{gd}$) show a good fit: the estimations have a correlation coefficient adjusted for degrees of freedom of above 0.75. Higher order autocorrelation (not shown) could be rejected as well. In estimations (2) to (5) all coefficients of explanatory variables are significant or almost significant at the conventional levels, with the notable exception of expected prices, and all have the right sign. Expected price, however, is clearly significant and has the right sign if expected price of three periods ahead is used. The restriction that the coefficient of current price and expected price is the same but with opposite sign, is tested. Values of the Likelihood Ratio statistic ($\chi^2_{restriction}$) indicate that this restriction cannot be rejected in equation (4), but should be rejected in the other equations. On the basis of goodness of fit (loglikelihood, R2adj) of restricted equations (not shown) we also select estimation (4) as the best.

Significant coefficients of price and expected price, and non rejection of the restriction on these coefficients, allows the conclusion that the hypothesis of speculative stock demand cannot be rejected. A lead structure in stock demand of

**Table 3.2**     Estimation results

dependent variable:    change in stocks at growers and dealers ($\Delta s_{gd}$)
estimation method:    2SLS
sample period:       1980.1-1989.12
no. of observations:   120

| | (1) | (2) | (3) | (4) | (5) |
|---|---|---|---|---|---|
| CT | 2456.5 | 2137.3 | 1841.9 | 1472.7 | 2025.2 |
| | (1.3) | (1.2) | (1.1) | (0.9) | (1.3) |
| $\Delta p$ | -1669.8 | -1444.2 | -1414.6 | -1455.8 | -1441.1 |
| | (2.8) | (2.9) | (3.0) | (2.9) | (2.9) |
| $_t\Delta p^e_{t+1}$ | -235.3 | 61.0 | | | |
| | (0.4) | (0.2) | | | |
| $_t\Delta p^e_{t+2}$ | -568.4 | | 228.9 | | |
| | (0.8) | | (0.7) | | |
| $_t\Delta p^e_{t+3}$ | 1867.9 | | | 737.6 | |
| | (2.4) | | | (1.9) | |
| $_t\Delta p^e_{t+4}$ | -392.3 | | | | 172.3 |
| | (0.6) | | | | (0.5) |
| $_t\Delta p^e_{t+5}$ | -826.3 | | | | |
| | (1.1) | | | | |
| $_t\Delta p^e_{t+6}$ | 412.8 | | | | |
| | (0.7) | | | | |
| $\Delta q$ | 0.452 | 0.445 | 0.450 | 0.462 | 0.450 |
| | (4.8) | (5.2) | (5.2) | (5.4) | (5.2) |
| $s_{gd,t-1}$ | -0.077 | -0.082 | -0.079 | -0.064 | -0.079 |
| | (2.1) | (2.6) | (2.5) | (2.0) | (2.4) |
| $q_{t-1}$ | 0.115 | 0.114 | 0.117 | 0.113 | 0.112 |
| | (1.5) | (1.7) | (1.8) | (1.7) | (1.7) |
| log(L) | - | -1081.6 | -1081.9 | -1082.0 | -1082.0 |
| $\chi^2_{restriction}$ | - | 4.50 | 5.56 | 2.70 | 6.78 |
| R2adj | 0.750 | 0.785 | 0.784 | 0.783 | 0.783 |

$\chi^2_{restriction}$ is the likelihood ratio test statistic on the restriction on prices and expected prices, and is $\chi^2$ distributed with one degree of freedom (5% critical value: 3.841).

NB: Not reported in the table are the coefficients of a complete set of monthly dummy variables, included additional to the above explanatory variables, in all behavioral equations except the equation of consumption.

three months is in accordance with what is known from local dealers and their representative organizations (eg. the Kerala State Cooperative Rubber Marketing Federation Ltd.). Evaluated at the mean the elasticity of demand with respect to current and expected prices has a value of 0.8.[5] Elasticity with respect to production, evaluated at the mean, is 0.3 in the short run. Long run or equilibrium elasticity with respect to production, also evaluated at the mean, is around 1.4. A level of somewhat more than 2 months of production is kept in stock. A large part of stock formation by growers and dealers is due to fluctuations in the production process, both in the short run and in the long run. This latter relationship corroborates the view that carrying stocks generates a convenience yield.

### 3.6.4   Estimation of behavioral equations: stocks at manufacturers

In Table 3.3 selected estimations of stock demand by manufacturers are presented. Estimations are based on equation (10). Including values of consumption in first differences did not turn out to give good results (not significant) and this variable is therefore skipped from the list of explanatory variables. Again the first column, estimation (1), the estimation result of a specification with a sequence of expected prices is given, while the other columns report estimations with just one expected price. Analogous to the estimations the table reports the likelihood ratio statistic ($\chi^2_{restriction}$) on the restriction that the coefficients of current and expected price are equal but with opposite sign, using the same assumption with respect to discounting.

Estimations of stock demand by manufacturers ($s_{mf}$) perform substantially less compared to estimations of stock demand by growers and dealers. Adjusted R2 has a value ranging from 0.385 to 0.392 (ignoring estimation (1)). Higher order autocorrelation could be rejected. In estimation (1) we see significant (positive) coefficients for nearby expected prices. From estimations (2) to (4) it is seen that the restriction imposed on current and expected price is rejected in all estimations: only estimation (3) comes close to non-rejection.[6]

---

5       Mean values of variables are: p=25.1; $p_{sr}$=29.5; q=17525; $s_{gd}$=28163; $s_{mf}$=20766; c=20631; inc=143.2.

6       The critical value at 5% significance and 1 degree of freedom is 3.841.

**Table 3.3**     Estimation results

dependent variable:   change in stocks at manufacturers ($\Delta s_{mf}$)
estimation method:   2SLS
sample period:       1980.1-1989.12
no. of observations:  120

|  | (1) | (2) | (3) | (4) |
|---|---|---|---|---|
| CT | 3374.4 | 3715.6 | 3069.3 | 3628.3 |
|  | (2.7) | (3.6) | (3.1) | (3.8) |
| $\Delta p$ | -1264.1 | -1315.7 | -1285.6 | -1358.3 |
|  | (2.6) | (3.5) | (3.6) | (3.6) |
| $_t\Delta p^e_{t+1}$ | -704.2 | 91.6 |  |  |
|  | (1.4) | (0.4) |  |  |
| $_t\Delta p^e_{t+2}$ | 1342.4 |  | 538.5 |  |
|  | (2.3) |  | (2.1) |  |
| $_t\Delta p^e_{t+3}$ | -91.1 |  |  | 237.1 |
|  | (0.1) |  |  | (0.8) |
| $_t\Delta p^e_{t+4}$ | -347.7 |  |  |  |
|  | (0.6) |  |  |  |
| $_t\Delta p^e_{t+5}$ | -568.6 |  |  |  |
|  | (0.9) |  |  |  |
| $_t\Delta p^e_{t+6}$ | 645.2 |  |  |  |
|  | (1.4) |  |  |  |
| $s_{mf,t-1}$ | -0.316 | -0.354 | -0.329 | -0.349 |
|  | (4.2) | (5.5) | (5.2) | (5.6) |
| $c_{t-1}$ | 0.259 | 0.281 | 0.278 | 0.282 |
|  | (3.7) | (4.9) | (4.9) | (4.9) |
| log(L) | - | -1048.6 | -1047.9 | -1048.6 |
| $\chi^2_{restriction}$ | - | 6.40 | 3.94 | 11.44 |
| R2adj | 0.230 | 0.386 | 0.392 | 0.385 |

NB: Not reported in the table are the coefficients of a complete set of monthly dummy variables, included additional to the above explanatory variables in all behavioral equations except the equation of consumption.

Based on goodness of fit (log(L), R2adj) estimation (3) performs best and this is also true for restricted specifications. Speculative behaviour in the stockholding activities of manufacturers is not rejected by these estimation results. The elasticity of demand with respect to current and expected price, evaluated at the mean, is around 0.9. Long run elasticity with respect to consumption is around 0.9. A level of somewhat less than 1 month of consumption is kept in stock.

### 3.6.5   Estimation of behavioral equations: production

In Table 3.4 selected estimation output of equations for production is shown. Estimations are based on equation (21). One explanatory variable needs some additional comment. We require monthly data on long run production ($q_{lr}$). Long run production is a constructed time series of production that accounts for the vintage composition and the yield profile of rubber trees: it embodies the typical long run dynamics of 'perennial crop' production. Time series on annual long run production are taken from Burger *et al.* (1995, see Burger *et al.* (1995), pp. 91-95). Transforming these annual series into monthly long run production is imple-mented by multiplying average monthly long run values with a weighing factor. The weighing factor is a three year moving average of the seasonal fluctuations in actual production; seasonal fluctuation is defined as actual production relative to average production. In formula this reads:

$$q_{lr,i,t} = \varphi_{i,t} * (q_{lr,annually,t}/12)$$

$$\text{where } \varphi_{i,t} = [\sum_{j=1}^{3} q_{monthly,i,t-j} / q_{monthly\ average,t-j}] / 3, \qquad \sum \varphi_i = 1$$

$$\text{and} \qquad q_{monthly\ average,t} = \sum_{i=1}^{12} q_{monthly,i,t}/12,$$

The estimated production equation has a high correlation coefficient: adjusted R2 moves around 0.88. Test statistics on (first and higher) order autocorrelation have acceptable values. Expected price for the current period conditional on the previous period information, expected prices one period ahead and one period lagged prices do have the right sign, but are all not significant. One to three months lagged rainfall has a positive, however, hardly significant impact. The instantaneous impact of the number of rainfall days per month is negative, as expected and significant. Error correction is highly significant.

The good statistical fit is to a large extent due to the high seasonality of production: recall that a complete set of monthly dummies is included to control

**Table 3.4**  Estimation results

dependent variable:   change in production ($\Delta q$)

estimation method:   OLS

sample period:   1980.1-1989.12

no. of observations:   120

|  | (1) | (2) | (3) | (4) |
|---|---|---|---|---|
| CT | 2706.0 | 2401.0 | 2719.2 | 2716.0 |
|  | (1.7) | (1.5) | (1.7) | (1.7) |
| $rfmm_{t-1}$ | 1.718 | 1.208 | 1.824 | 1.779 |
|  | (0.9) | (0.6) | (1.0) | (1.0) |
| $rfmm_{t-2}$ | 1.801 | 1.205 | 1.771 | 1.845 |
|  | (1.1) | (0.7) | (1.1) | (1.1) |
| $rfmm_{t-3}$ | 0.724 | 0.177 | 0.779 | 0.791 |
|  | (0.4) | (0.1) | (0.5) | (0.5) |
| rfnd | -186.5 | -184.1 | -186.0 | -187.0 |
|  | (3.6) | (3.6) | (3.6) | (3.7) |
| $_{t-1}\Delta p^e_t$ | 58.7 |  |  |  |
|  | (0.2) |  |  |  |
| $_{t}\Delta p^e_{t+1}$ |  | 479.0 |  |  |
|  |  | (1.4) |  |  |
| $\Delta p_{t-1}$ |  |  | 146.4 |  |
|  |  |  | (0.4) |  |
| $q_{t-1}$ | -0.726 | -0.749 | -0.696 | -0.720 |
|  | (5.8) | (6.5) | (5.9) | (6.3) |
| $q_{lr,t-1}$ | 0.691 | 0.736 | 0.660 | 0.682 |
|  | (5.0) | (5.5) | (5.0) | (5.3) |
| log(L) | -1071.6 | -1070.4 | -1071.2 | -1071.6 |
| R2adj | 0.880 | 0.882 | 0.880 | 0.881 |

NB: Not reported in the table are the coefficients (of a complete set) of monthly dummy variables, included additional to the above explanatory variables in all behavioral equations except the equation of consumption.

for systematic monthly influences. If equation (1) is assumed to represent the actual short run response of growers on expected price, the elasticity of production, evaluated at the mean, has a value of 0.08. Despite the low t-statistic we are inclined to consider such a low elasticity acceptable. In the long run production will tend to follow the trend in production, as calculated with the vintage approach.

### 3.6.6 Estimation of behavioral equations: consumption

In Table 3.5 selected estimation output of equations for consumption is shown. Estimations are based on equation (22). The price of synthetic rubber is a weighted average of domestic price of different grades of synthetic rubber, with the production share as weight. The income variable is approximated with real gross domestic product (source: CSO/India). Short term response to prices is shown to have the proper sign and to be almost significant. Elasticity of consumption with respect to price, evaluated at the mean, is around 0.3. Long run price elasticity is lower. Coefficients of prices of synthetic rubber have the right sign in the long run, but are not significant. Finally, gross industrial product influences consumption of rubber significantly both in the short run (short run elasticity: around 0.4) as well as in the long run (long run elasticity: 0.9).

Using price series of different grades of synthetic rubber instead of a weighted average (not shown) did not generate substantial improvement in the significance of the coefficient of synthetic rubber prices. A possible explanation for this poor result is that the inter-commodity substitution is blurred due to the level of aggregation. Estimations with annual data of specific end-products and with prices of different grades of both synthetic and natural rubber, do show significant, however, low substitution elasticities of synthetic rubber for natural rubber (not shown). Low and insignificant substitution elasticities can also be explained by the large difference in domestic prices of natural relative to synthetic rubber in the sample period (see Chapter 2): quantities are only sensitive if synthetic rubber prices move within a limited range of natural rubber prices. Coefficients of prices become more significant if estimations are run for a longer sample period (78.09-91.12; estimations not shown): these estimations indicate a significant short run price elasticity of 0.5, a significant long run price elasticity of 0.6, and a nearly significant long run elasticity with respect to synthetic rubber prices of 0.3, all evaluated at the mean.

**Table 3.5**     Estimation results

dependent variable:   change in consumption ($\Delta c$)

estimation method:    2SLS

sample period:        1980.1-1989.12

no. of observations:  120

| | (1) | (2) | (3) | (4) |
|---|---|---|---|---|
| CT | 755.0 | 755.6 | 885.3 | 967.0 |
| | (0.4) | (0.4) | (0.5) | (0.5) |
| $\Delta p$ | -222.0 | -249.8 | -229.4 | -246.1 |
| | (1.5) | (1.7) | (1.5) | (1.7) |
| $\Delta p_{sr}$ | -17.6 | | -18.9 | |
| | (0.3) | | (0.3) | |
| $\Delta inc$ | 58.5 | 58.3 | 58.3 | 58.4 |
| | (5.1) | (5.1) | (5.1) | (5.1) |
| $c_{t-1}$ | -0.341 | -0.339 | -0.342 | -0.340 |
| | (4.1) | (4.1) | (4.1) | (4.1) |
| $inc_{t-1}$ | 47.3 | 46.5 | 47.3 | 46.8 |
| | (3.5) | (3.4) | (3.5) | (3.5) |
| $p_{t-1}$ | -20.9 | -26.2 | -21.5 | -23.5 |
| | (0.4) | (0.5) | (0.4) | (0.5) |
| $p_{sr,t-1}$ | 3.6 | 10.4 | | |
| | (0.1) | (0.2) | | |
| log(L) | - | - | | |
| R2adj | 0.171 | 0.168 | 0.176 | 0.176 |

### 3.6.7   Estimation of behavioral equations: system estimations

As mentioned in Section 3.3 it is likely that the disturbances in behavioral equations will be correlated. With system estimation we are able to control for these effects. The estimated system of equations contains four behavioral equations (stockholding by growers and dealers (equation (9)), stockholding by manufacturers (equation (10)), production (equation (21)) and consumption (equation (23))), and five identities (the accounting identity (equation (24)), and four identities relating levels of endogenous variables to first differences). The system has nine endogenous variables: stockholding by growers and dealers, stockholding by manufacturers, production and consumption, all in level and in first differences, and prices in first differences. Levels of variables are required because the accounting identity is in levels. In the system estimation, expected prices are derived iteratively. Expected price is calculated according to equation (37) and contains all the cross equation restrictions: all parameters appearing in the expected price equation are in fact parameters appearing in the four behavioral equations. Once convergence in estimation is realized the estimated parameters of the behavioral equations are used to construct a new expected price variable. With the new expected price variable the FIML estimation is implemented again. This process is repeated until the value of the loglikelihood function does not change. Eventually the parameters that are used in the construction of expected price are identical to the parameters that are generated as estimation result of the behavioral equations.

Some additional assumptions are required. Short term elasticity of supply is fixed to 0 in the estimations. As in earlier estimations ρ has a fixed value of 1.005. FIML estimations did not converge without additional restrictions. Therefore the short run coefficient of price in the consumption equation has been constrained on the level of the single equation estimations. FIML estimation of the resulting system did converge and the iterative procedure to calculate expected price also generated stable outcomes.

Estimation results are presented in Table 3.6. Production is relatively well explained. Rainfall has a positive effect but it is, however, hardly significant. The instantaneous impact of the number of rainfall days per month is negative, as expected and significant. Long run production is significant because of the error correction mechanism. The estimation result for production is similar to the single equation estimation. In stockholding the estimation result is slightly different compared to single equation estimations. Again, speculative behaviour in stockholding activities of growers and dealers isnot rejected. However, the elasticity of demand with respect to current and expected price, evaluated at the mean, is some what higher, around 2.1. Equilibrium elasticity with respect to production is around 1. On the manufacturing side speculative behaviour is also not rejected by these estimation results. The elasticity of demand with respect to current and expected price, evaluated at the mean, is around 2.2. Long run elasticity with respect to consumption is significant and also come near to a value of 1. In consumption short term response to prices is, as noted above, constrained to a value that corresponds with the single equation estimations (and implies an elasticity of 0.3 evaluated at the mean). Coefficients of prices of synthetic rubber do have the right sign, but are hardly significant. Gross industrial product influences consumption of rubber significantly both in the short run as well as in the long run (short run and long run elasticity is around 0.4).

**Table 3.6**      Estimation results

estimation method:              FIML
sample period:                  1980.1-1989.12
no. of observations:            120
log likelihood function:        -3229.8

| dependent variable | $\Delta q$ | $\Delta s_{gd}$ | $\Delta s_{mf}$ | $\Delta c$ |
|---|---|---|---|---|
| CT | 2978.1  (1.1) | -1976.7 (0.4) | 2088.8 (0.7) | -776.0 (0.3) |
| $rfmm_{t-1}$ | 0.980  (0.3) | | | |
| $rfmm_{t-2}$ | 1.561  (0.7) | | | |
| $rfmm_{t-3}$ | 1.711  (0.9) | | | |
| rfnd | -199.7  (3.4) | | | |
| $\Delta q$ | | 0.266 (0.7) | | |
| $\Delta p$ | | -3771.4 (1.9) | -2814.1 (2.5) | -250.0 (-) |
| $\Delta p^e_{t+3}$ | | 859.6 (1.1) | | |
| $\Delta p^e_{t+2}$ | | | 815.2 (1.2) | |
| $\Delta inc$ | | | | 60.2 (3.7) |
| $q_{t-1}$ | -0.822  (5.4) | 0.096 (0.5) | | |
| $q_{lr,t-1}$ | 0.783  (4.3) | | | |
| $s_{gd,t-1}$ | | -0.057 (0.8) | | |
| $s_{mf,t-1}$ | | | -0.361 (2.9) | |
| $c_{t-1}$ | | | 0.344 (2.2) | -0.384 (3.8) |
| $inc_{t-1}$ | | | | 57.5 (3.7) |
| $p_{t-1}$ | | | | 21.2 (0.4) |
| $p_{sr,t-1}$ | | | | 12.6 (0.2) |
| R2adj | 0.896 | 0.534 | 0.129 | 0.203 |

NB: Not reported in the table are the coefficients of a complete set of monthly dummy variables, included additional to the above explanatory variables, in all behavioral equations except the equation for consumption. The equation of price expectation is implicit in the coefficients of the behavioral equations and is not reported separately in the table.

The most striking difference between the single equation estimations and the system estimation is the size of the elasticity of speculative stock demand.

This elasticity increases from slightly above 0.9 to 2.1 in case of stockholding by growers and dealers, and to 2.2 in case of stockholding by manufacturers. This is presumably caused by the correlation of the errors in the behavioral equations. The elasticities on the basis of the system estimations come closer to what is reported in the empirical literature: Miranda and Glauber (1993) report an elasticity of stock demand in the US soy-bean market of 4.8.

## 3.7    Summary and conclusion

In this chapter stock behaviour in commodity markets is investigated with a small rational expectation error correction model of the Indian natural rubber market, covering the period from January 1980 to December 1989. During this period the Indian natural rubber market was relatively isolated from the world market so that price data can be considered as the outcome of domestic market clearing. 2SLS and FIML estimations provide clear evidence of speculative behaviour in stockholding. The error correction framework provides a helpful device in distinguishing speculative behaviour, a typical short run activity, from other types of stockholding behaviour. Transaction demand is strongly reflected in equilibrium behaviour of manufacturers. The relatively simple empirical framework developed in this chapter allows to identify different types of stock behaviour and gives plausible outcomes for speculative behaviour. In this respect it compares reasonably well to the competitive storage model. With a perennial crop like natural rubber, a rather small, but nevertheless non-zero, short run elasticity of production with respect to prices should be expected. However, we are unable to confirm a (significant) short term price responsiveness of production with the current estimations. Consumption of natural rubber is to some extent price elastic in the short run, but the price elasticity is much lower than the price elasticities of speculative stock demand. With the size of the elasticities of all groups we conclude that most short run responsiveness to prices is by arbitrage activities of stockholders (growers, dealers and manufacturers), and not by increasing or decreasing production or consumption. Hence, by far the largest quantity adjustments induced by prices and price expectations are due to behaviour of stockholders. Substantial inter-temporal arbitrage in this market by stockholders points at a huge potential to stabilize prices without government intervention. This conclusion will also apply to other commodity markets with similar features. In particular we refer to commodity markets of perennial crops with a price formation that is to a large extent independent of the world market. Although in the era of trade liberalization few domestic markets can be claimed to be isolated from the world market, the conclusion also applies to domestic markets where domestic supply more or less balances domestic demand for prolonged stretches of time, or markets where goods are traded that are not traded in the world market. High elasticities of speculative demand for stocks in such markets of 'non-traded' commodities or 'non-tradeables' suggest that a bandwidth price policy intended to stabilize prices might be superfluous or even counter-effective (cf. Gilbert (1993)): this matter will be investigated in Chapter 5.

## Appendix 3.1

### Data, (co)integration tests and dynamic specification

Most data are published in the Indian Rubber Statistics. For more details on data and their sources, see Chapter 2. Stock variables are measured at the end of the period. The data meet the market clearing identity as formulated in equation (24), apart from minor errors that are negligible compared with the magnitude of the variables.[7] The price of natural rubber and synthetic rubber is deflated by the general consumer price index. Calculated values for long run production are available on an annual basis, and, hence, a monthly seasonal pattern is super-imposed.

In Table 3.7 the augmented Dickey Fuller test statistics are reported, to find the order of integration of the variables used. These are calculated as the t-statistic of $\alpha$ in the test equation $\triangle x_t = (\text{constant} +)\alpha x_{t-1} + \beta_j \Sigma \triangle x_{t-j-1} \ (+\gamma t)$ in the upper panel and $\triangle \triangle x_t = (\text{constant} +) \ \alpha \triangle x_{t-1} + \beta_j \Sigma \triangle \triangle x_{t-j-1} \ (+\gamma t)$ in the lower panel. Equations with and without constant term and trend variable are reported separately. Every first column reports the ADF test statistic with one lagged variable (j=0). Testing for higher order serial auto-correlation on the basis of an LM test for AR(p)/MA(p) disturbances with a maximum lag length of 12, revealed serious higher order serial correlation, almost without exception. Reducing this by adding lags was, unfortunately, not effective in all cases (rejection of higher order serial autocorrelation at the 5% level is indicated in Table 3.7 with an asterisk): however, changing the sample period in order to do away with outliers showed that this test outcome is due to outliers and does not invalidate the ADF tests.

From the upper panel of Table 3.7 we cannot reject the null hypothesis of integration ($H_0$: $x_t \sim I(1)$) for all variables, with some exceptions. ADF statistics of rfmm and rfnd indicate rejection of the null hypothesis of integration: however, both rainfall and number of rainfall days should be I(0). Additionally $s_{gd}$ (ct,t, one lag), $s_{mf}$ (ct,t, one lag) point at rejection. It should be noted that the extended test equations, with 12 lags, indicate that we cannot reject the null. From the lower panel of Table 3.7, reporting test statistics on variables in first differences, the null hypothesis ($H_0$: $x_t \sim I(2)$) is rejected for all variables (with the exception of

---

7      If market clearing is characterized with an error of less than 1% of consumption of natural rubber, and after some minor and obvious corrections, the original monthly series fulfil the market clearing identity in around 50% of all periods (for details see appendix to Chapter 2).

**Table 3.7**     Testing the order of integration of variables (period: 80.01-90.12)

$H_0$: $x_t \sim I(1)$ against $H_A$: $x_t \sim I(0)$; in levels

| variable | ADF,nct,nt | | ADF,ct | | ADF,ct,t | |
|---|---|---|---|---|---|---|
| lags | 1 | 12 | 1 | 12 | 1 | 12 |
| $q$ | -1.5 | 4.3 | [-5.0] | 2.5 | [-7.5] | -0.5 |
| $q_{lr}$ | -1.3 | 0.9 * | [-5.0] | 3.2 * | [-7.6] | [2.7] (*) |
| $s_{gd}$ | -0.9 | 0.6 * | [-3.9] | -1.1 * | -5.8 | -2.2 |
| $s_{mf}$ | 0.0 | 1.3 | [-2.5] | -0.3 | -4.8 | -2.1 (*) |
| $c$ | 1.6 | 3.9 * | -0.0 | 2.2 * | [-4.4] | -1.3 (*) |
| $p$ | -0.5 | 2.9 | [-2.4] | -0.5 | [-5.0] | [-2.9] |
| $p_{sr}$ | 0.3 * | 0.8 * | [-3.0] * | -1.5 | [-3.1] | -1.5 |
| inc | 1.4 | 5.0 * | -0.4 | 3.1 * | [-5.2] | [-1.0] (*) |
| rfmm | -3.4 | -0.4 * | [-5.7] | [-2.4] * | -5.7 | [-2.5] (*) |
| rfnd | -2.8 | -0.6 * | [-5.4] | -1.7 * | [-5.4] | [-2.3] (*) |

$H_0$: $x_t \sim I(2)$ against $H_A$: $x_t \sim I(1)$; in first differences

| variable | ADF,nct,nt | | ADF,ct | | ADF,ct,t | |
|---|---|---|---|---|---|---|
| lags | 1 | 12 | 1 | 12 | 1 | 12 |
| $q$ | -9.8 | -6.1 * | -9.7 | [-7.4] | -9.7 | [-8.3] |
| $q_{lr}$ | -10.2 | -5.9 * | -10.1 | 0.4 * | -10.2 | [-2.3] |
| $s_{gd}$ | -8.2 | -2.8 | -8.2 | -2.9 | -8.2 | -2.9 |
| $s_{mf}$ | -9.2 | -3.7 | -9.2 | -3.9 | -9.2 | -4.0 |
| $c$ | -11.9 | -1.9 | [-12.3] | [-3.6] | -12.4 | -4.4 |
| $p$ | -8.5 | -4.3 | -8.5 | -4.4 | -8.5 | -4.5 |
| $p_{sr}$ | -9.7 * | -3.5 | -9.7 * | -3.6 | -9.7 (*) | -3.5 |
| inc | -11.1 | -1.6 * | -11.3 | [-3.3] * | -11.3 | -4.0 (*) |

where: ADF,(n)ct,(n)t = Augmented Dickey Fuller statistic, test equation with(out) a constant term (ct) and with(out) a trend variable (t); brackets around the ADF statistic indicate significance of the constant term which invalidates the critical values; rejection of higher order serial autocorrelation at the 5% level is indicated with an asterisk (*). The variables rfmm (= rainfall in mm) and rfnd (= number of days with rainfall) need to be stationary (I(0)), hence, these variables are only evaluated in levels); MacKinnon critical values (5%) are: ADF(nct,nt)-1.94; ADF(ct)-2.87; ADF(ct,t)-3.44.

$q_{lr}$ (ct, 12 lags), inc(nct,nt, 12 lags), $s_{gd}$ (ct,t, 12 lags). To summarize, we can conclude that the level of all variables except the weather variables are integrated of the order 1 (I(1)) or stationary if differenced one time. Weather variables (rfmm, rfnd) are integrated of the order 0 (I(0)) or stationary.

The derived specifications of behavioral equations presume normality, a constant variance, and no autocorrelation of the disturbances. Therefore we assess the statistical adequacy of the dynamic specification of the structural equations by executing some diagnostic checks. These checks are implemented using estimations (3) of Table 3.2 and 3.3, and (1) in Table 3.4 and 3.5, and are reported in Table 3.8. The lag length in testing for serial correlation is set at 1 and 12. There is some indication of higher order autocorrelation and heteroscedasticity in the equation of consumption ($\Delta c$), but this can be attributed to a number of outliers; the same applies to non-normality in the production equation ($\Delta q$) and the equation of stocks at growers and dealers ($\Delta s_{gd}$).

**Table 3.8**    Diagnostic checks on dynamic specification

| test statistic | $\Delta q$ | $\Delta s_{gd}$ | $\Delta s_{mf}$ | $\Delta c$ |
|---|---|---|---|---|
| AR/MA(1) | 2.28 | 0.01 | 0.85 | 0.02 |
| AR/MA(12) | 11.9 | 11.8 | 13.4 | 37.9* |
| ARCH(1) | 1.98 | 0.02 | 0.14 | 4.83* |
| N | 22.6* | 23.0* | 0.20 | 4.95 |

The test statistics are AR/MA(n): Breusch/Godfrey LM test for n-order AR/MA disturbances; N: Jarque-Bera LM test for normality; ARCH(1): first order ARCH test; * significant at the 5% level

Finally, in order to find the relevant equilibrium equation or to cancel out the irrelevant equilibrium specifications, test results for the cointegrating variables are presented in Table 3.9. Boswijk (1992,1994) proposes to test the null hypothesis of no cointegration using the Wald test statistic $\xi$ for the restrictions of $\lambda=0$ and $\delta=0$ in the test equation: $\Delta y_t = \lambda y_{t-1} + \delta z_{t-1} + \gamma \Delta z_t$.

The Wald statistic can be calculated as $\xi = nF$, where F is the F-statistic for these restrictions and n the number of restrictions. Critical values are taken from Boswijk (1994). From the table we infer that the null of no cointegration is accepted in a number of cases (marked with an asterisk): the corresponding combinations of cointegrating variables can safely be skipped from the list of possible relationships. The remaining values of test statistics indicate rejection of the null of no cointegration and indicate possible combinations of cointegrating variables. Further selection has been made on the basis of statistical performance in the estimation of the behavioral relationships and economic plausibility.

**Table 3.9**  Testing for Cointegrating Variables

| equation | | stocks at growers and dealers ($s_{gd}$) | | | | |
|---|---|---|---|---|---|---|
| integrating variables | | c | c,p | q | q,p | p |
| test statistic ($\xi$) | (-) | 9.46 * | 8.76 * | 74.43 | 78.84 | 3.72 * |
| | (ct) | 9.38 * | 14.18 * | 87.46 | 87.88 | 13.78 |
| | (ct,t) | 14.89 | 17.3 | 102.4 | 99.10 | 14.30 |

| equation | | stocks at manufacturers ($s_{mf}$) | | |
|---|---|---|---|---|
| integrating variables | | c | c,p | p |
| test statistic ($\xi$) | (-) | 21.40 | 22.60 | 2.36 * |
| | (ct) | 22.57 | 22.74 | 12.49 |
| | (ct,t) | 32.16 | 35.91 | 16.43 |

| equation | | consumption (c) | | | | | |
|---|---|---|---|---|---|---|---|
| integrating variables | | inc | $p_{sr}$ | p | inc,$p_{sr}$ | inc,p | inc,$p_{sr}$,p |
| test statistic ($\xi$) | (-) | 19.46 | 1.97 * | 0.98 * | 19.63 | 19.49 | 19.77 |
| | (ct) | 18.04 | 0.00 * | 4.00 * | 18.30 | 18.13 | 18.33 |
| | (ct,t) | 29.84 | 21.06 | 22.99 | 29.50 | 29.64 | 29.23 |

Sample period: 1980.1-1989.12

Critical values (5%) (see Boswijk (1994)):

without constant term (-):          9.64 (k=1); 13.34 (k=2) and 16.42 (k=3);

with constant term (ct):          11.41 (k=1); 14.38 (k=2) and 17.18 (k=3);

with constant term and trend (ct,t):  14.28 (k=1); 17.20 (k=2) and 19.81 (k=3);

## Appendix 3.2

## Deriving a specification of a rational expectation of prices of natural rubber

To derive a price equation that can be estimated we apply standard rational expectation techniques. We use the following equation as a starting point:

$$\Delta p_t = \lambda \Delta_t p^e_{t+1} + Z' \Delta X_t + V' Y_{t-1} \tag{1}$$

Taking expectations from both sides, yields:

$$E_t \Delta p_t = \lambda E_t \Delta p_{t+1} + Z' E_t \Delta X_t + V' E_t Y_{t-1} \tag{2}$$

For expositional reasons we maintain the term $V' E_t Y_{t-1}$, instead of simplifying with $V' E_t Y_{t-1} = V' Y_{t-1}$.

Forwarding equation (1) and taking expectations yields:

$$E_t \Delta p_{t+1} = \lambda E_t \Delta p_{t+2} + Z' E_t \Delta X_{t+1} + V' E_t Y_t \tag{3}$$

If we substitute equation (3) into (2) we have:

$$E_t \Delta p_t = \lambda [\lambda E_t \Delta p_{t+2} + Z' E_t \Delta X_{t+1} + V' E_t Y_t] +$$
$$Z' E_t \Delta X_t + V' E_t Y_{t-1} \tag{4}$$

If equation (1) is forwarded another time and, again, expectations are taken, we get:

$$E_t \Delta p_{t+2} = \lambda E_t \Delta p_{t+3} + Z' E_t \Delta X_{t+2} + V' E_t Y_{t+1} \tag{5}$$

Substituting this expression into equation (4) yields:

$$E_t \Delta p_t = \lambda [\lambda [\lambda E_t \Delta p_{t+3} + Z' E_t \Delta X_{t+2} + V' E_t Y_{t+1}] +$$
$$Z' E_t \Delta X_{t+1} + V' E_t Y_t]$$
$$Z' E_t \Delta X_t + V' E_t Y_{t-1} \tag{6}$$

With $V' E_t Y_t = V' Y_t$ and $V' E_t Y_{t-1} = V' Y_{t-1}$ this is simplified to:

$$E_t \Delta p_t = \lambda [\lambda [\lambda E_t \Delta p_{t+3} + Z' E_t \Delta X_{t+2} + V' E_t Y_{t+1}] +$$
$$Z' E_t \Delta X_{t+1} + V' Y_t]$$
$$Z' E_t \Delta X_t + V' Y_{t-1} \tag{7}$$

Further substitution of forwarded expected price is straightforward.

The general expression of this equation is:

$$E_t \Delta p_t = \lambda^{k+1} E_t \Delta p_{t+k+1} + \sum_{n=0}^{k} \lambda^n [Z' E_t \Delta X_{t+n} + V' E_t Y_{t+n1}] \tag{8}$$

For a large value of k, $\lambda^{k+1} \to 0$, and we can approximate equation (8) with:

$$E_t \Delta p_t = \sum_{n=0}^{k} \lambda^n [Z' E_t \Delta X_{t+n} + V' E_t Y_{t+n-1}] \tag{9}$$

This equation cannot be estimated due to the endogeneity of the term

$$V' E_t Y_{t+n-1} \text{ for } n>0 \tag{10}$$

This can be solved by expressing all endogenous variables in exogenous variables. We will make some steps by evaluating the first three components of this term (cf. equation (7)). Recall that:

$$V'Y_{t-1} = \theta_4 c_{t-1} + \theta_5 inc_{t-1} + \theta_6 P_{t-1} + \theta_7 P_{sr,t-1} + \theta_8 s_{mf,t-1} + \theta_9 s_{gd,t-1} + \theta_{10} q_{t-1} \quad (11)$$

This implies that:

$$V'E_t Y_{t-1} = \theta_4 c_{t-1} + \theta_5 inc_{t-1} + \theta_6 P_{t-1} + \theta_7 P_{sr,t-1} + \theta_8 s_{mf,t-1} + \theta_9 s_{gd,t-1} + \theta_{10} q_{t-1} \quad (12)$$

$$V'E_t Y_t = \theta_4 c_t + \theta_5 inc_t + \theta_6 P_t + \theta_7 P_{sr,t} + \theta_8 s_{mf,t} + \theta_9 s_{gd,t} + \theta_{10} q_t \quad (13)$$

$$V'E_t Y_{t+1} = E_t[\theta_4 c_{t+1} + \theta_5 inc_{t+1} + \theta_6 P_{t+1} + \theta_7 P_{sr,t+1} + \theta_8 s_{mf,t+1} + \theta_9 s_{gd,t+1} + \theta_{10} q_{t+1}] \quad (14)$$

Equation (12) contains only predetermined variables and is not problematic for estimation. Equation (13), however, contains current endogenous ($c_t$, $P_t$, $s_{mf,t}$, $s_{gd,t}$) and current exogenous variables ($inc_t$, $P_{sr,t}$, $q_t$). Likewise equation (14) contains expectations of future endogenous variables $E_t(c_{t+1}, P_{t+1}, s_{mf,t+1}, s_{gd,t+1})$ and expectations of future exogenous variables $E_t(inc_{t+1}, P_{sr,t+1}, q_{t+1})$. Specification of more terms of equation (10) involve expectations of endogenous and exogenous variables of a more distant future. The original behavioral equations need to be substituted for (expectations on) endogenous variables.

Even after specifying only a few terms and making a few steps, it is clear that substituting the original behavioral equations in equation (13), (14) and any subsequent component of equation (10) generates a mass of additional coefficients to be included in estimation of equation (9). Note that both stock equations also have a complete set of monthly dummies as explanatory variables. To avoid the tedious series of substitutions involved we propose to estimate an restricted version of equation (9)[8], in particular:

$$E_t \Delta p_t = \sum_{n=0}^{k} \lambda^n Z'E_t \Delta X_{t+n} + V'Y_{t-1} \quad (15)$$

It is implicitly assumed that:

$$\sum_{n=1}^{k} \lambda^n V'E_t Y_{t+n-1} \approx 0 \quad (16)$$

No attempt is made to elaborate this issue further.

---

8     Another option would be to postulate that the outcome of these substitutions will be an equation identical to equation (15) but without the term $\lambda^n$ and without restrictions on the parameters ($Z'$ becomes $Z'_{t+n}$). We have tried this but with little success.

# 4    RATIONAL EXPECTATIONS OF BOUNDED PRICES

## 4.1    Introduction

For a number of years in the period from 1965 to 1995 - in particular from 1984 to 1989 - a bandwidth price policy, the so-called Buffer Stocking Scheme (BSS) has been operational in the Indian natural rubber market. The Buffer Stocking Scheme is a standard bandwidth price policy. A ceiling price and a floor price, as well as an upper trigger price and a lower trigger price, are determined at a predetermined distance on either side of a bench mark price. The bench mark price is determined by the central government on the basis of costs of producing natural rubber. If the price decreases below the lower trigger price or the floor price the State Trading Corporation (STC) may buy, respectively, is obliged to buy natural rubber on the market until the market forces move the price above the lower trigger price. Likewise, if the price increases above the upper trigger price, or above the ceiling price, the STC may sell, respectively, is obliged to sell natural rubber from stocks, or releases imports on the market, until the market forces move the price below the upper trigger price (see Chapter 2 for a more extensive description). Figure 4.1 shows ceiling and floor prices and market price during BSS.

In Chapter 3 it was shown in what way this price policy changes the formalization of the accounting identity and the price equation (see Chapter 3, equation (26'), (31) and (32)). However, in the empirical work of Chapter 3 the impact of the bandwidth price policy was ignored. The purpose of this chapter is to incorporate the bandwidth price policy into the model. Agents in the market, faced with a bandwidth price policy will adjust their expectations of future prices. To calculate these adjusted expectations, an estimation procedure is needed that incorporates the truncation of prices and expected prices, and, subsequently, applies these adjusted expectations to the behavior of agents in the market.

In order to implement this, we first present in Section 4.2 a summary of the literature on estimation of equations with censored endogenous variables. On the basis of this summary a technique is selected for our purpose. In fact, a modified version of the major estimation strategy, the limited dependent rational expectation of prices (Pesaran and Samiei (1992,1995)) is developed in Section 4.3. In Section 4.4 estimation results of price equations with bounded prices are presented. The resulting estimated price equation is used to construct expected

**Figure 4.1**    Domestic market price and maximum & minimum prices of BSS

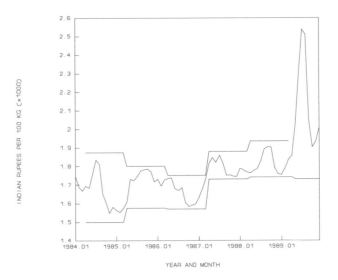

Source:        Indian Rubber Statistics, Rubber Board of India

prices. These are subsequently used to estimate the structural equations, the stock demand equations. In Section 4.5 estimation results of stock demand equations are presented and evaluated. In Section 4.6 a summary of the main findings is given.

## 4.2    Estimation with bounded variables: a survey of literature[1]

The estimation of models with bounded variables has been studied by a number of authors and has led to the development of the limited dependent rational expectation model, the LD-RE model (e.g. Maddala (1983a), Chanda and Maddala (1983), Shonkwiler and Maddala (1985), Holt and Johnson (1989), Maddala (1990), Pesaran (1990), Donald and Maddala (1992), Pesaran and Samiei (1992(a,b), 1993, 1995), Pesaran and Ruge-Murcia (1996)). In a number of papers Pesaran *et al.* (Pesaran and Samiei (1992(a,b), 1993, 1995), Pesaran and Ruge-

---

1        The focus of this review is the literature on estimating variables with bounded variation. Substantial parts of the literature on (price) expectations discuss the justifiability of the rational expectation hypothesis, as opposed to other assumptions with respect to expectation formation (e.g. adaptive expectations, survey data on expectations, futures prices). Despite its relevance this issue will not be considered here (see e.g. Pesaran (1987)).

Murcia (1996)) address the problem of estimating linear rational expectation models with expectations of the endogenous variable that are bounded. This subject is of particular relevance to price or expected price with bounded variation, but the derivations are presented in a general formulation and are intended for a wider range of problems.[2] A model with expectations of a current price, based on the information one period earlier is studied in Pesaran and Samiei (1992a). Essential to their model is that the bounds imposed on the fluctuation of prices, for example as a part of a fully credible policy, do not only have an impact on the price variable, but also through the expectation of this variable. Consequently, the policy that sets bounds - or the announcement of such a policy - has an impact even if these bounds are not effective. Roughly their model states that expected price is the product of the probability to be in a regime and the price in that regime, summed over the regimes, while at the same time these probabilities are also a function of price and expected price. As a result it is not possible to give an explicit solution of this model. However, under some assumptions the model is shown to have a unique solution. Different estimation techniques are tested and evaluated with the help of a Monte Carlo simulation.[3] Estimation results confirm the importance of taking account of the bounds of both the dependent variable and its expectation. Estimation techniques that do not take account of price bounds are shown to generate parameters that are seriously misleading. Two-step maximum likelihood estimation (first estimate expectational values of exogenous variables; next, use estimated values of these expectational variables as regressors, together with other regressors, to explain the truncated dependent variable) is shown to generate almost the same estimation outcome as the one step ML estimation, and has the advantage to be computationally less demanding. Both ML estimates are close to their true values. An extension for the two-limit situation is developed and applied to data of Deutsch mark / French franc exchange rate within the exchange rate mechanism of the EMS.[4]

---

2      Estimation techniques for models with rational expectations and bounded variation of the endogenous variable, have empirical applications in a number of different areas. Most prominent of all is the work on target zones of exchange rates. Other fields of applications are the modelling of non-negativity of stocks, liquidity constraints and credit demand.

3      The Monte Carlo experiment is implemented by creating a set of observations using plausible values of the parameters and varying proportions of censored observations.

4      Determination of exchange rates subject to target zones is a prominent example of LD-RE models with *future* expectations (as opposed to *current* expectations in their 1992a article) as they claim, surprisingly, in a later article (Pesaran and Samiei (1995)).

In Pesaran and Samiei (1993, 1995) models with expectations of future prices based on the current information set, as opposed to models with expectation of current prices, based on the past information set (as in Pesaran and Samiei (1992a)) are investigated. The dependent variable, censored above and below, is determined by its own future expectations, which in its turn is also censored above and below, next to a set of exogenous variables that are labelled 'fundamentals'. Without bounded prices, and if the appropriate transversality condition is satisfied the solution is easily calculated as an infinite sum of expected future values of the fundamentals. With bounded prices this solution is not valid because it does not take account of the truncation of prices. Finding an analytical solution is now realized by truncating the horizon and calculating the solution for the last period of the horizon. Subsequently, through (repeated) backward recursion an expression is found for each expected future value, starting in the period of truncation and proceeding backwards. Hence, an analytical solution is obtained. With serially correlated disturbances the derivation becomes extremely complicated mainly due to the revisions of the expectations. It is shown that in this case a numerical solution can be obtained through stochastic simulation. If the disturbance term is assumed to be a normal random variable, calculations proceed as in the case of serially independent errors and an (approximate) solution can be found. After an extension of the model for intra marginal interventions, a Monte Carlo simulation is again implemented to assess the properties of the model. The results of this exercise confirm the importance of taking account of bounds in estimations. The proof of uniqueness of the rational expectation solution is further generalized in Lee (1994): in particular serially independent disturbances are shown not to be required.

In Pesaran and Ruge-Murcia (1996) the analysis (with expectation of current variables) is extended to allow for stochastic variations in the bounds. With the help of Monte Carlo simulation it is shown that assuming bounds not to be fully predictable to the agents in the market, has only a negligible effect on parameter estimates if the variability of the bound is small compared with the other sources of uncertainty in the model. Not taking account of the stochastic character of the bounds will bias the estimation results. Then it is shown that the rational expectation solution becomes less non-linear, if the uncertainty about future values of the bounds increases.

The formalization of the impact of price bounds on expected price and on behavior of agents in the market, as described in Pesaran and Samiei (1995), has great intuitive appeal. The method formalizes that this impact could be felt before price bounds are hit. And it allows an impact of these price bounds even if these bounds are not hit. For these reasons we have chosen to implement a variant of the Pesaran and Samiei (1995) model.[5]


## 4.3    Implementing estimation with bounded prices

The derivation below is developed with the assumption that current and all future values of the price bounds are known with certainty. Other assumptions with respect to the determination of these bounds e.g. bounds that follow a specific rule or stochastic bounds, are not considered. This is only done for practical reasons: the available empirical material does not allow the testing of these alternatives, despite its intuitive appeal (see e.g. Pesaran and Ruge-Murcia (1996) for a treatment of stochastic varying upper and lower bounds in LD-RE models). The centrally imposed price policy is also taken to be fully credible. The ceiling price of the BSS would be vulnerable to speculative attack from private stockholders without this assumption (see Salant (1983)). The STC is able through its monopoly position on the import of natural rubber (see Section 2.1) and with world market prices in Indian Rupees continuously below domestic market prices, to earn money by selling these imports in the domestic market. Their income earned in this way will generate sufficient funding for open market operations to defend minimum prices and to maintain sufficient stocks. An additional point needs to be mentioned in this respect: it appears that private stockholding in the Indian natural rubber market, a rather small-scale activity, is to a large extent taking place as a side activity of either natural rubber growers or the rubber products manufacturing industry, and not so much as an independent income earning trading activity. Even in the aggregate it will be doubtful if the 'trading sector' will be financially strong enough to generate a speculative attack (i.e. to buy all government stocks). The financially most powerful stockholders are concentrated at the rubber products manufacturing industry and this industry has little incentive to promote a speculative attack, as it is more interested in low prices of their major input.

As a starting point a simplified version of the model of Chapter 3 is considered without a buffer stock or floor prices and ceiling prices. A formal

---

5       It is not difficult to foresee that with increasing complexity, an increasing number of problems will appear to have no analytical solution and numerical techniques will be the only way to solve these problems. This is reflected in some contributions on the subject at hand (see e.g. Pesaran and Samiei (1995), and Holt and Johnson (1989); see also Deaton and Laroque (1991, 1994a,1994b on a related subject) and also points at the limitations of the technique used in the current chapter.

derivation of the behavioral relationships of producers, consumers and stockholders proceeds along the lines as set out in Chapter 3. The model can also be interpreted as a fairly general specification of a commodity market of a perennial crop: zero (or negligibly low) short run price elasticity of supply, short run supply mainly determined by seasonal influences and combined with non-zero price elasticities in consumption and stockholding.

$$\Delta q_t \quad = \quad \alpha_0 + \alpha_1 w_t + \alpha_2 q_{t-1} + \alpha_3 q_{lr,t-1} + u_{t,1} \tag{1}$$

$$\Delta s_t \quad = \quad \beta_0 + \beta_1 (\Delta p_t - \Delta_t p^e_{t+1}) + \beta_2 s_{t-1} + \beta_3 q_{t-1} + \beta_4 c_{t-1} + u_{t,2} \tag{2}$$

$$\Delta c_t \quad = \quad \gamma_0 + \gamma_1 \Delta z_t + \gamma_2 \Delta p_t + \gamma_3 c_{t-1} + \gamma_4 z_{t-1} + \gamma_5 p_{t-1} + u_{t,3} \tag{3}$$

$$q_t \quad = \quad \Delta s_t + c_t \tag{4}$$

where $q$ = production, $\Delta s$ = stock demand and $c$ = final demand; $w$ and $z$ represent supply and demand shifters; $q_{lr}$ = long run production, i.e. production controlled for vintage composition; $p$ = the (real) market price, and $p^e_{t+1}$ represents the current rational expectation of future market (real) price(s) in $t+1$, conditional on information in period $t$; the disturbance terms $u_j$ are assumed to be IID $(0, \sigma_j^2)$ with $j = q, s, c$;

A number of simplifications are made purely for expositional reasons. The most important simplifications, compared with the model of Chapter 3, are that stockholders are taken together as one group instead of two and that all exogenous demand and supply determinants are taken together as supply and demand shifters. These simplifications are not essential to the derivation of rational expectation of bounded prices. In the empirical work of this chapter we maintain the disaggregation of Chapter 3. Extension of the derivation to such detailed and disaggregated specifications is straightforward.

Analogous to that model short run demand for stocks, as formalized in equation (2), is determined by arbitrage opportunities $(\Delta p_t - \Delta p^e_{t+1})$, while long run behavior is either due to precautionary demand, transaction demand, forced stockholding, or long run speculative type of considerations $(\beta_2 s_{t-1} + \beta_3 q_{t-1} + \beta_4 c_{t-1})$. Expected prices in demand for stocks are related to speculative behavior and are short run in character: this contrasts with typically long run expected prices in production.[6] These long run expected prices - the focus of analysis in work on supply response models as e.g. in Shonkwiler and Maddala (1985) - are exogenous in the current model. This is immediately obvious in the equation for production, equation (1). Production $(q_t)$ is determined by exogenous supply shifters, mainly seasonal influences $(w_t)$, and long run equilibrium production, related to the vintage composition of trees $(q_{lr,t-1})$. Consumption $(c_t)$, as formalized in equation (3), is determined by demand shifters $(z_t)$ and the current price $(p_t)$. The system is closed with an equilibrium equation (equation (4)), indicating that production is equal to the change in stocks plus consumption. Model-consistent expectations refer to current expectations of future prices, and not to past expectations of current prices as in Shonkwiler and Maddala (1985), Pesaran (1990) and Pesaran and Samiei (1992).

Solving the above system for current price gives the following expression:

$$\Delta p_t = \lambda \, \Delta_t p^e_{t+1} + Z' \Delta X_t + V' Y_{t-1} + u_t \tag{5}$$

where $Z' \Delta X_t$ represent current values of explanatory variables, $V' Y_{t-1}$ predetermined values of explanatory variables and $u_t$ a composite error term that is, by implication, IID $(0, \sigma^2)$ (see Chapter 3, equation 36). Taking expectations of both sides yields:

$$\Delta_t p^e_t = \lambda \, \Delta_t p^e_{t+1} + Z' \Delta_t X^e_t + V' Y_{t-1} \tag{6}$$

By repeated substitution of forwarded equations the following approximation of this equation is obtained:

$$\Delta_t p^e_t = \lambda^{k+1} \, \Delta_t p^e_{t+k+1} + \sum_{n=0}^{k} \lambda^n Z' \Delta_t X^e_{t+n} + V' Y_{t-1} \tag{7}$$

where $n = 0, 1, .. , k$

Note that we have made the simplifying assumption that $E(V' Y_{t+j}) = 0$, where $j = 0, 1, .. \infty$. See Chapter 3 for a number of comments on this assumption. Assuming that the transversality condition

---

6       For a perennial crop like natural rubber price expectations in production extend over a much larger period than for annual crops. See also Section 4.

$$\lim_{m \to \infty} \lambda^m \Delta_t p^e_{t+m} = 0$$

is satisfied,[7] the unique solution of expected price is given by:

$$\Delta_t p^e_t = \sum \lambda^n Z' \Delta_t X^e_{t+n} + V'Y_{t-1} \tag{8}$$

This equation is a familiar equation expressing expected future price as a geometrically declining function of expected current and future variables and a number of lagged terms that represent the error correction term. Equation (8) is the expression for $\Delta_t p^e_t$ that we would use without a price floor and a ceiling price (see also Chapter 3).

If a market with a buffer stock or both floor prices and ceiling prices is considered, this outcome no longer holds. Prices are truncated and so are expected prices. The whole process of repeated substitution of forwarded expected price equation cannot be implemented, at least not in this way. To derive a rational expected price, assumptions are required with respect to the distribution of disturbances. The truncation of prices affects the distribution of disturbances. Introduction of bounded variation in prices yields:

$$\Delta p_t = \begin{cases} \Delta p_{max,t} & \text{if} \quad \Delta p_t & \geq & \Delta p_{max,t} \\ \Delta p_{1,t} & \text{if} \quad \Delta p_{min,t} & < \quad \Delta p_t \quad < & \Delta p_{max,t} \\ \Delta p_{min,t} & \text{if} \quad \Delta p_t & \leq & \Delta p_{min,t} \end{cases} \tag{9}$$

where

$p_{max}$ = exogenous price ceiling;
$p_{min}$ = exogenous price floor;
$\Delta p_{max,t} = p_{max,t} - p_{t-1}$;
$\Delta p_{min,t} = p_{min,t} - p_{t-1}$;

To further simplify the presentation we omit the predetermined term on the right hand side of equation (6), $V'Y_{t-1}$. The remaining part of the right hand side of equation (8) is assumed to represent the driving forces of the latent variable ($\Delta p_{1,t}$). Substitution in equation (9) yields:

---

[7]     In Chapter 3 it was shown that $\lambda$ takes a value between 0 and 1 for reasonable values of the underlying parameters, and, hence, this condition for the uniqueness of the rational expectations solution is satisfied.

$\Delta p_t \quad =$

$$\begin{cases} \Delta p_{max,t} & \text{if } u_t \geq \Delta p_{max,t} - \lambda \, \Delta \, _t p^e_{t+1} - Z'\Delta X_t \\ \lambda \, \Delta \, _t p^e_{t+1} + Z'\Delta X_t + u_t & \text{if } \Delta p_{min,t} - \lambda \Delta_t p^e_{t+1} - Z'\Delta X_t < u_t < \Delta p_{max,t} - \lambda \Delta_t p^e_{t+1} - Z'\Delta X_t \\ \Delta p_{min,t} & \text{if } u_t \leq \Delta p_{min,t} - \lambda \, \Delta \, _t p^e_{t+1} - Z'\Delta X_t \end{cases} \quad (10)$$

where $u_t$ is assumed to be IID $(0,\sigma^2)$

The above equation formalizes the notion that the observed dependent variable is truncated normally distributed, if the disturbance term in the equation of the latent variable is normally distributed. Such a problem can be solved with the standard two-limit Tobit technique (see e.g. Maddala (1983a), Chapter 6). Expressions can be obtained for the (un)conditional expected price by making use of the properties of the standard normal distribution. The probabilities to be in a specific regime are formalized: the expected price is the sum of the products of the probability to be in a particular regime and the price in that particular regime, or:

$$\begin{aligned} E\Delta p_t = \quad & P(\Delta p_t = \Delta p_{max,t}). \; \Delta p_{max,t} \; + \\ & P(\Delta p_{min,t} < \Delta p_t < \Delta p_{max,t}). \; \Delta p_{1,t} \; + \\ & P(\Delta p_t = \Delta p_{min,t}). \; \Delta p_{min,t} \end{aligned} \quad (11)$$

where $P(.)$ is the probability operator

It can be shown that the Tobit technique gives consistent estimates of the parameters of the model (including the standard error which is also estimated). If there are no observations at the bounds the estimation degenerates to OLS.

The problem is, however, somewhat more complicated compared with the standard two-limit Tobit as the Tobit technique only takes account of truncation of the dependent variable and not of the truncation of the explanatory variables. To allow for this, we first rewrite equation (11) by specifying the probabilities. Probabilities can be expressed as the values of the standard normal distribution, evaluated at the relevant truncation. This yields:

$\Delta_t p^e_t \quad =$

$$[1-\Phi(C_{max,t})] \, \Delta p_{max,t} + [\Phi(C_{max,t}) - \Phi(C_{min,t})] \, \Delta p_{1,t} + [\Phi(C_{min,t})] \, \Delta p_{min,t} \quad (12)$$

and

$$C_{min,t} = (\Delta p_{min,t} - \lambda \Delta_t p^e_{t+1} - Z' \Delta_t X^e_t)/\sigma, \quad (13)$$

$$C_{max,t} = (\Delta p_{max,t} - \lambda \Delta_t p^e_{t+1} - Z' \Delta_t X^e_t)/\sigma, \quad (14)$$

where $\Phi(.)$ is the distribution function of the standard normal variable;

$\Delta p_{1,t}$ is now the (expected) price $\Delta p_t$ conditional on $\Delta p_t$ being between the maximum and minimum price and its expected value is given by:

$$\Delta p_{1,t} = \lambda \, \Delta \, _t p^e_{t+1} + Z' \Delta_t X^e_t - \sigma \, \{\phi(C_{max,t}) - \phi(C_{min,t})\} \, / \, \{\Phi(C_{max,t}) - \Phi(C_{min,t})\}$$

where                                                                                          (15)

$\sigma^2 = Var(u)$

$\phi(.)$ is the density function of the standard normal variable

The first part of equation (15), $\lambda \, \Delta \, _t p^e_{t+1} + Z' \Delta X^e_t$, is the price in the absence of the price ceiling and price floor and the last part ($- \sigma \, \{\phi(C_{max,t}) - \phi(C_{min,t})\}$ / $\{\Phi(C_{max,t}) - \Phi(C_{min,t})\}$) is due to the truncation of $u_t$.

The problem is now to determine what $\Delta_t p^e_{t+1}$ in equation (13), (14) and (15) should be under these constraints: both the probability of being in a specific regime, and the actual price depend on expected future prices, which are themselves also truncated. Note that the derivation is made under the assumption that the agents in the market have an information set that contains current and past values of all variables, as well as values of the price ceiling and price floor for all futures periods. Shonkwiler and Maddala (1985) suggest two alternatives out of this problem: a Tobit approximation and a perfect foresight technique. The Tobit approximation, not advocated by the authors as a satisfactory solution, assumes that the reduced form (expected) price equation is either the minimum price, or a quadratic function of the minimum price and demand and supply shifters. This equation is estimated using the standard Tobit technique. The second method is based on a perfect prediction of the period when the price support is going to be effective and is labelled as the perfect foresight model. In addition to the suggested specifications of expected prices, appropriate futures quotations are used as a proxy for expected prices in order to provide a reference of the rationally expected price generated by the model. In terms of goodness of fit the Tobit approximation and the futures price specification are outperformed by the perfect foresight model.

A more elegant method, that avoids the extreme assumption of perfect foresight, suggested by Pesaran and Samiei (1995), runs as follows. Forward equation (12) analogous to the derivation without bounds:

$$\Delta \, _t p^e_{t+1} = \quad [\Phi(C_{max,t+1}) - \Phi(C_{min,t+1})] \cdot \Delta p_{1,t+1} +$$
$$[\Phi(C_{min,t+1})] \cdot \Delta p_{min,t+1} + [1 - \Phi(C_{max,t+1})] \cdot \Delta p_{max,t+1} \qquad (16)$$

and substitute this expression in equation (13),(14) and (15), which yields an expression of

$\Delta p_{1,t}$ in terms of $\Delta p_{1,t+1}$, $\Delta p_{min,t+1}$ and $\Delta p_{max,t+1}$:

$$\Delta p_{1,t} = \lambda \left[ [\Phi(C_{max,t+1}) - \Phi(C_{min,t+1})] \cdot \Delta p_{1,t+1} + \right.$$
$$[\Phi(C_{min,t+1})] \Delta p_{min,t+1} + [1-\Phi(C_{max,t+1})] \Delta p_{max,t+1} \left. \right]$$
$$+ Z'\Delta X_t - \sigma \{\phi(C_{max,t})-\phi(C_{min,t})\} / \{\Phi(C_{max,t})-\Phi(C_{min,t})\} \quad (17)$$

Then, forwarding equation (15) yields:

$$\Delta p_{1,t+1} = \lambda \Delta_t p^e_{t+2} + Z'\Delta_t X^e_{t+1} -$$
$$\sigma\{\phi(C_{max,t+1})-\phi(C_{min,t+1})\}/\{\Phi(C_{max,t+1})-\Phi(C_{min,t+1})\} \quad (18)$$

Equation (18) is used to eliminate the term $\Delta p_{1,t+1}$ in equation (16). The resulting equation expresses (expected) truncated price as a function of exogenous variables and the truncated expected price of two periods ahead, $\Delta p^e_{t+2}$. The sequence of steps can then be repeated to eliminate $\Delta p^e_{t+2}$, and subsequently $\Delta p^e_{t+3}$, etc. etc. These substitutions are repeated until expected prices of periods in a more distant future do not matter.

We omit the presentation of a general expression of expected price with bounded prices as it will be rather uncomfortable to read. If we assume, for the sake of exposition, that prices of two periods ahead do not matter or that $\lambda$ is sufficiently small, equation (18) simplifies to:

$$\Delta_t p_{1,t+1} = Z'\Delta_t X^e_{t+1} - \sigma\{\phi(C_{max,t+1})-\phi(C_{min,t+1})\}/\{\Phi(C_{max,t+1})-\Phi(C_{min,t+1})\} \quad (19)$$

And, likewise:

$$C_{min,t+1} = (\Delta p_{min,t+1}-Z'\Delta_t X^e_{t+1})/\sigma, \quad (20)$$
$$C_{max,t+1} = (\Delta p_{max,t+1}-Z'\Delta_t X^e_{t+1})/\sigma, \quad (21)$$

An impact of price bounds is guaranteed through expected future prices even if prices do not touch upper or lower bounds. Existence and uniqueness of the solution of this price equation are studied by others and will not be considered here (see Donald and Maddala (1992), Lee (1994), Pesaran and Samiei (1992a,b, 1995)).

The loglikelihood function is given by the following equation, combined with equations (16) and (19) to (21):

$$\log L = \sum_0 \log(\Phi(C_{min,t})) +$$
$$-n_1/2\log(2\pi\sigma_u^2)+1/(2\sigma_u^2)\sum_1[\Delta p_t - \lambda\Delta_t p^e_{t+1} - Z'\Delta X^e_t]^2 +$$
$$\sum_2 \log(1-\Phi(C_{max,t})) \qquad\qquad (22)$$

$$C_{min,t} = (\Delta p_{min,t} - \lambda \Delta_t p^e_{t+1} - Z'\Delta X^e)/\sigma, \qquad\qquad (23)$$
$$C_{max,t} = (\Delta p_{max,t} - \lambda \Delta_t p^e_{t+1} - Z'\Delta X^e)/\sigma, \qquad\qquad (24)$$

where the indices 0, 1 and 2 respectively refer to observations below or equal to the price floor, between (future expected) price floor and ceiling, and above or equal to the (future expected) price ceiling.

This system of equations is estimated. The specification of $X_t$ (and $V_{t-1}$) is given in Chapter 3, equation 36. Note that $\Delta_t p^e_t$ is a function of all parameters to be estimated through equation (12), (13) and (14). Hence, even without observations below or equal to the floor price, and above or equal to the ceiling price, as is the case in our data-set - and, thus, without the first and the last part of the likelihood function - the truncation has an impact on the likelihood. This corresponds with the intuition that price bounds have an impact on expectations even if these price bounds are not effective (see also Pesaran and Samiei (1992), p. 142) and is in line with recent developments in exchange rate research on the impact of target zones (see e.g. Krugman (1991)). Note also that both Tobit estimation as well as the method suggested by Shonkwiler and Maddala require observations that hit the bounds.

The model developed in the above section captures the features of the estimation method for expected prices with bounded variation of (expected) prices. As mentioned above, estimations presented in the sections below make use of detailed specifications of explanatory variables and disaggregates between groups of stockholders, both along the lines of Chapter 3, but are equivalent with the above derivation.


## 4.4    Estimations of price expectations

Equations are estimated by Full Information Maximum Likelihood (FIML) in the 'no-bounds' price equation, by Maximum Likelihood (ML) in case of the limited dependent - limited rational expectation formulation, and by Two Stage Least

**Table 4.1** Estimating expected prices in the Indian natural rubber market

| dependent variable: | first difference of price ($\Delta p$) |
| sample period: | 1980.01-1989.12 (120 obs.) |

| | formation of expected future prices | | | |
|---|---|---|---|---|
| | no bounds | | LD-RE | |
| | | | Pesaran & Samiei (1995) | |
| estimation method | FIML | | ML | |
| explanatory variables | | | | |
| constant | 3.982 | (2.7) | 1.244 | (2.4) |
| $\Delta p^e_{t+j}$ ($\lambda$) | 0.633 | (6.7) | 0.673 | (5.7) |
| $blc^e_t$ | 0.343E-4 | (1.6) | 0.442E-4 | (1.8) |
| $\Delta q^e_t$ | -0.845E-4 | (2.2) | -0.434E-4 | (1.2) |
| $\Delta inc^e_t$ | -0.019 | (0.9) | -0.024 | (0.9) |
| $s_{gd,t-1}$ | -0.624E-4 | (2.9) | -0.281E-4 | (0.9) |
| $q_{t-1}$ | -0.715E-4 | (1.9) | -0.524E-4 | (1.2) |
| $s_{mf,t-1}$ | -0.115E-3 | (2.7) | -0.134E-3 | (2.7) |
| $c_{t-1}$ | 0.163E-3 | (1.6) | 0.208E-3 | (1.5) |
| $inc_{t-1}$ | -0.0052 | (0.3) | 0.0013 | (0.1) |
| $p_{t-1}$ | -0.318 | (5.4) | -0.206 | (4.1) |
| $p_{sr,t-1}$ | 0.077 | (1.4) | 0.165 | (3.9) |
| log(L) | -168.637 | | -174.832 | |
| R2 adjusted | 0.270 | | | |

See Chapter 3 for the explanation of variable names; log(L) = log of the likelihood function; R2 adjusted = coefficient of correlation adjusted for degrees of freedom; (absolute) t-statistics are presented in parentheses next to the coefficients.

Squares (2SLS) in case of the behavioral stock equations. With 2SLS instruments are chosen as in Chapter 3: next to all exogenous explanatory variables of the specific estimated equation, the following variables are used as instruments: production ($q_t$), lagged stocks with growers & dealers ($s_{gd,t-1}$) and manufacturers ($s_{mf,t-1}$) and lagged consumption ($c_{t-1}$). Equations are estimated with error-correction. Tests on the (co)integration of variables were given in the appendix 3.1 of Chapter 3. Contrary to the derivation in Section 4.3 the horizon of economic agents in their short run behavior is not truncated at future prices of two months ahead, but at future prices of six months ahead, similar to the specification in Chapter 3. Note from Figure 4.1 at the start of this chapter that prices never actually hit the price floor or price ceiling. In Table 4.1 the estimation results for the price equations are reported. The first column of Table 4.1 reports estimation results of the price equation 'as if there are no bounds', the second column reports estimation results of the limited dependent - rational expectation method (LD-RE, Pesaran and Samiei (1995)). The estimates of the LD-RE method are obtained by maximizing the loglikelihood function given in equation (22).

The estimation results show that taking account of price bounds marginally reduces the value of the log of the likelihood function. The coefficient of the expected future price is significant with both estimation techniques and have values that come close to each other: the estimated $\lambda$ has a value of .673 with LD-RE as compared to 0.633 in the 'no bounds' estimate. Significant coefficients of other explanatory variables differ slightly in size. If coefficients differ substantially, either one of them or both are insignificant.

## 4.5    Estimations of stock demand

In Table 4.2 the estimation results of the behavioral stock equations are reported: the first four columns report estimation results for stockholding by growers and dealers and the last two columns estimation results on stockholding by manufacturers. The likelihood ratio statistic of a restriction on the parameters price and expected price (see also equation (1) and Chapter 3) is reported in the table.[8] The statistics, which are chi-squared distributed, confirm that this restriction cannot be rejected at conventional levels of significance. This result applies to all equations except the 'no bounds' equation of stock demand by manufacturers where the restriction is near to acceptance. From the tables it is observed that the estimation technique that takes account of price bound in expected prices, generates marginally different estimation results in the structural stock demand equations. The value of the likelihoodfunction is approximately unchanged in the equation of stockholding by growers and dealers, and improves slightly in the equation of stockholding by manufacturers. The coefficient of expected price

---

[8]    From the theory on speculative behavior a restriction on the parameters can be derived. In particular this implies an equal but opposite sign for price, and (the sum of the coefficients of) expected future prices (in formula: $\Sigma\gamma_{1,i}=-\Sigma\gamma_{2,j}$ and $\Sigma\zeta_{1,m}=-\Sigma\zeta_{2,n}$).

**Table 4.2**    Estimations of stock demand in the Indian natural rubber market: stocks at growers and dealers, and stocks at manufacturers

sample period:    1980.01-1989.12 (120 obs.)  estimation method:    2SLS

dependent variable (first differences):

| | stocks at growers and dealers ($\Delta s_{gd}$) | | stocks at manufacturers ($\Delta s_{mf}$) | |
| --- | --- | --- | --- | --- |
| | formation of expected future prices | | | |
| explanatory variables | no bounds | LD-RE | no bounds | LD-RE |
| constant | 1472.7 | 1814.0 | 3069.3 | 3229.4 |
| | (0.9) | (1.1) | (3.1) | (3.5) |
| $\Delta p^e_{t+2}$ | | | 538.5 | 868.1 |
| | | | (2.1) | (3.2) |
| $\Delta p^e_{t+3}$ | 737.6 | 588.3 | | |
| | (1.9) | (1.5) | | |
| $\Delta p_t$ | -1455.8 | -1440.0 | -1285.6 | -1319.3 |
| | (2.9) | (3.0) | (3.6) | (3.9) |
| $\Delta q_t$ | 0.462 | 0.453 | | |
| | (5.4) | (5.3) | | |
| $s_{gd,t-1}$ | -0.064 | -0.078 | | |
| | (2.0) | (2.5) | | |
| $q_{t-1}$ | 0.113 | 0.121 | | |
| | (1.7) | (1.8) | | |
| $s_{mf,t-1}$ | | | -0.329 | -0.369 |
| | | | (5.2) | (6.2) |
| $c_{t-1}$ | | | 0.278 | 0.305 |
| | | | (4.9) | (5.6) |
| log(L) | -1081.95 | -1081.84 | -1049.9 | -1041.94 |
| R2 adj. | 0.783 | 0.784 | 0.378 | 0.450 |
| $\chi^2_{restr.}$ | 2.76 | 3.04 | 3.94 | 1.10 |

decreases in the equation of stockholding by growers and dealers, and increases in the equation of stockholding by manufacturers. All other coefficients do not change dramatically. It should be concluded that in the current study taking account of price-bounds in the estimation method hardly matters if behavioral equations are estimated with calculated expected future prices.

How should we interpret the outcome that using estimation techniques that adequately account for price bounds hardly changes the estimation result? The marginal changes in the estimation results of the behavioral equations are perhaps due to the fact that the price policy has not been entirely credible. From the description in Chapter 2 it is clear that especially among manufacturers of rubber products (the consumers in the model) it has been doubted whether the State Trading Corporation would strictly act according to the rules of BSS. The relatively short period in which the BSS has been  operational (60 months) may also be a (purely statistical) reason for these poor results. Perhaps the impact of price policies is felt in another way: buffer stocks might influence the behavior of groups in the market drastically, in particular the behavior of stockholders. For that reason it is highly questionable to assume that the parameters of the model remain fixed over the entire period and it seems, hence, more appropriate to investigate if behavior is different with and without a price policy. This will be implemented in the next chapter.


## 4.6    Summary and conclusion

In this Chapter we have reviewed a number of ways to model rational expectations of bounded prices. A variant of the limited dependent rational expectation model (LD-RE), as formalized by Pesaran and Samiei (1995), is used to modify our model. A most appealing feature of the limited dependent - rational expectation method is that coefficients in the current and expected (bounded) prices are estimated simultaneously and, related to this, price bounds are modelled to have an impact on prices even if these price bounds are not effective. Estimations of LD-RE and 'no-bounds' price expectations were used in estimations of stock demand equations. The 'no bounds' price equation and the LD-RE price equation have similar estimation outcome. Estimates of structural stock demand are marginally affected by taking account of price bounds. The use of different expected prices in the estimation of behavioral equations does not generate a drastic improvement in the goodness of fit. Despite the intuitively appealing features of the LD-RE method and the reasonably promising estimation results for the price equation, we were unable to confirm substantial changes in the estimations of behavioral equations. Possible explanations for the marginal changes in the estimation results are the low credibility of BSS, the short operational period of BSS, offering limited opportunities to test different hypotheses, and structural breaks in the parameters of the model due to BSS. The latter will be investigated in the next chapter.

# 5    STABILIZING PRICES IN COMMODITY MARKETS:
       PRICE BOUNDS VERSUS PRIVATE STOCKHOLDING[1]

## 5.1    Introduction

In Newbery and Stiglitz (1981, Chapter 14 and Part VII) the interaction between price stabilization and private stockholders is investigated. Newbery and Stiglitz assert that successful attempts of a buffer stock manager to reduce the fluctuations of prices, diminish potential arbitrage returns from stockholding and, consequently, lead to reductions in private stockholding. The reduction of private stockholding will make the costs of the buffer stock manager higher as she has to store more to achieve a given degree of price stabilization. The purpose of the current chapter is to explore the interaction between a domestic price stabilization scheme and private stockholders with our data of the Indian natural rubber market. Specifically we investigate empirically if and to what extent the behavior of private stockholders in the Indian natural rubber market is affected by the existence of the Buffer Stocking Scheme. We hypothesize that its impact is felt through a decreased propensity to arbitrage and not (only) through diminished arbitrage opportunities. Next it is analyzed with the help of a simulation exercise to what extent private stockholding contributes to price stabilization as compared to a centrally imposed bandwidth price policy.

The chapter is organized as follows. In Section 5.2 some preliminary empirical evidence is presented: it is explored if estimated coefficients that reflect arbitrage behavior differ with and without price policy and it is attempted to identify the date of a structural break in such behavior. In Section 5.3 it is formally tested if behavior with respect to arbitrage activities changes with and without price policy. Finally, in Section 5.4 with the help of a number of simulation experiments it is assessed if pure private stockholding realizes a higher reduction in price fluctuation than a centrally imposed price policy. In Section 5.5 the main findings are summarized.

---

1    This chapter is a revised version of Zant (1997).

## 5.2    Structural breaks due to the Buffer Stocking Scheme

If the behavioral relationship of stock demand is estimated on the basis of the entire sample period it is implicitly assumed that the behavior of stockholders, reflected in the coefficients of the equation, remains unchanged throughout this period. This proposition, however, is challenged in this chapter. In particular, we investigate if the propensity to arbitrage is less during the period of a centrally imposed price band scheme, the Buffer Stocking Scheme (BSS).

To see how such a change in behavior may come about, we make use of the behavior of risk averse stockholders as derived in Chapter 7 (the reasoning for risk neutral stockholders as derived in Chapter 3 is analogous):

$$s_{t-1} = \frac{E_{t-1}(p_t) - \rho p_{t-1} + z_s \cdot (\bar{s}_{t-1} + \varepsilon_{s,t-1})}{z_s + A_s \cdot VAR_{t-1}(p_t)}$$

Assuming $\rho=1$ and omitting the disturbance term, we rewrite this equation as follows:

$$s_t = \alpha_1 [E_t(p_{t+1}) - p_t] + \alpha_2 \bar{s}_t$$

where

$$\alpha_1 = 1 / [z_s + A_s \cdot VAR_t(p_{t+1})]$$
$$\alpha_2 = z_s / [z_s + A_s \cdot VAR_t(p_{t+1})]$$

Our proposition is that a part of the group of stockholders behaves differently during a price band scheme: we partition the population of stockholders into two groups. The first group behaves according to equation above, regardless of whether a price band scheme is in operation. Members of the other group, however, only engage in arbitrage activities if a certain threshold return is earned per unit of stockholding; otherwise their marginal propensity to hold stocks will be zero ($\alpha_1 = 0$). If a price band scheme is in operation this threshold value withholds the members of this group from entering into arbitrage activities as the government interventions keep $[E_t(p_{t+1}) - p_t]$ below the per unit threshold return. In the aggregate this shows in a decreased propensity to store under a price band scheme (or formally $\alpha_{1,\text{price band scheme}} < \alpha_{1,\text{ no price band scheme}}$) where the aggregate propensity to store is a weighted average of the propensity to store of the two groups with their relative size as weights. It should be noted that the price band scheme also affects the riskiness of the arbitrage activity: the variance of prices ($VAR_t(p_{t+1})$) decreases, and hence the propensity to store becomes larger.

It has to be determined empirically which of these two effects dominates the other. Note that the potential arbitrage opportunities will obviously be lower during a price band scheme: this relates to the interaction between private stockholders and a price band scheme mentioned in the introduction. Such an influence does, however, not affect the coefficients of the behavioral equation.

Prior to testing for a structural break we have to determine how we split up the sample in a pre BSS, a BSS and a post BSS period. The beginning and ending of BSS is, in this respect, related to the behavior of stockholders, and not to the formal start and end of the BSS in, respectively, March 1984 and March 1989: formal start and structural break in behavior do not necessarily coincide. It could be either earlier or later, depending on how the price policy is interpreted by these agents. Additionally, these structural breaks do not necessarily coincide for the different groups of stockholders. This could be caused by different access to information or different assessment of information. However, how is the exact date of the structural break identified?

As the exact timing of the BSS, or perhaps better, as the timing of the change in the behavior of stockholders due to the BSS is not clear, we first apply techniques that are specifically designed to identify structural breaks if the break point is unknown, namely recursive least squares (RLS), CUSUM and CUSUM of squares. The technique of recursive least squares implies the estimation of the same equation repeatedly, using ever larger subsets of the sample data. We have applied the recursive least squares technique on the coefficient that reflects arbitrage activities. Large fluctuations in the value of parameters are, in general, an indication of parameter instability. Structural breaks early in the sample will be identified much more clear than breaks late in the sample, due to the fact that more observations of different regimes will dampen the change in the coefficient. The equations used to implement this technique are taken from Chapter 3 and are repeated below:

$$\Delta s_{gd,t} = \gamma_0 + \gamma_1 \, \Delta \, {}_t p^e_{t+3} + \gamma_2 \rho \, \Delta p_t + \gamma_3 \, \Delta q_t + \gamma_4 \, s_{gd,t-1} + \gamma_5 \, q_{t-1} + \varepsilon_{gd}$$
$$\Delta s_{mf,t} = \zeta_0 + \zeta_1 \, \Delta \, {}_t p^e_{t+2} + \zeta_2 \rho \, \Delta p_t + \zeta_3 \, \Delta c_t + \zeta_4 \, s_{mf,t-1} + \zeta_5 \, c_{t-1} + \varepsilon_{mf}$$

where:

$s_{gd}$ = stocks of natural rubber with growers and dealers;

$s_{mf}$ = stocks of natural rubber with manufacturers of rubber products;

${}_t p^e_{t+i}$ = expected price for t+i, conditional on the information at time t;

$p$ = price;

$q$ = production;

$c$ = consumption.

The coefficients that are of particular interest to the objective of this chapter are $\gamma_1$ and $\gamma_2$ in the case of stockholding by growers and dealers, and $\zeta_1$ and $\zeta_2$ in the case of stockholding by manufacturers. In Chapter 3 it is derived that $\gamma_1 = -\rho\,\gamma_2$ and $\zeta_1 = -\rho\,\zeta_2$ which simplifies to $\gamma_1 = -\gamma_2$ and $\zeta_1 = -\zeta_2$ if we assume that $\rho$ is approximately equal to 1. In the estimation of these equations a complete set of monthly dummies has been included to account for systematic monthly influences not captured with other explanatory variables. To focus the attention on the coefficients of interest and because coefficients of some of these monthly dummies show substantial fluctuation if estimated for different periods, significant coefficients have been fixed at their full sample estimates. In appendix 5.1 the estimation of these equations using the full sample are reported.

The results of RLS, showing the development of the coefficient that reflects arbitrage activities with ever increasing sample size within a two standard error band, is presented in Figure 5.1 (upper panel for the coefficient in the equation of stocks at growers and dealers($s_{gd}$)) and lower panel for the coefficient in the equation of manufacturers ($s_{mf}$)). To some extent the figures confirm the stability of the coefficient, in the sense that the standard error gets smaller the longer the period on which the estimation is based. Also, a number of abrupt deviations from a smooth development of the coefficient can be identified:

From the upper panel of Figure 5.1 (stockholding by growers and dealers) a sudden decrease at the start of 1984 is seen. The further development over time of the coefficient shows, however, a number of erratic jumps, both up and down, and do not allow any conclusion in favor of our proposition. In particular an increase in the coefficient at the start of 1986 and a decrease at the end of 1987 do not fit in our story. However, if the figure is looked at from an overall perspective, we do observe a slightly lower value of the coefficient during BSS.

From the lower panel of Figure 5.1 (stockholding by manufacturers) a decrease of the coefficient starting halfway 1983 can be observed: possibly the estimated equation tries to digest a structural break during this period. After this decrease the coefficient stays more or less at the same level till the end of 1987 and the end of 1988, that both show two mild upward jumps. Again, we feel that the figure only provides weak evidence and does not allow firm conclusions in favor of our proposition. Like in the case of stockholding by growers and dealers, we do observe a slightly lower value of the coefficient during BSS, if an overall perspective is taken.

It should be noted that breaks in later periods will be more difficult to detect as periods with different regimes contaminate the same estimation. A structural break at the start of the Buffer Stocking Scheme is weakly captured

**Figure 5.1**

Recursive estimation of the coefficient of arbitrage behavior of stockholders (growers and dealers ($s_{gd}$): upper panel; manufacturers ($s_{mf}$): lower panel); the dotted lines represent two standard error lines above and below the coefficient

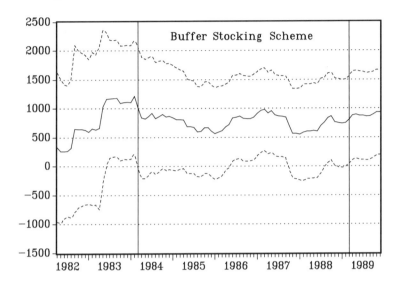

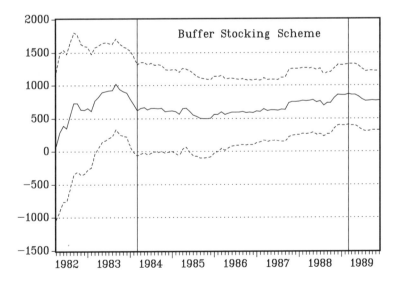

with the RLS technique. It also seems that stockholding by manufacturers reacts slightly earlier than stockholding by growers and dealers: the coefficient of the former starts to decrease in October 1983 and the decrease is completed in March 1984, while the coefficient of the latter starts to decrease in February 1984, and this decrease is completed in April 1984. We feel that the remaining part of the RLS figures does not allow firm conclusions, although a rough overview of the two figures suggest that the coefficients indeed are lower during BSS.

Another technique to identify structural breaks, if the exact date of the structural break is uncertain, is the CUSUM test and the CUSUM of squares test. Both tests are based on the ex-post prediction error in period t ($e_t$), using t-1 observations to estimate the equation. The test statistic of the CUSUM test is based on the cumulated sum of the (scaled) residuals, $w_r$ (see Greene (1993), pp. 216-217):

$$\text{CUSUM} = \sum_{r=K+1}^{r=t} (w_r / \hat{\sigma})$$

where

$$\hat{\sigma}^2 = 1/(T-K-1) \sum_{r=K+1}^{r=T} (w_r - w^*)^2$$

$$w^* = 1/(T-K) \sum_{r=K+1}^{r=T} w_r$$

If the parameters are stable the CUSUM test statistic has a zero mean and a variance of approximately the number of residuals being summed. In practice the statistic is plotted between confidence bounds: if the statistic falls outside these bounds the hypothesis is rejected. A similar alternative is the CUSUM of squares test. The test statistic of the CUSUM of squares test is:

$$\text{CUSUMSQ} = \sum_{r=K+1}^{r=t} (w_r^2) / \sum_{r=K+1}^{r=T} (w_r^2)$$

This test statistic is also presented with confidence bounds: if the test statistic falls outside these bounds parameter stability is questionable. Both the CUSUM and CUSUM of squares test are appropriate for time series, and are in particular attractive if the exact date of the structural break is uncertain. The test, however, does have a rather low power compared to the Chow test (see below).

The test results of the CUSUM and CUSUM of squares tests are reported in the appendices to this chapter (see Appendix 5.2, Figures 5.2 to 5.5). The evidence presented in these figures is mixed: all CUSUM tests do not reject parameter stability, and all CUSUM of squares tests indicate parameter instability or parameters that are on the fringe of being unstable. The timing of the parameter instability, however, is far from uniform. In the case of stockholding by growers and dealers the CUSUM of squares test indicates coefficient instability from mid 1984 to the end of 1987 (see Appendix 5.2, Figure 5.2, lower panel). With a simplified specification (see below), parameter instability is much less apparent (see Appendix 5.2, Figure 5.3, lower panel). In the case of stockholding by manufacturers the outcome of the CUSUM of squares test indicate parameter instability in 1986 and 1987 (see Appendix 5.2, Figure 5.4, lower panel). Again this is weakened with a simplified specification. For both groups of stockholders, and for both tests, it is observed that parameter stability is substantially higher before 1984 and from 1988 onwards.

In summary we conclude that the presented evidence of these recursive estimation techniques confirm to some extent the instability of the parameter that reflect arbitrage behavior: the evidence points at possible structural breaks, in particular a structural break at the start of BSS is corroborated. Nevertheless, evidence from these recursive estimation techniques is not always convincing and uniform about these breaks.

Because the results of our search of the exact timing of the structural break with RLS, CUSUM and CUSUM of squares are not in all respects satisfactory, it has been decided to find the exact date of the structural break by maximizing the F statistic of the Chow test. Therefore, we have split the sample period into three parts: from the start of the sample period (1980.01) to the beginning of the BSS, the period of the BSS and the period from the end of the BSS to the end of the sample period (1989.12). We propose that the structural break for both groups of stockholders, if any, should lie somewhere in an interval of less than one year before the formal beginning of BSS, implying forward looking behavior of stockholders. Likewise, another structural break should lie somewhere in an interval of less than a year before the ending of BSS. We proceed by calculating F values of the Chow test for all possible dates of structural breaks. This procedure yielded 1984.02/03 and 1988.06/07 as dates of structural break in the case of stockholding by growers and dealers and 1983.09/10 and 1988.06/07 in the case of stockholding by manufacturers. The selected dates for the structural break are to some extent corroborated by the recursive least squares (see below and Figure 5.1). Finally it is noted that the structural breaks are attributed to the Buffer Stocking Scheme: other causes of breaks in behavior are assumed to be controlled for through the inclusion of the other explanatory variables.

### 5.3    Testing for breaks in the behavior of stockholders

A statistically more rigorous approach to test for breaks is desirable. Therefore, we proceed with applying a number of tests on structural breaks of the coefficients. The tests in the current section all assume the exact date of the structural break to be known. Practically this is implemented by maximizing the significance of a Chow test within a range of one year before the formal beginning (ending) of the price policy. Tests are based on estimation results for the stock demand equation for the sub-periods as presented in Table 5.2 and 5.3. The test statistic of the Chow test is:

$$CHOW(J,n-K) = ((RSS_r-RSS_1-RSS_2-RSS_3)/J) / (RSS_1+RSS_2+RSS_3)/(n_1+n_2+n_3-3*K)$$

where

RSS(.) = sum of squared residuals

J      = number of restrictions

n      = number of observations

K      = number of explanatory variables (including constant term)

r refers to the restricted estimation (parameters constant throughout the complete sample period), while 1,2 and 3 refer to the different sub periods

The Chow test has a F distribution, to be evaluated at $(J,n-K)$.

Next a likelihood ratio test is reported. In order to implement this test, two dummy variables are introduced: the first one takes a value of 1 during the Buffer Stocking Scheme, and 0 in other periods $(D_{BSS})$, the second one takes a value of 1 in the post-BSS period, and 0 in other periods $(D_{POST})$. The equation estimated on the basis of the complete sample (the restricted equation) is compared to the estimation outcome of a test equation. In the test equation all explanatory variables are included three times: the first time, as in the ordinary specification, the second time in combination with the BSS dummy and the third time in combination with the post-BSS dummy. The test equation is:

$$\Delta s_{gd,t} = \gamma_0 + \gamma_1 \, \Delta \, _tp^e_{t+3} + \gamma_2 \, \rho \Delta p_t + \gamma_3 \, \Delta q_t + \gamma_4 s_{gd,t-1} + \gamma_5 q_{t-1}$$
$$\gamma_6 \cdot D_{BSS} + \gamma_7 \cdot D_{BSS} \, \Delta \, _tp^e_{t+3} + \gamma_8 \cdot D_{BSS} \, \rho \Delta p_t + \gamma_9 \cdot D_{BSS} \, \Delta q_t +$$
$$\gamma_{10} \cdot D_{BSS} \, s_{gd,t-1} + \gamma_{11} \cdot D_{BSS} q_{t-1} +$$
$$\gamma_{12} \cdot D_{POST} + \gamma_{13} \cdot D_{POST} \, \Delta \, _tp^e_{t+3} + \gamma_{14} \cdot D_{POST} \, \rho \Delta p_t + \gamma_{15} \cdot D_{POST} \, \Delta q_t +$$
$$\gamma_{16} \cdot D_{POST} \, s_{gd,t-1} + \gamma_{17} \cdot D_{POST} q_{t-1} + \varepsilon_{gd}$$

Likewise we can construct a test equation for $\Delta s_{mf,t}$, which is, however, not presented to save space. The test statistic of the Likelihood Ratio test is:

$$LR = 2.(L_u - L_r)$$

where

$L_u$ = maximum of the log of the likelihood function of unrestricted equation
$L_r$ = maximum of the log of the likelihood function of the restricted equation

and this statistic has a $\chi^2$ distribution, to be evaluated at the number of restrictions imposed.

A final test is an ordinary t-test on the coefficient of a dummy variable for the BSS period defined as above and combined with, respectively, price and expected price. The significance of the coefficient of this dummy variable, represented by its t-value, can also be interpreted as a test on a structural break. The test equations run as follows:

$$\Delta s_{gd,t} = \gamma_0 + \gamma_1 \, \Delta \, _t p^e_{t+3} + \gamma_2 \, \rho \, \Delta p_t + \gamma_3 \, D_{BSS} \, \Delta \, _t p^e_{t+3} + \gamma_4 \, \rho \, D_{BSS} \, \Delta p_t +$$
$$\gamma_5 \, D_{POST} \, \Delta \, _t p^e_{t+3} + \gamma_6 \, \rho \, D_{POST} \, \Delta p_t + \gamma_7 \, \Delta q_t + \gamma_8 s_{gd,t-1} + \gamma_9 q_{t-1} + \varepsilon_{gd}$$

$$\Delta s_{mf,t} = \zeta_0 + \zeta_1 \, \Delta \, _t p^e_{t+2} + \zeta_2 \, \rho \, \Delta p_t + \zeta_3 \, D_{BSS} \, \Delta \, _t p^e_{t+2} + \zeta_4 \, \rho \, D_{BSS} \, \Delta p_t +$$
$$\zeta_5 \, D_{POST} \, \Delta \, _t p^e_{t+2} + \zeta_6 \, \rho \, D_{POST} \, \Delta p_t + \zeta_7 \, \Delta c_t + \zeta_8 \, s_{mf,t-1} + \zeta_9 \, c_{t-1} + \varepsilon_{mf}$$

The t-test has the obvious advantage that it focuses on the very coefficient of interest. It does, however, assume at the same time that all other coefficients are unaffected by the BSS. The t-test requires the pre- and post-BSS values of the coefficients of all explanatory variables other than the coefficients of $\Delta \, _t p^e_{t+j}$ and $\Delta p_t$, to be equal. This is a strong assumption and different from the Chow and the Likelihood Ratio test, that allow the pre- and post-BSS values of the coefficients of all explanatory variables to be different. The test results from the Chow test, the Likelihood Ratio test and the t-test are given in Table 5.1.

From Table 5.1 it is observed that the null hypothesis of no structural break has to be rejected in almost all tests for both groups of stockholders. Note that the t-test indicates rejection of the null only through the coefficient of price and not through the coefficient of expected price.

Finally we take a closer look at the actual estimation results of stock demand equations for the different periods. These estimation results are presented in Table 5.2 and Table 5.3. From the estimations for the three different periods (and

**Table 5.1**    Test statistics for structural breaks

|  | $S_{gd}$ | | $S_{mf}$ | |
|---|---|---|---|---|
|  | (1) | (2) | (1) | (2) |
| CHOW (F) | 2.58 (2.22) | 3.06 (3.21) | 3.06 (2.22) | 4.26 (3.21) |
| Likelihood ratio ($\chi^2$) | 54.94 (27.59) | 13.84 (9.49) | 62.70 (26.30) | 22.30 (11.07) |
| t-values $_t p^e_{t+j}$ | 0.3 | 0.4 | 0.3 | 0.2 |
| t-values $\Delta p_t$ | 1.9 | 1.9 | 1.8 | 2.1 |

(1):    free estimation;

(2):    estimation with the value of some coefficients fixed at the value of the
80.01-89.12 estimates (see below, Table 5.2 and 5.3).

Critical values at 5% confidence levels for the Chow test (respectively F(15,100)
and F(5,100)), and the Likelihood Ratio test are presented in brackets next to the
coefficient.

focusing on the upper part of Tables 5.2 and 5.3), we can observe that the
coefficients that reflect arbitrage behavior - the coefficients of price ($\Delta$p) and
expected price ($\Delta p^e_{t+j}$) - evolve over time as hypothesized: in particular we
observe relatively large and highly significant coefficients in the pre- and post-
BSS period, and relatively low and often insignificant coefficients in the BSS
period. In the case of stockholding by growers and dealers the pre-BSS, BSS and
post-BSS values of these coefficients are, respectively, -2252.1, -630.2 and -887.4
for price ($\Delta$p), and 1124.7, 682.6 and 1633.2 for expected price ($\Delta p^e_{t+3}$). In the
case of stockholding by manufactures the pre-BSS, BSS and post-BSS values of
these coefficients are, respectively, -1356.1, -475.0 and -1658.6 for price ($\Delta$p),
and 934.9, 613.8 and -2051.0 for expected price ($\Delta p^e_{t+2}$). Apart from the last
coefficient (which has the wrong sign, probably due to the fact that there are only
2 degrees of freedom in this estimation), the estimated values of these coefficients
clearly indicate a decreased marginal propensity to arbitrage during BSS. Note
also that the coefficients of price and expected price during BSS are insignificant.

The estimated equations in the upper part of Tables 5.2 and 5.3 contain a
large number of explanatory variables that will not or negligibly be affected by a
price policy. Coefficients of these explanatory variables, however, do change,
when estimations are run for different sample periods. For this reason we have re-
estimated the equations with a number of coefficients fixed at their values
estimated with the large sample (1980.01-1989.12). This procedure enables us also

**Table 5.2**  Estimations of stock demand: stocks at growers and dealers

dependent variable: $\Delta s_{gd}$ estimation method: 2SLS

sample period (no of obs.)  80.01-84.02 (50) 84.03-88.06 (52) 88.07-89.12 (18)

independent variables

| | | | |
|---|---|---|---|
| constant | -8665.3 (1.8) | 2919.1 (0.6) | 1276.3 (0.1) |
| $\Delta p$ | -2252.1 (2.8) | -630.2 (0.7) | -887.4 (1.1) |
| $\Delta p^e_{t+3}$ | 1124.7 (2.3) | 682.6 (0.9) | 1633.2 (0.8) |
| $\Delta q$ | 0.598 (3.9) | 0.671 (2.9) | 0.581 (3.4) |
| $s_{gd,t-1}$ | -0.044 (0.6) | -0.100 (1.5) | -0.299 (0.9) |
| $q_{t-1}$ | 0.634 (3.3) | 0.086 (1.5) | 0.348 (2.2) |
| log(L) | -428.75 | -460.29 | -124.11 |
| SSR | 0.821E8 | 0.149E9 | 0.103E7 |
| R2 adjusted | 0.848 | 0.812 | 0.968 |
| DW | 1.91 | 1.60 | 2.26 |
| $\chi^2_{restriction}$ | 3.714 | 0.004 | 2.750 |
| constant | 1329.0 (5.5) | 1493.3 (4.8) | 547.8 (1.1) |
| $\Delta p$ | -1855.1 (5.1) | -819.6 (2.2) | -1101.5 (2.5) |
| $\Delta p^e_{t+3}$ | 760.6 (2.5) | 433.3 (0.9) | 1573.7 (2.2) |
| $\Delta q$ | 0.449 (9.7) | 0.553 (11.4) | 0.532 (8.2) |
| $s_{gd,t-1}$ | -0.065 (-) | -0.065 (-) | -0.065 (-) |
| $q_{t-1}$ | 0.109 (-) | 0.109 (-) | 0.109 (-) |
| log(L) | -439.82 | -463.55 | -159.44 |
| SSR | 0.128E9 | 0.168E9 | 0.520E8 |
| R2 adjusted | 0.830 | 0.846 | 0.887 |
| DW | 1.81 | 1.75 | 2.33 |
| $\chi^2_{restriction}$ | 5.52 | 0.614 | 0.506 |

Absolute t-values are reported in brackets next to the coefficients; log(L) = Log of Likelihood function; SSR = sum of squared residuals; R2 adjusted = coefficient of correlation adjusted for degrees of freedom; DW = Durbin-Watson statistic; $\chi^2_{restriction}$ is the likelihood ratio test statistic on the restriction that the coefficient of prices($\Delta p$) and expected prices($\Delta p^e_{t+3}$) is of equal but opposite sign, and is $\chi^2$ distributed with one degree of freedom.

**Table 5.3**     Estimations of stock demand market: stocks at manufacturers

dependent variable: $\Delta s_{mf}$          estimation method:          2SLS

sample period (no of obs.)  80.01-83.09 (45) 83.10-88.06 (57) 88.07-89.12 (18)

independent variables

| | | | |
|---|---|---|---|
| constant | -5332.8 (1.4) | -3173.2 (1.8) | 76709 (11.7) |
| $\Delta p$ | -1356.1 (1.8) | -475.0 (0.8) | -1658.6 (9.2) |
| $\Delta p^e_{t+2}$ | 934.9 (2.4) | 613.8 (1.4) | -2051.0 (6.1) |
| $s_{mf,t-1}$ | -0.401 (2.7) | -0.414 (3.6) | -1.261 (11.6) |
| $c_{t-1}$ | 0.834 (3.7) | 0.621 (4.2) | -1.350 (10.0) |
| log(L) | -377.71 | -486.70 | -111.570 |
| SSR | 0.514E8 | 0.871E8 | 255049 |
| R2 adjusted | 0.441 | 0.459 | 0.985 |
| DW | 2.12 | 2.30 | 1.78 |
| $\chi^2_{restriction}$ | 0.404 | 0.044 | 65.222 |
| | | | |
| constant | -3993.1 (1.4) | -2220.0 (1.5) | 9856.6 (1.1) |
| $\Delta p$ | -667.7 (2.2) | -701.2 (2.7) | -1590.4 (3.8) |
| $\Delta p^e_{t+2}$ | 802.5 (2.7) | 240.9 (0.8) | 1017.5 (1.7) |
| $s_{mf,t-1}$ | -0.185 (2.1) | -0.387 (4.2) | -0.303 (2.7) |
| $c_{t-1}$ | 0.566 (3.4) | 0.573 (4.6) | -0.018 (0.1) |
| log(L) | -382.767 | 489.427 | 156.847 |
| SSR | 0.644E8 | 0.958E8 | 0.390E8 |
| R2 adjusted | 0.493 | 0.535 | 0.651 |
| DW | 2.09 | 2.38 | 2.23 |
| $\chi^2_{restriction}$ | 0.112 | 1.932 | 1.130 |

Absolute t-values are reported in brackets next to the coefficients; log(L) = Log of Likelihood function; SSR = sum of squared residuals; R2 adjusted = coefficient of correlation adjusted for degrees of freedom; DW = Durbin-Watson statistic; $\chi^2_{restriction}$ is the likelihood ratio test statistic on the restriction that the coefficient of prices($\Delta p$) and expected prices($\Delta p^e_{t+3}$) is of equal but opposite sign, and is $\chi^2$ distributed with one degree of freedom.

Note with Table 5.2 and 5.3: Not reported in the tables are the coefficients of a complete set of monthly dummy variables, included additional to the above explanatory variables. In the lower part of the tables the specification is as in the upper part except that the values of some coefficients are fixed at their 80.01-89.12 estimates.

to focus more effectively on the parameters of interest, namely the parameters on price ($\Delta p$) and expected price ($\Delta p^e_{t+j}$). Incidentally it also solves the degree of freedom problem in the post-BSS sample period. The explanatory variables that are fixed are monthly dummy variables, whenever significant in the free estimation, and the long-run variables in the case of growers and dealers. The estimation results reported in the lower part of Tables 5.2 and 5.3 confirm our earlier observations even more convincingly: in the pre- and post-BSS period coefficient of price ($\Delta p$) and expected price ($\Delta p^e_{t+j}$) have the proper sign, are all significant and have equal or much larger values than their BSS counterparts. In the BSS period the coefficient of expected price ($\Delta p^e_{t+j}$) is insignificant for both groups of stockholders.

If the coefficient of price ($\Delta p$) is equal but opposite in sign to expected price ($\Delta p^e_{t+j}$), the elasticity of stock demand for arbitrage purposes, evaluated at the mean, has a value of 1.07-1.08 in the pre and post-BSS period and 0.61 during BSS in the case of stocks at growers and dealers. These elasticities are 0.89-1.73 in the pre and post-BSS period and 0.63 during BSS, in the case of manufacturers. Hence, the price elasticity of stock demand for arbitrage purposes is almost twice as high before BSS and after the BSS in the case of stockholding by growers and dealers. In the case of manufacturers a comparable pattern is observed: the elasticity is almost 1.5 times as high as before and almost three times as high as after BSS.

To summarize the results of this section, we note that the test outcome clearly indicates a structural break in the behavior of stockholders due to BSS. Additionally, the estimation results of Tables 5.2 and 5.3 show to what extent arbitrage behavior is different during the sub-periods: the elasticity of stock demand for arbitrage purposes, before the BSS and after the BSS, is almost twice as high in the case of growers and dealers and almost one and a half to three times as high in the case of stocks at manufacturers.

## 5.4    Simulating price volatility with and without price policy

Having established a significantly increased elasticity of stock demand for arbitrage purposes before and after the period of the BSS, compared to the period of the BSS itself, it is interesting to relate this information to the variability of prices during these sub-periods. The development of both nominal and real prices is presented in Figure 5.6 (see Appendix 5.2). From the figures it is immediately obvious that nominal price variation is much less during the BSS compared to before and after the BSS. However, keeping in mind the eventual objective of the BSS (see Chapter 2), in particular, the periodical revision of minimum and maximum prices on the basis of studies on the costs of production, it is assumed that only real prices matter. The figure with real prices is much less clear about the extent of price variation during the respective sub-periods. For that reason the coefficients of variation have been calculated and these are presented in Table 5.4.

If we look in Table 5.4 at the row of nominal prices, the observation from Figure 5.6 is clearly confirmed: the coefficient of variation (CV) is three times higher before, and more than twice as high after the BSS (compared to the coefficient of variation during the BSS). However, if we look at the row of real prices, it seems that there is hardly any difference in variation between the respective periods. The CV for the period after the BSS is somewhat higher but this might very well be caused by the institutional changes taking place in the Indian economy (e.g. opening up). These calculations allow the conclusion that the actual variation in real prices has been more or less the same over the entire sample period, irrespective of whether a bandwidth price policy has been operative.

**Table 5.4**    Coefficient of variation of nominal and real price of natural rubber (RMA4) in India, in percentages

| period | pre-BSS | BSS | post-BSS |
|---|---|---|---|
| variable | 1980.01-1983.11 | 1983.12-1988.06 | 1988.07-1989.12 |
| actual nominal price | 15.7 | 4.8 | 11.6 |
| actual real price | 8.5 | 9.4 | 10.5 |

Of course other circumstances, like dramatic institutional changes or a drastic change in the gap between supply and demand could have enforced different potential price volatility. Here, we intend to suggest that without the BSS the price fluctuations would have been much larger. With respect to institutional changes we note that, apart from the opening-up policy introduced in the beginning of the 1990s which perhaps causes additional volatility in prices due to uncertainty, we are not aware of any other major institutional change in this market that could have influenced the volatility of prices (apart, of course, of the BSS itself). For all sub-periods India had a net shortage of natural rubber every year. Hence, India did not change from a net-importer of natural rubber to a net exporter during any of the sub-periods (see also Chapter 2). Domestic prices are far below world market prices for the larger period of the period considered, with one exception and that is some months during 1988 (see Chapter 2).

    A rigorous way to assess the different impact of the elasticity of stock demand for arbitrage purposes while controlling for exogenous shocks is to simulate prices. Prices are found by imposing equilibrium. Three simulation outcomes are presented: in the first simulation (simulation 1) the estimation results over the whole sample period have been inserted, i.e. the elasticity of stock demand for arbitrage purposes is taken to be 0.88 and 0.85 respectively for growers and dealers, and for manufacturers. In the second simulation (simulation 2) this elasticity is 1.1 for stockholding by growers and dealers and 1.3 for stockholding by manufacturers i.e. the size of the elasticity outside the BSS, see Table 5.2 and 5.3. In the third simulation (simulation 3) the size of the elasticity during the BSS has been used, 0.6 and 0.6, see also Table 5.2 and 5.3, and the accompanying text of that section.

**Table 5.5**    Coefficient of variation of simulated real price of natural rubber (RMA4) in India, in percentages

| period | 1983.12-1988.06 (BSS) |
|---|---|
| variable | |
| simulated real price (1)[*] | 36.9 |
| simulated real price (2)[*] | 31.2 |
| simulated real price (3)[*] | 47.3 |

[*] elasticity of arbitrage stock demand for

|  | simulation 1 | simulation 2 | simulation 3 |
|---|---|---|---|
| growers and dealers | 0.88 | 1.1 | 0.6 |
| manufacturers | 0.85 | 1.3 | 0.6 |

The coefficients of variation reported in Table 5.5 show that the price variation with the lower elasticities, i.e. the BSS elasticities (simulation 3), is substantially higher compared to the price variation with the higher elasticities, i.e. the pre- and post-BSS elasticities (simulation 2). For these reasons we can conclude that arbitrage behavior of stockholders will provide a larger contribution to stable prices compared to the bandwidth price policy.


## 5.5    Summary and conclusion

In this chapter we investigated if a centrally imposed bandwidth price policy is more effective in reducing price fluctuations in commodity markets than the arbitrage activities of private stockholders. The Indian natural rubber market offers an opportunity to compare periods with and without centrally imposed price band policy: centrally imposed price bounds - the so-called Buffer Stocking Scheme (BSS) - were in effect from March 1984 to March 1989. A small error correction rational expectation model of this market, and in particular of stockholding by growers and dealers, and by manufacturers, has been estimated with monthly data covering the period 1978-1992. We have shown that the propensity to arbitrage differs substantially between the respective sub-periods: the elasticity of stock demand for arbitrage purposes, before and after the BSS, is almost twice as high as in the BSS period in the case of growers and dealers and one and a half to three times as high in the case of manufacturers. The change in the behaviour is different from the standard assertion about the interaction between private stockholding and a price band scheme, namely that during a price band scheme the arbitrage opportunities diminish. Simulated prices confirm the stabilizing impact of arbitrage stock behavior measured with the coefficient of variation: simulations with pre- or post-BSS elasticities generate price series with lower coefficients of variation during BSS compared to simulations with BSS elasticities. No other causes of price volatility could be identified: the net external position in this market has been similar throughout all periods and no institutional changes (other than the BSS) have taken place. Hence, the conclusion is allowed that arbitrage behavior of stockholders will provide a larger contribution to the reduction of reducing price fluctuations than a bandwidth price policy.

## Appendix 5.1
## Estimations of stock demand using the entire sample period

| | | | |
|---|---|---|---|
| sample period | 80.01-89.12 | estimation method: | 2SLS |
| sample period | 80.01-89.12 | | |
| dependent variable | $\Delta s_{gd}$ | $\Delta s_{mf}$ | |
| independent variables | | | |
| constant | 2448.9 (1.7) | 2823.9 (3.0) | |
| $\Delta p$ | -1631.3 (3.6) | -1173.7 (3.5) | |
| $\Delta p^e_{t+2}$ | | 490.7 (2.0) | |
| $\Delta p^e_{t+3}$ | 751.0 (2.2) | | |
| $\Delta q$ | 0.475 (6.1) | | |
| $s_{gd,t-1}$ | -0.072 (2.4) | | |
| $q_{t-1}$ | 0.085 (1.4) | | |
| $s_{mf,t-1}$ | | -0.296 (4.8) | |
| $c_{t-1}$ | | 0.257 (4.7) | |
| log(L) | -1069.08 | -1042.04 | |
| SSR | 0.392E9 | 0.245E9 | |
| R2 adjusted | 0.840 | 0.443 | |
| DW | 1.94 | 2.04 | |
| $\chi^2_{restriction}$ | 2.74 | 3.620 | |

Absolute t-values are reported in brackets next to the coefficients; log(L) = Log of Likelihood function; SSR = sum of squared residuals; R2 adjusted = coefficient of correlation adjusted for degrees of freedom; DW = Durbin-Watson statistic; $\chi^2_{restriction}$ is the likelihood ratio test statistic on the restriction that the coefficient of prices($\Delta p$) and expected prices($\Delta p^e_{t+3}$) is of equal but opposite sign, and is $\chi^2$ distributed with one degree of freedom.

**Appendix 5.2**
**CUSUM and CUSUM of squares tests**

**Figure 5.2**
CUSUM (upper panel) and CUSUM of squares test (lower panel): stockholding
by growers and dealers, free estimation; dotted lines indicate 5% critical lines

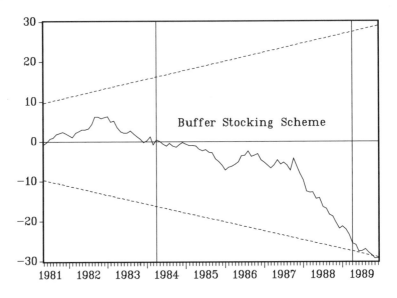

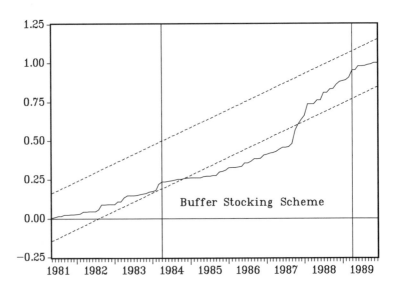

**Figure 5.3**

CUSUM (upper panel) and CUSUM of squares test (lower panel): stockholding by growers and dealers, with fixed coefficients (see Section 5.3) dotted lines indicate 5% critical lines

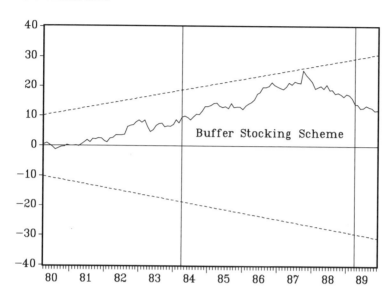

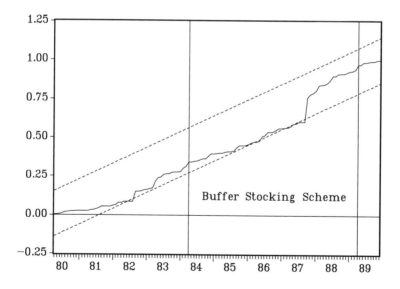

**Figure 5.4**

CUSUM (upper panel) and CUSUM of squares test (lower panel): stockholding by manufacturers, free estimation dotted lines indicate 5% critical lines

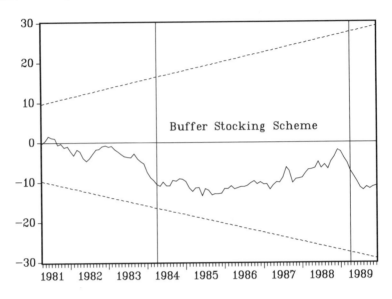

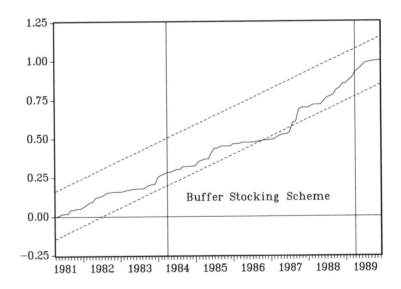

**Figure 5.5**

CUSUM (upper panel) and CUSUM of squares test (lower panel): stockholding by manufacturers, with fixed coefficients (see Section 5.3) dotted lines indicate 5% critical lines

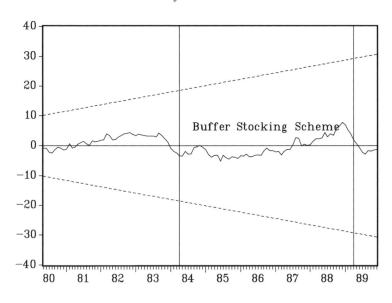

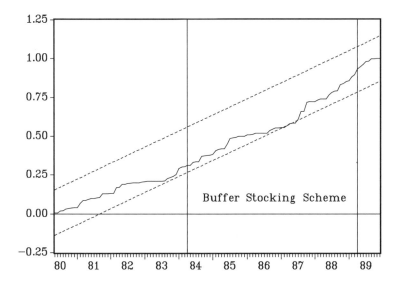

**Figure 5.6**

Nominal price (upper panel) and real market-price (lower panel) of natural rubber (RMA4) in India

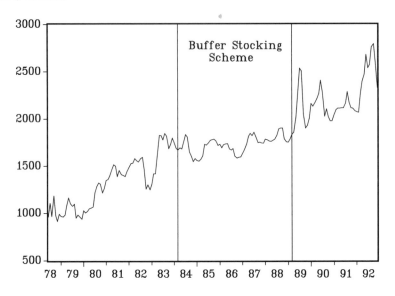

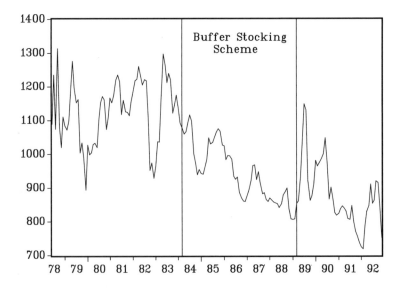

# 6 MANAGING COMMODITY PRICE RISKS IN DEVELOPING COUNTRIES

## 6.1 Introduction

For a number of years financial risk management instruments, like futures, options and swaps, have been suggested as effective instruments to reduce price uncertainty in commodity markets (see eg. Claessens and Duncan (1993), UNCTAD (1994(a,b),1995)). At the beginning of the 1990s both the World Bank and UNCTAD took up an active policy to promote the use of financial instruments to manage commodity price exposure in developing countries. As far as UNCTAD is concerned this is laid down in Cartagena Commitment (UNCTAD VIII meeting in Cartagena, Columbia, February 1992, paragraph 205):

'.. *Where appropriate, developing countries should be provided with technical assistance and policy advice on mechanisms, such as the use financial instruments, to manage price and other commodity related risk.*'

Protection against price fluctuations and setting reference prices for trade are regarded as the main benefits of these financial instruments. UNCTAD's work focuses on the question if these markets are indeed proper, well functioning price formation mechanisms, and if developing countries have access to financial risk management instruments, and, if not, how to achieve such access. The World Bank embarked on a policy to stimulate the use of financial risk management instruments as a part of the Bank's broader program of financial technical assistance to developing countries. In an early stage the World Bank only took up research on problems to be resolved in order to be able to make use of financial risk management instruments, later to be followed by a technical assistance program. The work by the World Bank has been particularly motivated by the limited use of these instruments by developing countries, despite their potential to hedge price risks.

The purpose of this chapter is to investigate if and how financial risk management instruments can play a role in the Indian natural rubber market. The chapter is intended to set the stage for a quantitative assessment in Chapter 7. As a first step in this investigation in Section 6.2 the main financial instruments are listed, their characteristics summarized and, for each instrument, a typical hedging operation is explained. Most of these instruments can only be used effectively if they are traded on smoothly operating commodity exchanges, which are characterized by substantial flows of trade. Therefore, the issue of liquidity and participation on the commodity exchanges is also considered in this section. Subsequently, a number of potential applications of risk management strategies that are reviewed in the literature, are summarized in Section 6.3. Despite the desirability of hedging price risk, actual use of financial risk management instruments is limited. This is partly due to a number of constraints on implementation of hedging activities. These constraints and related problems are elaborated in Section 6.4. Finally, in Section 6.5, current futures trading practices in India are considered. In Section 6.6 the main findings are summarized.

## 6.2    Financial risk management instruments, hedging operations and liquidity[1]

### 6.2.1    Financial risk management instruments and hedging operations

Financial risk management contracts are available as tailor-made contracts, typically referred to as over-the-counter contracts, or in a standardized form. The standardized type of financial instrument requires little or no negotiation about contract specifications. Such financial instruments are usually traded on organized exchanges. On these exchanges the terms of contracts (quantity of the commodity per contract, quality of the commodity, delivery terms, etc.) are determined by the exchange itself. A particular trader cannot individually construct a contract that nicely fits his needs, but instead must buy or sell a number of futures of a specific type in order to approximate the desired quantity of the commodity. A tailor-made contract, on the other hand, is designed to match specific needs of both parties involved and is, hence, not traded, or not made to be traded on organized exchanges. As a result price formation of over-the-counter contracts will not be transparent, contrary to price formation of standardized contracts. Commission costs of over-the-counter transactions are usually lower compared to these costs on organized exchanges. A number of different types of financial instruments are used in exchanges: the most important of these instruments, namely forward contracts, futures, options, swaps and commodity loans will be treated below.

---

[1]    The material in this section is not particularly 'new' and is documented exhaustively elsewhere. It is nevertheless needed to understand the remaining sections of this chapter and Chapter 7. Extensive use is made of Masuoka (1993), Claessens (1993) and the excellent survey of UNCTAD on this subject (UNCTAD (1994)).

A *forward contract* is an agreement to purchase or sell a given commodity at a future date at a preset price. If the spot-price at the time of maturity is higher than the price in the contract the buyer makes a profit and the seller suffers a loss, and where spot-prices are lower than the contracted price, the reverse will be the case: profits of one side of the market are mirrored by losses of the other side. The value of a specific quantity of a commodity to be delivered in the future can be fixed by means of a forward contract. Physical delivery of the contracted quantity of the commodity is expected at the time of maturity and it is not possible to close out a contract before maturity (unless the contract is traded on a organized exchange).[2] Contracts are made for periods of up to one year. There are no initial cash transfers required: cash transfers only occur at maturity. There are no other costs apart from transaction costs. Most transactions are over-the-counter and do not take place on organized exchanges: only a few exchanges of forward contracts are known (notably some oil contracts). Transactions of over-the-counter contracts are made directly by buyer and seller and, hence, are adapted to the specific needs and desires of the buyer and seller. With forward contracts both trading partners face a default risk: either partner could be unable to comply with the contract obligations and might be tempted to default if prices on the spot-market move away from the contracted price.

A typical hedging operation with a forward contract (forward cover) runs as follows: if one holds or purchases a specific quantity of a commodity, the same quantity of that commodity is sold forward at a pre-specified price. At maturity of the contract the contracted quantity of the commodity is sold/delivered at the agreed price. Absence of cash payments up front and the possibility to construct tailor-made contracts are major advantages of forward contracts. A major drawback of a forward contract is the high two sided default risk.

In a number of respects a *futures contract* is much like a forward contract. A futures contract is also an agreement to purchase or sell a given commodity at a future date at a preset price. Future contracts, however, are standardized and traded on organized exchanges. The counterpart of a future transaction is the clearinghouse of the future exchange. Contrary to forward contracts, futures contracts can easily be reversed or closed out before maturity and physical delivery is not necessarily implied. As a matter of fact, physical delivery at

---

2      Closing out a contract involves the purchase and sale of two identical contracts at different times.

maturity of futures contracts is rather unusual.[3] Contracts mature in at most 18 months, in some cases 36 months. On average contracts mature between 6 and 12 months. Futures transactions involve payments, the so-called margin payments, in order to avoid default risk. An initial cash transfer (initial margin) is required as collateral, the size of which differs by exchange, contract and price level of contracts, and varies from 10 to 25%. Being collateral the initial margin is refunded after closing out the futures contract. On top of the initial margin additional daily cash transfers (margin calls) are required if the price of the contract moves in a way adverse to the holder of a futures contract. This avoids accumulation of large losses and profits over longer periods. The size of the margin payments is determined by the exchange. Margin payments guarantee fulfilment of the contract and futures contracts therefore have a substantially lower default risk compared to forward contracts. Coverage of the costs of operating on a futures exchange (margin payments) requires either liquid funds available at the user of the exchange, or access to credit. Credit lines for trading on a futures exchange are usually offered by banks or trading houses. Nevertheless margin payments entail a problem of access to credit and create interest costs.[4]

A typical hedge operation with futures involves the execution of a number of reverse transactions on the spot and futures market: a producer who plans to sell a physical quantity of a commodity in the future, sells futures for the same quantity of this commodity, maturing in the period of physical delivery or later. The value of the future develops over time to the spot-price at maturity. At the time of maturity the producer sells his physical production on the spot-market and simultaneously reverses (or closes out) his position on the futures exchange. With rising prices a loss on the futures exchange is offset by an equally sized profit on the physical transaction, and hence the realized price (revenue) is fixed. Likewise, with falling prices a profit on the futures transaction is offset by a loss on the physical market. In practice these losses and profits are for a number of reasons not exactly offset, but only approximately. Price development on the (domestic) physical market, for example, could be slightly different from that on the futures exchange. Or the physical production (size, quality) does not match exactly with

---

3    In general turnover in futures markets is around ten times the volume of the underlying commodities. However, for some commodities this is lower (e.g. crude oil and robusta coffee turnover is five times the volume of the underlying physical market).

4    Note also that credit becomes cheaper if the collateral is secured, i.e. in case of credit required for a hedging operation.

the quantity traded on the futures exchange. Also, exchange rate changes may cause divergences. The extent to which profits and losses do not cancel out is called basis risk. The size of basis risk should be small, and, hence, should be assessed adequately before entering into a hedging strategy. A major advantage of a futures contract is the small default risk due to the margin payments. Trading in futures, however, does require sufficient liquidity or access to credit from the trading partners to meet these margin payments.

An *option* is a right (but not the obligation) to purchase or sell a specific commodity or a commodity future, on or before a specified future date at a preset price. This price is known in option jargon as the strike or exercise price. A buyer of an option purchases the right to buy or sell. A seller (writer) of an option sells this right to the buyer. At the time of contracting the buyer pays a premium, the price of the option, to the seller. If a buyer of an option actually makes use of the right to buy or sell, the option is exercised. An option to buy is called a call option and an option to sell a put option. A call option protects the buyer against price rises, and a put option protects the seller against price falls. An option will only be exercised if the option is in the money. A call option is in the money if the price of the underlying asset is higher compared to the strike price of the option. A put option is in the money if the price of the underlying asset is lower than the strike price of the option. Options are out of the money if the reverse is the case. If options are out of the money at maturity they will not be exercised but simply lapse. A very common construction is an option with futures as the underlying asset. In that case the date of maturity (expiration) of the option coincides with that of the future. The buyer of an option has to pay a premium at the time of contracting and this premium is incurred, irrespective of whether the option is exercised or not (cf. insurance premium). The size of the premium varies: out of the money options are relatively inexpensive (around 5%). The writer of an option is required to pay margin, not the one who purchases the option. In practice the amount of margin payments is shared between buyer and seller, depending on whether the option is out of the money or in the money. Margin payments on options are always less than those on comparable futures positions. Deep out of the money put options are sometimes suggested as attractive insurance against declining prices (see Gilbert (1988, 1995): because these options are deep out of the money they are less costly than other put options, and certainly compared to futures. Additionally, and unlike forward and futures contracts that fix a future price, options limit the size of the maximum loss, and leave open the possibility of gaining a profit. The degree of protection of such a hedging strategy comes very close to a market version of a traditional floor price guarantee. More sophisticated strategies with options are suggested that avoid the cost of the premium (see Powell and Gilbert (1988)). Options are both traded in organized option exchange markets as well as over-the-counter. In the case of over-the-counter transactions the buyer faces a default risk: the seller might not meet his commitment. The seller is on the liability side of the transaction and, hence, there is no default risk for the seller.

*Commodity swaps* are constructed to meet the demand for longer-term risk management instruments. The maturity of swap contracts varies from 6 months to 15 years, but the majority of commodity swaps lasts 1 to 7 years. A commodity swap is an agreement to exchange (or swap) specified cash flows at fixed intervals: a commodity swap is a series of forward contracts spread over time in a pre-specified way, with the slight difference that a commodity swap is a purely financial transaction that does not involve physical delivery of commodities. An example of a commodity swap is the following arrangement: a producer agrees with a bank or financial intermediary that the bank pays for a number of years, say 5 years, a specified and fixed annual amount of money in exchange for the value (i.e. a varying amount of money) of a specified quantity of a commodity, calculated at the world market spot-price of that moment and paid by the producer. In practice only net amounts will be paid. Such a hedging set-up eliminates producer price risk for a period of 5 years. Being a series of forward contracts a swap has properties comparable to forward contracts: in particular there is also two sided default risk and there are no initial cash transfers. Contracts match the specific needs of a producer or consumer. Swaps are made between producers or consumers on the one hand, and a bank or large trader on the other hand. The bank or large trader will attempt to reduce its risk by seeking an offsetting swap agreement or by hedging with futures. A commodity swap and commodity swap markets have been developed only recently. The major advantage of swaps is the total decoupling of the hedging operation and the physical trading activity and the possibility to manage long-term price risks. Stability of producer revenues improves the possibilities to obtain credit. A drawback of commodity swaps is that they require cash flow.

A *commodity linked loan* is an agreement to link the repayment of principal and interest to the price of a specific commodity or to an index of a number of commodity prices. It can be seen as a combination of a swap and a conventional bank loan. Commodity producers engage in commodity bonds or loans to raise investment capital in such a way that the return of investment is not influenced by fluctuations in the price of the commodity. Commodity bonds and commodity loans are not particularly made for risk management purposes but are much more related to investment projects: they play a role in obtaining access to the capital market (or in rescheduling external debts).

In the Indian natural rubber market a number of instruments are appropriate in hedging price risks. A long-term investment in a perennial crop like natural rubber will be most helped with a long-term hedging instrument, like a commodity swap. However, no swap contracts in rubber are currently known.[5] most likely due to poor capitalization of the supply side of the natural rubber market. Long-term hedging may also be realized by rolling over futures (see below). There are a number of international commodity exchanges trading natural rubber futures (Singapore, Tokyo, Kobe) and, hence, hedging with futures is possible at least on these exchanges.[6] The size of basis risk needs serious consideration if futures are used to hedge. Although options are no long-term hedging instrument, rolling over can be realized, if a future is the underlying asset of the option (a common combination). Out of the money put options are particularly attractive to Indian rubber growers and traders as they have the obvious advantage of protection against falling prices, leave open the opportunity of profiting from price increases and are relatively inexpensive. Such option contracts, however, are not known to be available.

### 6.2.2 Liquidity on commodity exchanges

Most financial risk management instruments can only be used effectively if they are traded on smoothly operating commodity exchanges, with substantial flows of trade.[7] The size of turnover on commodity exchanges, mostly referred to as liquidity, and access to these exchanges are important issues in this respect. Liquidity specifically refers to the volume of trading activity: a liquid market is a market with a high volume of transactions and (preferably) a large number of participants at both sides of the market. A liquid market implies that a counterpart for a transaction is easily and quickly found without having a major impact on prices of the particular instrument. Bid-ask spreads become smaller the more liquid the market. Large transactions can take place in a very short time and are absorbed by the market without affecting the price if markets are liquid. On the other hand, in markets with low liquidity, sometimes labelled as thin markets, it is difficult or at times even impossible to find counterparts for transactions and

---

[5] Most swap contracts are in highly capitalized sectors as oil or metals.
[6] See Section 6.4 for a discussion on whether to use an existing foreign exchange or to create a domestic one.
[7] Obviously this does not apply to over-the-counter risk management instruments.

prices of contracts are easily influenced by and susceptible to manipulations of individual traders. Thin markets are characterized by extreme and unpredictable fluctuations of prices in very short time spans. A high liquidity is required for the proper functioning of futures exchanges. Hedging operations should preferably be executed on liquid markets, and if markets are not liquid operating these markets should be done carefully and supported by knowledge on the underlying forces of price formation. Liquidity of risk management instruments in commodities is, in general, lower compared to liquidity of these instruments for interest rate and exchange rates. In particular long-term contracts suffer from low liquidity and are therefore also hardly available. Long-term risk management, however, can be implemented by chaining a number of short-term contracts: for example, a three year hedge may be implemented by buying six months futures, closing out at maturity and at the time of closing out buy futures for six months further. If this procedure is repeated 5 times in a row a three year hedge is obtained. Such an operation is called rolling-over.[8] Prices of futures in commodity exchange are usually higher for further-out futures contracts, reflecting the interest and storage costs of the commodity. The market is in that case referred to as being in contango. If the opposite is the case - further-out futures have a lower price than nearby futures - the market is called to be in backwardation. Backwardation is often attributed to the convenience yield of having a commodity at one's disposal and is regarded as an indication of a poorly functioning market. Whether a market is in backwardation or in contango has dramatic implications for long-term hedging by means of rolling-over. Depending on which side of the transaction you are on, rolling-over can lead to accumulation of losses or profits each time a contract is rolled over. To avoid losses with long-term hedging in such markets is difficult and requires, at the least, to make skilful use of temporary fluctuations in the market or to use over-the-counter transactions.

To improve liquidity obviously requires knowledge on potential market participants and possible obstacles for potential participants to get access to commodity exchanges. Data on market participation are, in general, not available and hence it is not possible to assess who accounts for the liquidity in markets or to analyze behaviour of agents with respect to risk. Some more general observations, however, can be made. The main users of commodity futures exchanges are the primary producers of the commodity, manufacturers of the processing industry and traders and speculators. Speculators are of particular

---

[8]    See Gardner (1989) for empirical evidence of the effectiveness of rollovers for long-term hedging.

importance as they are prepared to assume the risk and to take the opposite position of transactions desired by producers and manufacturers. However, their role is also played by more direct participants. Partly due to the complexity of using risk management instruments a large number of intermediaries are operating on commodity exchanges (eg. banks, trading houses, brokerage companies, commission houses, hedging departments of large companies, etc.[9]). In fact only very few users of commodity exchanges have direct access to these exchanges: membership of exchanges is mostly limited to these intermediaries. Although most users rely on far-away intermediaries to implement their hedging activities, some users choose a different organization of their hedging activities (see UNCTAD (1994a)), p.21):

'...*Some companies have their representatives close to the exchanges to arrange their risk management business, albeit by way of brokers. For example, Brazil's and Mexico's oil companies, Ghana's Cocoa Marketing Board and Cuba's sugar export organization have offices in London and/or New York responsible for futures and option transactions. This allows these institutions to follow quite advanced risk management strategies.*'

Financial risk management instruments have been developed, as noted above, in three fields, namely exchange rates, interest rates and commodities. The degree of development, expressed in terms of liquidity of the market, trade volume and number and type of contracts traded, is much higher in the case of interest rate and exchange rate instruments as compared to commodities. For example, the market for currency options is highly liquid and fairly well-developed, while the market for commodity options only came into being recently and is active for only a few commodities. India is known to make use of financial risk management instruments for interest rate and exchange rate risks (from Masuoka (1993), p.116). Experience with using these financial instruments is also important for hedging commodity price risk: hedging commodity price risk can be implemented on a foreign commodity exchange as well, and hence also requires to deal with the exchange rate risk.[10]

From the above considerations it is clear that the degree of liquidity should play a role in the choice of the commodity exchange. With commodity exchanges that are in backwardation or contango long-term hedges through rolling-over cause either losses or profits. Direct access to commodity exchanges is quite uncommon

---

[9]    There are even companies that offer complete comprehensive hedging packages to exporters (see Soumah (1995)).

[10]    Such a strategy is suggested in Chapter 7.

due to the complexity of hedging activities: most groups in the market do their risk management through intermediaries. Markets to hedge commodity price risk are less developed compared with markets to hedge foreign exchange rate and interest rate risks.

## 6.3    Applications of financial risk management instruments in commodity markets

There are no studies known that evaluate, ex post, the use of financial risk management in existing market set-ups and measure benefits of these risk management strategies. This is due to the fact that data on market participation in financial markets is lacking. There is some rough evidence on the very limited, nevertheless growing, participation of developing countries in commodity exchanges (see Varangis and Larson (1996)). On the other hand, studies that assess the potential ex-ante gains of using risk management instruments in specific commodity markets abound (e.g. Rolfo (1980), Gordon and Rausser (1984), Ouattara, Schroeder and Orlo Sorensen (1990), Claessens and Varangis (1993), Claessens, and Coleman (1993), Meyers (1993), Budd (1993), Savosnick and Sood (1993), Satyanarayan, Thigpen and Varangis (1993), Varangis, Thigpen and Akiyama (1993), Larson (1993), Thigpen and Satyanarayan (1994), Gazanfer (1995), UNCTAD (1995), UNCTAD / World Bank (1996), Faruquee and Coleman (1996)). A selection of these is reviewed below.

Ouattara, Schroeder and Orlo Sorensen (1990) calculate revenue from and optimal hedge ratios for coffee production and trade in Côte d'Ivoire, with both price and production uncertainty and for a range of values of the risk aversion parameter. Measures of price and production uncertainty are calculated as the difference between forecasts, based on information available before the harvest, and realized values. On the basis of these measures expressions for expectational values, variances and covariances of production and prices are derived (cf. Rolfo (1980)). The Ivorian Stabilization Fund, a parastatal agency, supervises the market operation, guarantees a fixed price to producers, and guarantees a CIF price to local licensed exporters. The Fund is exposed to price risk from the time it buys from producers to the time it sells coffee abroad. The futures at the New York Sugar, Coffee and Cocoa Exchange were chosen as hedging instrument as a larger volume is traded on this exchange as compared to London Robusta coffee futures market, and because the US is an important buyer of coffee. Using the coffee futures market to hedge coffee exports is shown to have reduced standard deviation but also the levels of revenues. Unfortunately an assessment of this strategy in terms of welfare is lacking. A complete welfare analysis is impossible as utility functions of agents in the market and compensating variations, relative to a situation without hedging, are not specified.

Meyers (1993) and Claessens and Varangis (1993) investigate exposure to price risk and potential hedging strategies for the coffee sector in Costa Rica. The main players in the coffee sector of Costa Rica are growers, mills and their representative organization, Federation of Cooperatives of Coffee Growers (FEDECOOP), exporters and a regulatory agency, the Instituto del Café de Costa Rica (ICAFE)). With margins and returns of the mills almost entirely administered, mills hardly face any risk. Risk is concentrated at the farmers level and at the exporters level. Exporters, however, are fairly well capable of hedging risk on the New York Exchange. The Central Bank seems to provide facilities to eliminate the additional exchange rate risk. That farmers bear the brunt of the price risks in this market, is also confirmed statistically. A transfer of risk from the farmer to the mill is suggested to improve the risk management. This can be realized by an increase of advance payments by mills to farmers, while at the same time offsetting the increased risk exposure of mills with a put option on the New York Exchange, providing downside price protection to farmers at minimum cost without adding to the risk of the mills. A number of institutional changes are suggested that pave the way for hedging strategies.[11] The benefits of hedging are calculated[12] and it is concluded that all strategies would have reduced intra-year price risk of coffee substantially.

A series of papers deal with hedging operations of cotton, making use of New York cotton futures contract, the only exchange where cotton futures are traded. Varangis, Thigpen and Akiyama (1993) examine the risk management possibilities for Egyptian cotton. Hedging through New York cotton futures is not advisable as domestic cotton prices are shown to be completely out of line with prices on the New York Cotton Exchange, creating a large basis risk. With a poorly developed physical market and substantial government regulations and intervention in the market, it is also not attractive to develop a domestic commodity exchange. Such a commodity exchange will also suffer most likely

---

[11]    Namely: allowing a fixed contract between mill and growers; regular announcement of reference prices by ICAFE based on the New York Exchange to serve a basis for these fixed contracts; increase of advances to growers; allowing domestic forward contracting by mills and exporters and making available forward exchange rate contracts.
[12]    Calculation of these benefits would require the specification of risk aversion in the utility functions of farmers, mills and exporters: we could not find any reference to this in their paper.

from a lack of liquidity. Instead, measures aiming at the development of a properly functioning physical market with market clearing and little government involvement in price formation are recommended. Satyanarayan, Thigpen and Varangis (1993) investigate cotton price risk and the possibilities for hedging for a number of African countries (Benin, Burkina Faso, Cameroon, Central African Republic, Chad, Côte d'Ivoire, Mali, Senegal and Togo). Parastatal marketing agencies usually sell forward 25-35% of the expected crop, at the time of planting and at market prices that bear little relation to world market prices. Simultaneously buffer funds are operated, accumulating funds if prices are high and serving as a buffer if prices are low. The forward sale is an instrument to stabilize intra-year price fluctuations and the fund is an instrument to stabilize inter-year price fluctuations. These funds, however, turned out to be insufficient to support prolonged periods of low prices: the deficit of the fund eventually had to be paid by government. With this marketing system the larger part of the price risk in these countries is for these marketing agencies and ultimately for the government. Hedging on the New York Cotton Exchange is shown to have acceptable basis risk for a specific contract. A hedging operation is suggested in which futures are sold in July and closed out next June, which corresponds to the cotton season in these countries. Risk minimizing and optimal hedge ratios at different levels of risk aversion are calculated on the basis of the years 1989, 1990 and 1990.[13] Hedging is shown to be effective in reducing price risk. In a slightly mechanical way the same exercise for a different set of countries (namely Uzbekistan, Pakistan, China, Turkey and the African countries of the former study) is implemented in Varangis, Thigpen and Satyanarayan (1994).

Faruqee and Coleman (1996) investigate the possibilities of hedging price risks in the Pakistan wheat market using US commodity exchanges. Import subsidies and procurement of domestic production are argued to distort price signals in this market and to constrain long-term growth. Releases from procurement agencies are sold at below market prices. By means of the import-, procurement- and release policy, the government has shifted the major part of the price risk to the government. Farmers are hardly exposed to price risk and, consequently, have little incentive to engage in risk management. The government is suggested to reduce its exposure to price risk by using hedging instruments.

---

[13]      For unbiased markets or if hedgers are infinitely risk averse the risk minimizing hedge ratio is easily derived by minimizing the variance of expected revenue. In practice this is calculated as the slope coefficient of a regression of futures prices on spot prices, both in first differences (see also Chapter 7).

Calculation of basis risk[14] shows that this risk is small when using futures prices of the Minneapolis Grain Exchange. Hedging strategies with futures, options and swaps, aiming at reducing price risk from import of wheat, indicate that market uncertainty could effectively be reduced. It is argued that future developments in the world grain market (decrease of subsidies in exporting countries, increase of price level and price volatility) make the use of hedging instruments in the Pakistan wheat market even more appropriate.

From all these studies it can be concluded that in many situations in which groups in the market are exposed to price risks appropriate hedging strategy can be designed. These strategies are shown to be economically attractive as they effectively reduce price risk. It is also apparent from these studies that an accurate characterization is needed of the process of price formation, the players in the market and the regulation regarding price formation. This is part of an investigation to identify price risk, i.e. to establish clearly who bears the price risk, and to measure the size of this risk. These issues need to be known, prior to suggesting any hedging strategy in a commodity market.

Measurement of price risk will only be possible with knowledge on risk aversion of market participants, and is beyond the scope of this section (see also Chapter 7). However, an assessment of the distribution of price risk in the Indian natural rubber market, based on the description in Chapter 2, is possible. Three groups of agents are active in the Indian natural rubber market, namely growers, traders and manufacturers of rubber products. Both growers and traders are in general very small and financially weak. Most growers, but also a large number of traders, are only engaged in natural rubber, and have little opportunity to diversify, which makes them particularly vulnerable to price fluctuations. On the other hand, the situation for manufacturers of rubber products is rather different: the major part of rubber supply (around 65%) is consumed by tire manufacturers. This is a small group of mainly large and highly capitalized enterprises: with respect to the diversification of risk, these enterprises are in a fundamentally different position relative to farmers and small scaled traders (access to credit, substitution, risk management). Hence, risk management strategies should focus on transferring price risk from growers and traders to others.

Actual use of financial risk management instruments in current commodity markets in developing countries is limited, despite the potential of these

---

14      A standard way to obtain a measure of basis risk is to regress domestic prices on futures prices (for statistical reason usually in first differences) and use 1 minus the degree of correlation (1-R2) as a measure of basis risk.

instruments to reduce price risk. The limited use is to a large extent due to a number of conditions required for the use of financial risk management instruments. In the next section it is indicated which conditions should be met to hedge price risks on commodity exchanges.

## 6.4    Implementing hedging strategies

### 6.4.1   Limitations to using financial instruments and problems with hedging activities

In a number of studies limitations to the use of financial instruments and problems with hedging activities are discussed (see e.g. Claessens (1993), Masuoka (1993), Varangis and Larson (1996)). These limitations and problems can be grouped under a few headings:

1.    financing international transactions (costs of financial instruments, credit worthiness, legal and regulatory framework);

2.    operating requirements for commodity exchanges (acceptable quality standardization, clearing house, equal access to information);

3.    government interference (restrictions imposed by the government in both physical and futures market).

We discuss the limitations and problems along these lines, to begin with the subject of financing international transactions. From the overview of financial instruments it is clear that the use of these instruments involves costs, or at least liquidity. Futures require margin payments (initial margin, paid at the start, and margin calls when the price of the future moves against the holder); in case of options a premium has to be paid up front; swaps also require substantial cash flows. In anticipation of future revenue it is common to acquire credit either from banks or brokers, to finance these costs. Banks and brokers, in their turn, are faced with customers making use of financial instruments that have a considerable risk of default. The possibilities to obtain credit depend much on the willingness to provide credit and the perception of the countries' credit worthiness. If financial markets have adverse perception of the countries credit worthiness, their possibilities to obtain credit will be severely limited. In an informative contribution Budd (1993) reviews the constraints in the legal and regulatory framework for financing export and hedging operations, in particular in African economies. Stock financing credit should be distinguished from credit for hedging purposes, covering margin payments, options premiums or other costs of financial instruments. The former is usually provided by banks and trading companies, the latter by banks and (to a small extent) brokers. The role of trading companies in providing credit has decreased somewhat due to a more careful approach by banks. Country credit limitations are determined by assessments of credit worthiness by banks and, hence, outside the scope of individual governments or exporters. However, there are local limitations to credit facilities that individual governments or exporters can do something about. Budd identifies three categories of structural impediments to the provision of credit: the commercial law, foreign exchange controls and export licenses, and political risk insurance.

The legal system that supports international finance is regarded as a first structural obstacle. Commercial financing requires a legal system that deals clearly and practically with acquisition and transfer of property rights, with property rights of bulk goods, with property rights over growing crops, with the issuing and transfer of documents on property rights, with creation and registration of security interests, with the creation of widely acceptable warehouse receipts and with seizure of collateral upon default (bankruptcy).

A second obstacle is the regulation with respect to foreign exchange and the issuing of export licenses. Authorization of foreign exchange purchases for hedging purposes should be made possible as well as the issuing of unrestricted export licenses. Restrictions in the specification of such licenses are e.g. the requirement that the physical commodity exists, the fixing of export price and the requirement of a letter of credit to the central bank. If these formalities are not arranged in a flexible way, their timing becomes extraordinary critical. Extension and transferability of export licenses also contribute to such flexibility.

The third obstacle to the provision of credit is (the lack of) political risk insurance: such an insurance covers the risk of non-delivery due to shortcoming of the obligations of the government or related organizations (contract repudiation), due to government operations or change in policy (contract frust-ration) or due to inability to observe the contract because of confiscation, expropriation, nationalization or deprivation. If such insurance is not available, or only at high cost, export financing will be more difficult. Availability of political risk insurance coverage is influenced by a number of circumstances: clarity of laws relating to export, export financing and property rights; permission to foreign companies to hold export licenses and to have property rights; early issuance of export licenses; continuation of government guarantees if exporters are privatized; official contact with providers of such insurance. Apart from these main obstacles there are a number of minor issues that enhance the provision of credit: property and casualty insurance, acceptance of other collateral, familiarity with comprehensive documentation, verification of collateral, demand for financial statements, other controls.

Next we come to the operating requirements for commodity exchanges. For the properly functioning of commodity exchanges a number of preconditions should be met. Most of these preconditions are related to improving the liquidity of the commodity exchange through promotion of confidence of potential users in trading and trading practices on the exchange. The commodity underlying the futures contract must be standardized in terms of size, grade and quality, place of delivery and month of maturity so that contracts become fungible and homogeneous. There should be clear and acceptable quality classification standards of the commodity that is traded. Without such a quality standard users of the commodity exchange will be reluctant to do business. Note that for some agricultural commodities quality classifications are difficult or impossible in which case a commodity exchange may not be feasible.[15] Before introducing a contract an accurate assessment of the market should be undertaken: availability and specifications of contracts should reflect risk management needs in the physical market. The commodity exchange should firmly establish rules for trading and procedures for resolving disputes and preventing manipulation. These arrangements should offer security to potential participants. They also should guarantee, among other things, equal access to market information. Essential to the good functioning of a commodity futures exchange is the presence of a clearing house with sufficient financial resources, capable to act as a counterpart in all transactions and to promote sufficient trading volume at both sides of the market. There should also be an adequate infrastructure for warehousing, transport, administration, communications and information processing and there should be sufficient expertise to support trade.

A final issue that limits the use of financial instruments and causes problems with hedging activities is government interference. Governments should, in general, abstain from interventions in both the physical and the futures market, so that prices are to a large extent determined by free market forces. The government should also remove regulations restricting the use of futures/options markets and/or the free flow of funds necessary to trade such markets (see above). Government agencies that deal with agriculture, agricultural commodities and agricultural policy, policy-makers in general and boards of directors etc. need to have some general understanding of these markets and of hedging operations to be able to take proper measures in creating opportunities to hedge commodity price risk.

---

[15]    For this reason there is no international commodity exchange for tea.

### 6.4.2  Intermediation or direct access?

If hedging is considered desirable the question arises: who is actually going to implement the hedging activities? From Section 6.2 it is clear that direct access of farmers or small traders is rare: an average farmer or local dealer in a 'developing' country commodity market usually does not have access to (international) financial markets. Farmers and local traders are usually too small, lack expertise, credit and credit worthiness (see Gilbert (1985)), or are on the whole reluctant to operate on these markets. In many instances access to foreign exchange is an important barrier to direct access to commodity exchanges. Also the continuous involvement in dealing with margin payments, and the accompanying claims on liquidity cause most groups in the market to be reluctant to implement hedging activities themselves. Even in the developed world most farmers are not doing the hedging operations themselves. From the perspective of the hedging operations it should be noted that there are economies of scale in undertaking hedging activities. If banks implement hedging strategies, this can also be combined with other types of commercial lending to the same customers. Local banks do assessments of credit worthiness of their customers as a standard business activity. For the above reasons it appears that intermediation is the best way to organize hedging operations. Gilbert (1995, p.10) states in this respect:

*'My view is that intermediated futures, relying on services of local banks, is in the ed the most effective means of hedging commodity revenues'.*

Institutionally one can also choose to create a government agency (marketing board) instead of making use of private sector agencies (cooperatives, brokers and banks). Government agencies, if empowered with the appropriate authorities will have less problems in acquiring foreign exchange and dealing with exchange rate risks. Commodity boards will have an acceptable credit status being supported (eventually) by the government, and, hence, have access to international financial markets. If private firms do the hedging operations an enforcement problem arises. Due to reputation effects, contract enforcement will be much less of a problem with intermediation through parastatal agencies. Gilbert (1995) notes in this respect:

*'.. For marketing boards reputation effects are generally sufficient to enforce compliance with contractual obligations.'.*

Finally, opting for government agencies to intermediate in hedging transactions on foreign commodity exchanges is politically more acceptable. Countries that are in the process of liberalization of the economy, have to shift all sorts of discretionary powers from the government to the private sector. Such processes often create painful adjustments for (markets and) institutions. For commodity boards a (gradual) transfer to less market distorting activities like intermediation in such hedging operations, offers a good opportunity to be of use to the market. In implementing these hedging operations, government agencies might act likewise as their market counterparts, again if empowered with the appropriate authorities. Hence, choosing for government agencies in intermediating hedging transactions, seems a nicer option in the process of liberalization of the economy.

### 6.4.3  Using existing foreign commodity exchanges or establishing a domestic one?

Establishing a domestic commodity exchange or using an existing commodity exchange abroad is another question that needs consideration. This also applies to India (UNCTAD/World Bank (1996)):

*'There is no economic reason for a country to insist that all its risk management activities take place through a domestic exchange. International markets could provide similar services. In fact, if a well-functioning international market already exists which adequately reflects Indian market conditions, Indian companies would gain little from the creation of a futures market in India. At least in theory, valuable foreign exchange may be saved if the local rather than the foreign market is used. On the other hand, interest in this market may well be limited, reducing its usefulness. However, risks associated with exchange rate fluctuations will generally involve trade-offs between basis and liquidity risks, unless instruments are available to hedge against exchange rate risks.'*

Such a matter should be considered for each country and each market separately. A number of issues may be used as guiding principles in coming to a conclusion. Futures markets perform two tasks: they provide a price discovery mechanism and a way to manage price risk. Price discovery allows improved planning, higher growth and a better allocation of resources. Price risk management allows domestic farmers and traders to guarantee their future income. Failure to perform either of these tasks is a clear indication of the choice that should be made.

There are two main benefits of using a domestic commodity exchange relative to foreign commodity exchange, namely the smaller basis risk and improved price discovery. These are due to the situation that contract specifications in a domestic commodity exchange will correspond more closely to supply on the domestic market. A range of accompanying and related issues favour a domestic commodity exchange: improved transmission of price and commodity related information, improved credit systems, more responsive capital markets, uniformity in repayment rules and market surveillance, reduced transaction costs and more accurate forward prices (Varangis and Larson (1996)).

It should be noted that using a domestic commodity exchange is also especially attractive because it avoids the need of often scarce foreign exchange resources, and, related to this, it avoids exchange rate risks. Another reason to develop a domestic commodity exchange is the absence of such exchanges abroad. This could also be a reason to further promote and enhance an already existing domestic commodity exchange. The Pepper Commodity Exchange in Cochin India, for example, is the only pepper futures exchange in the world. Attempts to further develop this commodity exchange are currently considered (see UNCTAD (1995), see also below). Also commodities, important in terms of contribution to GDP, mainly consumed domestically and with a price formation that may deviate from world market prices, are potential candidates for domestic commodity exchanges. In fact, it is most desirable that any commodity exchange should be supported by a sufficiently developed physical market in order to function properly.

Benefits of using a foreign commodity exchange relative to a domestic one are spelled out along the same lines. An obvious advantage of a foreign commodity exchange is the access to a larger number of users, and consequently a potentially higher liquidity. Foreign commodity exchanges usually exist already for a longer stretch of time: in terms of rules and regulations these exchanges are well established. An obvious drawback of using a foreign commodity exchange is the need for foreign exchange and, as a result, the need to deal with exchange rate risk. Some researchers even argue that foreign commodity exchanges may offer little opportunity for risk reduction, largely because of the size and unpredictability of the basis risk and exchange rate risk (see Vaillant *et al.* (1997), Bond and Thompson (1985,1987)). The availability of instruments to hedge exchange rate risks, however, is, in general, less of a problem than hedging commodity price risks. Exchange rate risks can also be eliminated completely by only allowing trade, even purely domestic trade, in foreign currency. Such a strategy is implemented in Kenya: since 1992 all coffee and tea trade is, by law, settled in US dollars (see Savosnick and Sood (1993)[16]). A final reason to choose for a foreign commodity exchange is the share of exports in domestic production: if commodities are mainly exported and the domestic market is small, the use of a foreign commodity exchange seems better defensible.

---

[16] This strategy, however, introduces another problem, namely limited access to foreign exchange. Savosnick and Sood (1993) regard the foreign exchange restriction the only effective (but nevertheless severe) restriction in the coffee and tea market in Kenya.

Although there is a substantial domestic market for (natural) rubber in India, an international commodity exchange is to be preferred over the establishment of a domestic commodity exchange for hedging the price risk of natural rubber for a number of reasons. It is doubtful whether a domestic commodity exchange will attract enough users to guarantee a acceptable level of liquidity. Current regulations in India (see Section 6.5) do not allow free access of insurance companies, pension funds and foreign investors to commodity exchanges. Also other institutional infrastructure is not particularly favourable for establishing domestic commodity exchanges. Even without such constraints, other Asian commodity exchanges (SICOM, Singapore) dealing in natural rubber futures have difficulties in generating sufficient liquidity.

A next issue to consider is which international exchange is most appropriate for hedging operations of Indian natural rubber producers and stockholders. This is an issue of liquidity: are size and scale of operations of the international futures exchange sufficient to  guarantee adequate functioning of the international futures exchange. We have chosen the Tokyo Commodity Exchange (TOCOM) as the international exchange where the commodity board buys or sells its futures contract: TOCOM is considered by participants to be sufficiently liquid and with a large enough turnover to absorb hedging activities of our Indian commodity board for natural rubber. This is confirmed by relating annual Indian production to annual turnover on TOCOM: this figure ranges from 1.0% (1994) to 4.4% (1992) with an average of 2.9%. The other two of the three international natural rubber markets that provide facilities for both futures as well as physical trading, namely the Singapore Commodity Exchange (SICOM) and the Kobe Rubber Exchange (KRE), are less liquid and have a smaller turnover.

## 6.5    Current futures trading practices in India

It is interesting to know the scope for hedging on commodity exchanges in India in view of the considerations discussed in the previous sections. A recent study by UNCTAD and the World Bank specifically focuses on the current futures trading practices in India (see UNCTAD/World Bank (1996)): India does have a regulatory framework that is suitable for futures trading: the Forward Contracts Regulation Act (1952, FCRA) controls all futures contracts; India also has a long tradition in the field of futures trading or more specifically India both has understanding of and experience with futures trading. There are good warehousing facilities and a banking and legal system that is capable of supporting futures trading. The physical infrastructure of commodity exchanges is adequate to support current needs. Although the regulatory framework is developed sufficiently, there is a rather severe restriction: futures trading and forward contracts is currently only allowed in a limited number of minor agricultural commodities (futures: raw jute and jute goods, black pepper, castorseed, gur, potatoes and turmeric; forward contracts: cotton lint, jute goods, raw jute and hessian). Futures trading and forward contracts in other commodities is prohibited, while options are prohibited for all commodities. Also limitations to contract specifications (transferability) make futures trading unattractive and together with regulations and controls on the operation of the commodity exchanges (contract approval process, price ceilings, margins and position limitations) cause most Indian futures markets to suffer from poor liquidity. Some regulations directly limit or restrict access to commodity exchanges. An example of this is the ban imposed by the Reserve Bank of India on the participation of pension funds or insurance companies. Additionally there are regulatory barriers to international users and agricultural cooperatives. Then the brokerage industry is perhaps well adapted to the current state of affairs in futures trading but poorly developed for a full-grown commodity exchange that is equipped to serve large-sized hedging needs in different markets and provide adequate informational services to its clients. Finally government intervenes in the physical market in a number of ways that prohibit a proper functioning of futures trading and in some cases completely eliminate the demand for risk management (storage and movement controls, selective credit controls by the Reserve Bank of India, external trade policies and government market interventions (eg. procurement in rice and wheat)).

The study makes a number of general recommendations for introduction of futures trading in commodity markets in India. These recommendations focus on the reduction of government interventions in physical markets in such a way that prices clear markets and trade is in the hands of the private sector. A major responsibility of the government should be the establishment of a stable and predictable environment. Also the restrictions on the functioning of futures exchanges should be abandoned (access of foreign users, profit repatriation, discretionary interventions), and the regulatory and institutional framework, although reasonably developed, should be improved. Finally attention should be given to the development of a proper infrastructure (brokerage industry, informational infrastructure). The Kabra report recommends the introduction of futures trading in basmati rice, seed cotton, cotton, raw jute and jute products, a number of oilseeds and their oils, major oilcakes, linseed, onions, gold and silver. UNCTAD/World Bank proposes some particular changes to improve the functioning of both current futures exchanges as well as exchanges that still have to be established/reopened.

In a follow-up study (UNCTAD (1995)) it is investigated if and how an international futures exchange for pepper should be established. Pepper prices are extremely unstable relative to other commodities: measured by the coefficient of variation, only sugar outstrips pepper in price volatility (UNCTAD (1995)). Pepper growers, domestic traders, exporters and importers and buyers are all exposed to price risks. Adequate facilities to hedge these risks would be most welcome. Estimates indicate that the aggregate level of pepper in the world-market is just sufficient to support one international futures exchange: with more international exchanges a lack of liquidity will prevail in all exchanges. Three possibilities are considered:

1. upgrading the currently existing Kochi futures exchange to an international one;
2. establishing independent futures exchanges in a number of countries;
3. establishing trading floors of a single futures exchange in a number of countries. Establishing independent futures exchanges in a number of countries is considered not viable, because of the most likely lack of liquidity. In view of a possible internationalization of the Kochi futures exchange, a number of problems related to the operation of the exchange and to government regulation are identified: no active promotion of services to potential customers; slow decision processes of committees of the exchange; no distribution of price information through Reuters or KnightRidder; access to exchange requires sales tax registration and is only available with some delay and under certain conditions; long trading hours for only a few contracts; primitive trading procedures (absence of time-stamping enabling brokers to abuse the exchange, there is no audit department to control floor practices) and clearing house arrangements are not up to (international) standard. The government intervenes in the physical market in a number of ways (e.g. by setting procurement prices, export). Also some regulations with respect to the operation of the Kochi futures exchange, that applies also to other Indian futures exchanges, are particularly unfavourable: foreign companies cannot become member; repatriation of earned income is impossible; pension funds, banks do not have access to commodity exchanges; hedging is not considered as a legitimate business activity. It is argued that the Kochi futures exchange is still some distance from becoming an international exchange: liquidity is shown to be too low for international traders/importers (most commodity markets trade more than 1,000 contracts a day, against 200 contracts of 2.5 MT currently in Cochin); foreign companies and domestic banks, pension funds and insurance companies should be allowed access to the foreign

exchange; standardization should be improved (ASTA is suggested as most appropriate candidate); concentration in trade is considered acceptable; there seems to be sufficient interest from domestic Indian speculators: they have a large share in turnover; service and infrastructure should be improved; warehousing should be established in importing countries; and, last but not least, there should be sufficient confidence in the role of the government (providing a stable environment, abstaining from intervention in the physical market and discretionary measures affecting the operation of the futures exchange).

Despite some attractive features of the current futures trading practices (experience with futures trading, regulatory framework) the infrastructure is not particularly favourable to establishment of domestic commodity markets and the use of financial risk management instruments in general. The most important constraints are no access to commodity exchanges of pension funds, insurance companies and foreign investors; poorly developed brokerage network; substantial government intervention in price formation in agricultural markets and a regulatory framework not fit for large scale hedging on commodity exchanges.

## 6.6    Summary and conclusion

In this chapter we have assessed the possibilities of risk reduction with financial risk management instruments in the Indian natural rubber market. A number of instruments are appropriate in hedging price risks. A long-term investment of a perennial crop like natural rubber will be most helped with a long-term hedging instrument, such as a swap. Long-term hedging is also realized by rolling over futures. Although no long-term instrument, options have the obvious advantage of protection against falling prices, and at the same time leave open the opportunity of profiting from price increases. In practice combinations of these instruments will provide an optimal hedging package. A major issue with respect to the use of these instruments is the liquidity of the markets in which these titles are traded: a hedging strategy should carefully take account of the liquidity of different commodity exchanges. Also basis risk - the issue if prices of a specific instrument sufficiently reflect local price developments - and exchange rate risk - if international commodity exchange are used - should be considered. A large number of studies show that hedging operations in commodity markets can be effective in reducing price risks. The limited use of financial risk management instruments is remarkable in view of this hedging potential and is explained by all the requirements that should be met to implement hedging strategies. The most important preconditions that need to be met, concern the establishment of an appropriate framework for international financial transactions, the establishment of a firm set of operating rules of the commodity exchange and the limited government involvement in price formation in commodity markets. India is shown not to be sufficiently equipped (yet) to meet these preconditions: in particular it is constrained because some firms are denied access to commodity exchanges, the brokerage network is not fit to modern hedging needs and the regulatory framework is inadequate. Intermediation, either through a government agency or through a private sector firm seem the most efficient way to implement hedging operations for individual farmers or traders. Potential liquidity and domestic infrastructure for commodity exchanges are the main determinants to choose for either establishing a domestic commodity exchange or to making use of a foreign one. In the case of natural rubber in India using a foreign one seems most appropriate.

## 7.1    Introduction

Financial risk management instruments are often suggested as an effective way to reduce price risk (see e.g. Claessens and Duncan (1993), UNCTAD (1994(a,b), 1995)). The purpose of this chapter is to quantify welfare gains of hedging price risks of domestic producers and local traders on an international futures exchange. A situation with and without such a hedging facility is compared with the help of a simulation exercise based on the Indian natural rubber market and the Tokyo Commodity Exchange. Under the proposed hedging scheme a commodity board in the domestic commodity market offers a forward contract to primary producers and stockholders against a fixed price. The board subsequently offsets its exposure by selling futures that correspond to its forward purchase commitments. At the time the primary producers and stockholders offer their production to the commodity board, the commodity board pays them the contracted price, closes out its futures positions and sells the physical commodity. Welfare effects of the risk averse players in the market, primary producers and stockholders, are estimated. Costs for the board of operating such a scheme are also calculated in order to quantify a break-even strategy and to assess its survival probability.

The impact of the introduction of futures markets in commodity markets has been studied extensively (e.g. McKinnon (1967), Danthine (1978), Newbery and Stiglitz (1981), Turnovsky (1983), Kawai (1983a), Turnovsky and Campbell (1985), Gilbert (1985,1989), and a number of more empirically oriented studies are Rolfo (1980), Claessens and Duncan (eds.,1993)). This literature was reviewed in Chapter 1. The main conclusion from the theory is that the introduction of futures markets increases welfare. However, little empirical work has been done in this area. We are not aware of empirical work in the literature in which welfare effects are quantified of providing forward contracts to producers and stockholders, based on empirically estimated risk aversion and cost parameters, and endogenous (futures) prices. The same applies to costs for a commodity board of operating such a scheme.

The chapter is organized as follows. In Section 7.2 we give details on the proposed hedging scheme and elaborate on the empirical underpinnings of the simulation. Section 7.3 addresses the derivation of the behaviour of the major agents. Section 7.4 relates the theoretical work to the data and in Section 7.5 the results of the simulation exercise are presented. The main findings are summarized in Section 7.6.

## 7.2    How to deal with domestic price risks

We assume that Indian natural rubber producers and stockholders can reduce their exposure to price risks by making use of a voluntary hedging scheme. A commodity board offers a forward contract to domestic primary producers and local traders. Prices of the forward contract offered to these groups are set by the board in the light of the prevailing futures prices at the international futures exchange, in our case the Tokyo Commodity Exchange (TOCOM). Producers and stockholders specify desired quantities to be sold forward. The board subsequently offsets its exposure by selling a quantity of futures on TOCOM that matches its forward purchase commitments. At delivery time the board pays producers and stockholders the contracted price, closes out its futures positions and sells the physical commodity in the market. Basis risk is borne by the commodity board.[1] The hedging scheme has no impact on the manufacturers of rubber products, the consumers in the market, as their welfare is unaffected and, hence, consumers will not be considered further. The empirical work in this chapter is based on quarterly data of the period 1990 to 1995.

If such a hedging scheme has to work effectively the natural rubber market in India must be sufficiently integrated within the world market so that price developments, but not necessarily price levels, are similar. A rough inspection of the data confirms this for the period from 1990 onwards (see Figure 7.1). Further, size and scale of operations in the international futures exchange should guarantee adequate functioning of the international futures exchange. We have chosen the Tokyo Commodity Exchange (TOCOM) as the international exchange where the commodity board buys or sells its futures contract primarily because of the adequate liquidity of this exchange (see Chapter 6 for more background information on this choice). Futures contracts traded on TOCOM have a contract period of six months, with one contract expiring each month. For most of our sample period (1990-1995) the six contracts that are traded at each moment in time are the contracts expiring in the current month and in each of the next five

---

1       Basis risk arises if the price development in the physical market is different from the price development on the futures market. With cash and futures prices moving parallel the basis risk is zero, and a hedge will be perfect: a loss on the paper transaction will be exactly offset by a profit on the physical transaction, or vice versa.

months. Hence, on the first of January 1995 there is trade in the January 1995, February 1995, March 1995, April 1995, May 1995 and June 1995 contracts, where the contracts are named after the date of expiration.

**Figure 7.1**    Domestic market price and world market price

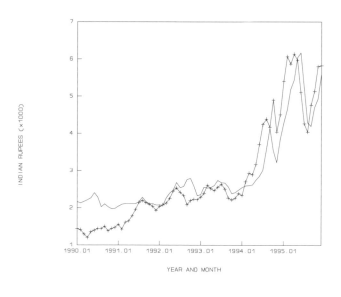

YEAR AND MONTH

---    RMA4    -+-    TOCOM (expiring contract)

Source: Indian Rubber Statistics, RBI; Tokyo Commodity Exchange.

Note: World market prices are monthly average quotations at the closing of the market of expiring contracts on TOCOM. Prices are in Indian Rupees. From the start of 1994 to March 1995 Indian prices lag two months behind world market prices, and from March 1995 onwards one month behind world market prices. We attribute this to the adjustment of the Indian economy to an increased international orientation.

Contracts expire seven days before the last day of the month. Quotations often fluctuate heavily during the last week before expiration due to reduced liquidity, with big traders playing around with each other trying to get either a favourable delivery or rolling over. The fluctuation of the price of a contract per day of trading (both upward and downward) is limited. These price limits are related to the standard price and are revised every now and then. The standard price is the average of closing prices for all contract months, except for the current month, on the previous day of business. Price limits do not apply to the current delivery month after the fifteenth. All market users have to deposit margin payments at the Tokyo Commodity Exchange. The margin per unit is also related to the standard price. Member or associate member margins are 50% of the general margin. Additional margin calls are required if prices change. Final payments are made at the time of closing the contract. It should be noted that margin payments are advance payments that eventually will be used to settle positions and should not be considered as costs: only the interest required to finance these payments generate costs. TOCOM provides contracts in only one grade (RSS3). Available information indicate that the bulk of Indian natural rubber consumption is RSS3. Import consists mainly of RSS3: from 1985 to 1992 between 70 and 85% of total natural rubber imports consisted of RSS3. However, somewhat outdated information indicates that Indian domestic production of ribbed smoked sheets consists mainly of RMA4 grade,[2] a grade that is of lower quality compared to the internationally used RSS3 grade. As long as the premium on RSS3 is sufficiently small (and as long as prices of these grades move parallel), this should not obstruct a hedging operation. Basis risk, however, will be slightly higher.

Figure 7.2 gives information on the development of futures prices of natural rubber on the Tokyo Commodity Exchange. The figure shows the difference in monthly average price of individual futures contract in the month that expiration is six months ahead and in the month of expiration, that is a difference in price of the same contract at two points in time. Positive values imply that the 'paper' part of a hedging transactions of producers is generating a loss while negative values imply the reverse. The figure also shows the difference in the average monthly price between a contract that will expire six months ahead and a contract that expires in the current month, that is a difference in price of two different contracts at one point in time. Positive values of this difference are known in futures market 'language' as a situation of contango, negative values as a situation of backwardation. From the figure it is observed that both situations

---

2      RMA is an Indian quality denomination that corresponds to the internationally used RSS4 denomination such that RMA1 equals RSS1, RMA2 equals RSS2 etc. Currently prices of natural rubber in the Indian domestic market are reported in terms of RSS quality denominations (see Indian Rubber Statistics (1996)).

alternate regularly,[3] implying, amongst other things, that no systematic basis risk loss or profit is evident.

**Figure 7.2**     Futures prices on the Tokyo Commodity Exchange

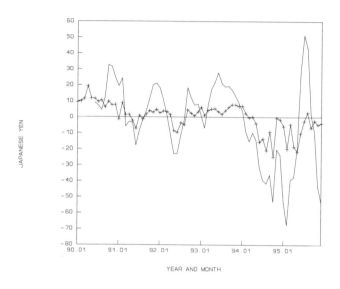

-----          price of futures contract (i) at time t-6 minus the price of futures contract (i) at time t

-+-           price of the six months ahead futures contract at time t minus the expiring contract at time t

Source: Tokyo Commodity Exchange.

Stockholders in the Indian natural rubber market tend to look two to three months ahead in their arbitrage behaviour (see Chapters 3, 4 and 5; Zant (1994a,b), (1996)). Hence, behaviour with respect to future variables is postulated to refer to three months ahead (expected) values of these variables. We assume additionally that growers have a comparable forward looking behaviour in their short term decisions of hiring tappers for tapping trees. In entering forward contracts these agents will, likewise, be interested in selling crop or stocks three months ahead. Therefore we assume that the board offers forward contracts for three months forward delivery. From the description above it is clear that the TOCOM allows hedging of such a contract. In order to keep the analysis technically feasible we

---

3       Because carrying commodities from one period to a future period entails costs, contango is seen as a normal situation, while backwardation is regarded as a temporary and abnormal situation on a futures exchange. Contango and backwardation have important implications in hedging long term commitments by rolling over contracts.

have transformed the data in this chapter to quarterly values and hence our sample stretches from the first quarter of 1990 (1990 I) to the last of 1995 (1995 IV). In case of futures prices we have used the average price of the 4, 5 and 6 months ahead futures contract (e.g. in the first quarter of 1990 the futures price for the second quarter is the average of the April90, May90 and June90 contract, as quoted in January, February and March).

We have chosen for intermediation by a commodity board because these boards may have easier access to foreign exchange, easier access to credit (as their credit status is supported eventually by the government) and easier access to international financial markets. Problems that account for limitations in credit markets like imperfect information, adverse selection and moral hazard, will most likely be smaller, as the board may have better opportunities to monitor potential users of the scheme. Due to reputation effects contract enforcement will also be easier with intermediation by a commodity board. Finally, it also seems most likely that such intermediation is an attractive outlet for commodity boards that might become redundant in a process of liberalization. Intermediation in hedging activities both nicely fits in the objectives of commodity boards to support marketing of the commodity and does not distort the functioning of the market. Nevertheless, the proposed hedging scheme might also be implemented by private sector intermediaries. Current circumstances in India, however, are not particularly favourable to private sector intermediation: the limited access of the private sector to international financial markets and to foreign exchange, as well as the sloppy infrastructure for hedging operations (see UNCTAD / World Bank (1996)) do not make this a viable option. We have chosen for hedging through futures because hedging with futures allows an elimination of price risk, futures markets are liquid and costs of futures trading are of acceptable proportions. It should be noted that such a hedging scheme does not obviate fluctuations of prices that reflect supply and demand conditions in the market. Considerations underlying these choices are further elaborated in Chapter 6.

If domestic market prices rise above the forward contract price at the time of delivery, producers and stockholders have an incentive not to perform the forward contract. Obviously the board needs to avoid such a default as it is a potential source of financial loss. We assume that the board has enough power to enforce implementation of contracts. In practise one can think of imposing a penalty on defaulting. For example, default can be punished by exclusion from forward contracts in the future. Individual forward contracts with the commodity board are not traded on an exchange. However, the board will be quoting prices continuously and clients will be able to buy back their own contracts at any moment they wish, at a price that equals the loss on the hedging operation. Non-tradability should be interpreted as a reflection of the absence of a futures exchange in the domestic market and not as a requirement for the analysis.

In addition to the assumptions on contract enforcement and non-tradability, we assume limits to the quantity sold forward. Individual producers are not allowed to hedge more than their production, and stockholders are not allowed to hedge more than their base period stocks. Such an assumption is in line with practises among private banks that finance hedging operations. These private banks usually request that the hedge is limited to a deliverable quantity: (future) production or stocks is used as collateral (see Ghosh *et al.* (1987), p.158; Gilbert (1989), p.158). There is also a policy ground not to allow more forward contracting than realised future supply. The board provides a facility to producers and stockholders to overcome price uncertainty. Hedging a larger quantity forward than physically available at the time of delivery is beyond the objective of the board. In order to implement this the board will stop buying forward contracts if the level of expected aggregate supply is realised. How is the board able to guarantee consistency between its expectation of aggregate supply and the sum of individual contracts? An individual producer will be uncertain about the exact level of his future production and the board will face even larger problems to estimate future production of an individual producer. Likewise, the board will also be unable to verify the level of base period stocks. Hence, implementation of this restriction will be difficult in the case of an individual producer or stockholder. Individual producers and stockholders will be urged not to sell forward more than their expected production, otherwise they might penalise their fellow producer or stockholder. The answer is moral persuasion and penalties. Individual producers and stockholders that do not behave according to this rule face a penalty of being excluded of forward contracting in the future. To summarize, individual producers or stockholders, consequently, cannot buy forward or take a long position. This is ruled out partly by regulation, partly by moral persuasion and partly by penalties.

## 7.3    Behavioral relationships

In this section we formalize the behaviour of major players in the market with respect to risk. We use the theoretical framework developed by Newbery and Stiglitz (1981), Turnovsky (1983), Kawai (1983a). We consider a domestic commodity market in a price-taking open economy. Three groups of players in the market are distinguished, namely producers (g, from 'growers'), stockholders (s), and the commodity board (b). Within our framework there is no need to discuss consumers, i.e. manufacturers of rubber products, as our hedging scheme has no effect on consumers prices and their welfare is unaffected. In the empirical work we do consider stockholding by manufacturers as manufacturers will arbitrage like all other stockholders. Producers earn an income by producing and selling a commodity. Stockholders store commodities and earn an income by exploiting differences in prices of the commodity over time. Stock demand is also assumed to be motivated by other considerations. The behaviour of these players is considered with and without a futures market in a two period model. In the first period producers decide on the size of planned crop. Both producers and stockholders can enter into forward contracts with the commodity board. Quantities per contract are determined by the producers and stockholders and prices are determined by the board. Simultaneously the commodity board sells futures on the international futures exchange. The second period is the harvesting period: farmers deliver their contracted quantities to the commodity board against the agreed price. Default is ruled out by assumption. Remaining production is sold in the market against the market price. Stockholders also deliver their contracted quantities to the board and sell the remaining part on the market. The commodity board settles its futures contracts on the international futures exchange and sells quantities of the commodity delivered by domestic producers and stockholders in the domestic market.[4] In the following sections we consider the behaviour of each of the players in the market in turn.

### 7.3.1  Producers

Price taking risk averse producers maximize expected utility of profit

$$\sum_{t=1}^{T} E_{t-1} \left( U_g(\pi_{g,t}) \right) \cdot \delta^t \tag{1}$$

where

$E_{t-1}()$ is the expectation conditional on the information at time t-1;

$U_i$ a strictly concave utility function of agent i; i = g (growers), s (stockholders);

$\pi_{i,t}$     = profit of agent i at time t;

$\delta$      = discounting factor,

---

4       The presumed sales of the commodity on the domestic market in this scheme, primarily reflect the situation on the Indian natural rubber market: selling on the domestic market is not a necessary requirement of such a scheme.

subject to a quadratic cost function. We assume that utility functions have the property of Constant Absolute Risk Aversion (CARA):

$$U_g(\pi_{g,t}) = -\exp(-A_g.\pi_{g,t}) \tag{2}$$

where A = coefficient of absolute risk aversion

We have chosen this function because it is useful for solving maximization problems, resulting in linear equations that can easily be aggregated. However, it has the implausible property that with normally distributed profits the absolute risk premium is independent of wealth. For our purpose this should not be a problem as wealth can be shown not to be important in the short run (Binswanger (1978)). Nevertheless, we are aware that the outcome of our simulation might be affected by the specification of the utility function (see e.g. Rolfo (1980)). If profits of producers $(\pi_{g,t})$ are distributed normally, maximization of the expected utility of profit is equivalent to maximization of

$$\sum_{t=1}^{T} [E_{t-1}(\pi_{g,t}) - \tfrac{1}{2} A_g.VAR_{t-1}(\pi_{g,t})] . \delta^t \tag{3}$$

where $VAR_{t-1}(.)$ is the variance conditional on information at time t-1

Profit of producers in a situation without forward contracts is characterized as

$$\pi_{g,t} = q_t.p_t - \rho.Z_g(q_t) \tag{4}$$

where

| | |
|---|---|
| $q_t$ | = production at time t; |
| $p_t$ | = real (spot) price at time t; |
| $\rho$ | = 1+interest rate; |
| $Z_i(.)$ | = cost function of agent i |

Maximization of expected utility of risky profit is calculated assuming certain production. In the case of a perennial crop like natural rubber such an assumption is fairly reasonable: natural rubber is harvested all year round, causing many shocks to be evened out during the year; natural rubber is not a 'fruit crop': fruit crops are to a much larger extent vulnerable to (the timing of) adverse weather conditions and, finally, the incidence of diseases, frost and storm damage is relatively low in the case of natural rubber. The certainty of natural rubber production is extensively treated in Chapter 2. Production costs are assumed to have a quadratic specification:

$$Z_g(q_t) = \tfrac{1}{2} z_g \cdot q_t^2 \tag{5}$$
where $z_g > 0$;

Moments of equation (4) are written as:

$$E_{t-1}(\pi_{g,t}) = q_t \cdot E_{t-1}(p_t) - \tfrac{1}{2}\rho z_g \cdot q_t^2 \tag{6}$$
$$VAR_{t-1}(\pi_{g,t}) = q_t^2 \cdot VAR(p_t) \tag{7}$$

For an optimum we require

$$\partial E_{t-1}(U_g)/\partial q_t = 0 \tag{8}$$

From equations (3) and (5) to (8) we derive optimal production as:

$$q_t = \frac{E_{t-1}(p_t)}{\rho.z_g + A_g \cdot VAR_{t-1}(p_t)} \tag{9}$$

Equation (9) is a familiar result saying that production is positively related to expected spot price ($E_{t-1}(p_t)$) and inversely to the discount factor ($\rho$), the cost parameter ($z_g$), the coefficient of absolute risk aversion ($A_g$) and the variance of spot price ($VAR_{t-1}(p_t)$). With risk neutrality ($A_g = 0$) production is only determined by expected price ($E_{t-1}(p_t)$) and not by its variance.[5]

In a situation with forward contracts, profit of producers is characterized as:

$$\pi_{g,t} = q_t \cdot p_t - \rho.Z_g(q_t) + fw_{g,t-1} \cdot (p_{fw,t-1} - p_t) \tag{10}$$
where

$fw_{t-1}$ = forward sales (quantity) at time t-1;

$p_{fw,t-1}$ = real forward price at time t-1 offered by the board to domestic producers and local traders (in domestic currency)

Moments of equation (10) are written as:

---

5       The comparison with optimal production with risk neuatral producers (see also Chapter 3) is straightforward. Optimal production is in that case:
$$q_t = 1/(\rho.z_p) \cdot E_{t-1}(p_t) - \varepsilon_{p,t-1}$$
Compared to equation (9) this equation suggests that risk averse producers will produce less than their risk neutral colleagues under equal conditions.

$$E_{t-1}(\pi_{g,t}) = q_t . E_{t-1}(p_t) - \rho . Z_g(q_t) + fw_{g,t-1} . (p_{fw,t-1} - E(p_t)) \qquad (11)$$
$$VAR_{t-1}(\pi_{g,t}) = (q_t - fw_{g,t-1})^2 . VAR(p_t) \qquad (12)$$

For an optimum we require:

$$\partial E_{t-1}(U_g)/\partial q_t = \partial E_{t-1}(U_g)/\partial fw_{g,t-1} = 0 \qquad (13)$$

From equations (3), (5) and (11) to (13) we derive optimal production and optimal forward sales as:

$$q_t = \frac{p_{fw,t-1}}{\rho . z_g} \quad \text{and} \qquad (14)$$

$$fw_{g,t-1} = q_t + \frac{p_{fw,t-1} - E_{t-1}(p_t)}{A_g . VAR_{t-1}(p_t)} \qquad (15)$$

and, due to the non-tradability of forward contracts and limits to forward sales[6] we have:

$$0 \leq fw_{g,t-1} \leq q_t \qquad (16)$$

From equation (14) it is seen that optimum production is equal to the forward price at time t-1 ($p_{fw,t-1}$) divided by the discounted cost parameter ($\rho . z_g$), while the optimum quantity of forward contracts is equal to production plus the difference of the forward price at time t-1 and the expected spot price at time t ($p_{fw,t-1} - E_{t-1}(p_t)$), divided by the coefficient of absolute risk aversion ($A_g$) and the variance of price at time t ($VAR_{t-1}(p_t)$). Optimum production is independent of the attitude towards risk and the distribution of spot prices, which contrasts with the optimum quantity of forward contracts. Note that production is the same with and without forward contracts if expected prices equal forward prices and producers are near risk neutral or the variance of prices is zero (see equation (14) and (9)). Equation (15) indicates that producers sell their entire future crop

---

6       Modelling private sector intermediation is, however, not without problems. Relaxing restrictions on forward contracting allows tradability of contracts and also uncovered forward contracting. Trade in contracts cannot take place due to the representative agent approach, unless we specify an additional agent. Unlimited forward contracting, on the other hand, affects the price formation on the international futures exchange which is assumed not to be affected by our scheme. The current welfare analysis will not be affected by private sector intermediation.

forward, unless the expectation of higher prices in the future compensates them enough for the increased uncertainty of future prices. Smaller values of the variance of prices $(VAR_{t-1}(p_t) \to 0)$ or the coefficient of absolute risk aversion $(A_g \to 0)$, will force the optimal quantities on the bounds (see equation (16)).

### 7.3.2  Stockholders

For stockholders we make similar assumptions as in the case of producers. Stockholders are also assumed to be risk averse price-takers, to maximize expected utility of profit, to have utility functions of the CARA type and quadratic costs. Likewise, if $\pi_{s,t}$ is distributed normally, maximization of the expected utility of profit

$$\sum_{t=1}^{T} E_{t-1} (U_s(\pi_{s,t})) \cdot \delta^t \tag{17}$$

is equivalent to maximization of

$$\sum_{t=1}^{T} [E_{t-1}(\pi_{s,t}) - \tfrac{1}{2} A_s . VAR_{t-1}(\pi_{s,t})] \cdot \delta^t \tag{18}$$

Profit of stockholders in a situation without forward contracts is characterized as:

$$\pi_{s,t} = s_{t-1} . (p_t - \rho.p_{t-1}) - Z_s(s_{t-1}) \tag{19}$$

where $s_{t-1}$ = purchases of stockholders at time t-1.

Costs of stockholding take the following quadratic form:

$$Z_s(s_{t-1}) = \tfrac{1}{2} z_s(s_{t-1} - \bar{s})^2 \tag{20}$$

where $z_s > 0$;   $\bar{s}$ = a target stockholding level

Costs of stockholding are postulated to be determined by the difference between direct carrying costs (warehouse costs, insurance fees, physical losses) and the benefits from having a larger stock reducing the probability of stock-out and loss of consumers, and reducing risk by exploiting the variation of prices over time (see Newbery and Stiglitz (1981), p.196). These latter two motivations are summarized in target stockholding (see e.g. Ghosh *et al.* (1987)). A more extensive account of the backgrounds of target stockholding is given in Chapter 3. Moments of equation (19) are written as:

$$E_{t-1}(\pi_{s,t}) = s_{t-1} . (E_{t-1}(p_t) - \rho.p_{t-1}) - Z_s(s_{t-1}) \tag{21}$$

$$VAR_{t-1}(\pi_{s,t}) = s_{t-1}^2 . VAR_{t-1}(p_t) \tag{22}$$

For an optimum we require

$$\partial E_{t-1}(U_s)/\partial s_{t-1} = 0 \tag{23}$$

From equations (18) and (20) to (22) we derive the following optimal stock demand for the situation without forward contracts:

$$s_{t-1} = \frac{E_{t-1}(p_t) - \rho p_{t-1} + z_s.\bar{s}}{z_s + A_s.VAR_{t-1}(p_t)} \tag{24}$$

Equation (24) is, again, a familiar result indicating that stockholding is positively related to the difference of expected spot price ($E_{t-1}(p_t)$) and discounted spot price in the base period ($\rho p_{t-1}$) and the target stockholding level ($\bar{s}$), and inversely to the cost parameter ($z_s$), the coefficient of absolute risk aversion ($A_s$) and the variance of spot price ($VAR_{t-1}(p_t)$). With identical arbitrage opportunities ($E_{t-1}(p_t) - \rho p_{t-1}$), a higher volatility of prices ($VAR_{t-1}(p_t)$) will create less stock demand. With risk neutral stockholders ($A_s=0$) or an infinitely small variance of price ($VAR_{t-1}(p_t) \rightarrow 0$), and expected price equal the discounted base period price ($E_{t-1}(p_t)=\rho p_{t-1}$) stockholding equals target-stockholding ($s_{t-1}=\bar{s}$). Both in a situation with and without forward contracts we impose non-negativity of stocks ($s_t \geq 0$ for all t). Note, however, that in the actual calculation this never has become effective due to sufficient target stockholding.[7]

In a situation with forward contracts profit of stockholders is formalized as:

$$\pi_{s,t} = s_{t-1}.(p_t - \rho.p_{t-1}) - Z_s(s_{t-1}) + fw_{s,t-1}.(p_{fw,t-1} - p_t) \tag{25}$$

Moments of equation (25) are written as:

$$E_{t-1}(\pi_{s,t}) = s_{t-1}.(E_{t-1}(p_t) - \rho.p_{t-1}) - Z_s(s_{t-1}) + fw_{s,t-1}.(p_{fw,t-1} - E_{t-1}(p_t)) \tag{26}$$

$$VAR_{t-1}(\pi_{s,t}) = (s_{t-1} - fw_{s,t-1})^2.VAR_{t-1}(p_t) \tag{27}$$

---

7    In Chapter 3 the behaviour of risk neutral stockholders is formalized. From this derivation we obtained the following expression for stockholding (see Chapter 3):

$s_{t-1} = 1/z_s.(E_{t-1}(p_t) - \rho p_{t-1}) + \bar{s}_{t-1} + \varepsilon_{s,t-1}$

Comparing this equation with equation (24) makes clear that risk averse stockholders will have a lower stock demand with equal arbitrage opportunities (ceteris paribus) compared to risk neutral stockholders.

For an optimum we require, again:

$$\partial E_{t-1}(U_g)/\partial s_{t-1} = \partial E_{t-1}(U_g)/\partial fw_{s,t-1} = 0 \tag{28}$$

From equations (18), (20) and (26) to (28) we derive optimal stockholding and optimal forward sales as:

$$s_{t-1} = \bar{s} + \frac{p_{fw,t-1} - \rho \cdot p_{t-1}}{z_s} \tag{29}$$

and the optimal quantity of forward contracts as

$$fw_{s,t-1} = s_{t-1} + \frac{p_{fw,t-1} - E_{t-1}(p_t)}{A_s \cdot VAR_{t-1}(p_t)} \tag{30}$$

and, due to the non-tradability of forward contracts and limits to forward sales[8]:

$$0 \le fw_{s,t-1} \le s_{t-1} \tag{31}$$

From equation (29) and (30) it follows that optimal purchases of stocks are positively determined by target stockholding ($\bar{s}$) and the difference between the forward price and the (discounted) price at time t-1 ($p_{fw,t-1} - \rho \cdot p_{t-1}$), and inversely with the cost parameter. The optimal quantity of forward contracts is positively determined by the optimal purchases of stocks and the difference of the forward price and the expected spot price ($p_{fw,t-1} - E_{t-1}(p_t)$), and inversely by the coefficient of absolute risk aversion ($A_g$) and the variance of price at time t ($VAR_{t-1}(p_t)$). Hence, physical stock demand differs from the quantity of forward contracts depending on expectations. As in the case of producers, only the optimal quantity of forward contracts (and not purchases of stocks) is influenced by the probability distribution of spot prices and the coefficient of absolute risk aversion.

### 7.3.3  The commodity board

In a situation with forward contracts the commodity board covers the quantity of forward contracts with domestic producers and local stockholders on the international futures exchange by selling futures. The board purely functions as an intermediary to the international futures exchange and has no other activities. The exact matching of the forward commitments of the commodity board depends on

---

8        Private sector intermediation requires the relaxing of this assumption. See the section on producers for details.

size and timing of the futures contract on the international futures exchange. In the model, however, we will assume that the commitment of the board is covered perfectly, or:

$$ft_t = fw_{g,t} + fw_{s,t} \tag{32}$$

where $ft_t$ = futures sales (quantity) at time t.

Forward prices are determined by the international futures exchange. Futures prices in our empirical application are denominated in Japanese yen. Prices of forward contracts offered by the board to domestic producers and local traders are, hence:

$$P_{fw,t} = (1+\tau_t).rer_{RY,t+1}.P_{ft,t} \tag{33}$$

where

$rer_{RY,t} = er_{RY,t} / cpi_t$

$rer_{RY,t}$ = real Indian rupee / Japanese yen exchange rate at time t;

$er_{RY,t}$ = Indian rupee / Japanese yen exchange rate at time t;

$cpi_t$ = consumer price index for India at time t;

$\tau_t$ = surcharge at time t;

$P_{ft,t}$ = futures price (for period t+1) at time t;

Upper case and lower case letters for prices refer to nominal and real prices.

Equation (33) defines the forward price offered to domestic producers and local traders, as the product of futures price in Japanese yen, the rupee / yen exchange rate and a surcharge imposed by the board. It should be noted that equation (33) does not imply that one has to pay a surcharge for trading on the international futures exchange. However, it does offer the board a possibility to impose a surcharge on the forward price offered to growers and stockholders in order to increase the durability of the scheme or to maximize long run welfare (or to do both). Futures prices on the international futures exchange are assumed not to be affected by the transactions of our commodity board. We assume perfect foresight with respect to future exchange rates in real terms. As far as exchange rate risks are concerned, this assumption is justified by the possibilities to hedge exchange rate risks effectively: dollar-yen risks could be managed easily by the board and there is an over-the-counter forward market for the rupee-dollar exchange rate, which the board could be authorized to use.[9] In practice such a hedging of

---

9      See Kofman (1991) for a discussion of exchange rate risks in commodity trade.

exchange rate risks may increase the basis risk of the complete hedging operation slightly. However, possible difficulties caused by real exchange rate fluctuations are assumed absent in our exercise which allows to focus on the impact of the use of forward contracts.

The commodity board has taken over the basis risk, and, hence, it is of interest if the commodity board breaks even and what is the size of losses and profits. The basis risk of the hedging operation, i.e. the income of the board in our exercise, is defined as:

$$y_{b,t} = ft_{t-1} \cdot [(rer_{RY,t} \cdot P_{ft,t-1} - rer_{RY,t} \cdot P_{ftexp,t}) - (p_{fw,t-1} - p_t)] \qquad (34)$$

where

$y_{b,t}$    = income of the board at time t in constant prices;

$P_{ftexp,t}$ = futures price at delivery at time t

The first part of equation (34), $ft_{t-1} \cdot [(er_{RY,t} \cdot P_{ft,t-1} - er_{RY,t} \cdot P_{ftexp,t})$, represents the paper transaction on the international futures exchange. The second part, $ft_{t-1} \cdot [(p_{fw,t-1} - p_t)]$, represents the physical transaction on the domestic market. Together these terms constitute the basis risk of the operation.

Basis risk will be zero with forward prices determined by futures prices (and if $\tau_t = 0$ for all t, see equation (33)), and if domestic spot prices are equal to world market spot prices converted at the relevant exchange rate (note that futures prices at the time of expiration of contracts are equal to world market spot prices). Together with the endogenization of world market prices (both spot and futures) this implies that both income and expected income of the board in the model degenerates to zero in all periods. Fortunately actually observed domestic prices and futures prices of expiring contracts differ from the model prediction, leaving some scope for further analysis. Finally we note that without forward contracts income of the board ($y_b$) is zero and the board has no economic existence. It should be noted that interest costs due to margin payments, omitted in the current study, could easily be incorporated in the above formalisation.


## 7.4    Empirical implementation

### 7.4.1  Expectation and variance of prices

In this section we establish the relationship that describes expectation and variance of prices, which are determinants of the behaviour of producers and stockholders. Shocks are assumed to originate from the world market, and the stochastic process describing these shocks is a subsidiary outcome of this work. We consider a domestic market in a small open economy: in contrast with the situation in Chapters 3, 4 and 5, domestic supply and demand conditions do not matter in the determination of domestic prices. These domestic prices are assumed to be completely determined on the world market. This, consequently, also applies to expectation and variance of domestic prices.

Time series properties of world market prices in our model ($P_w$), the world market price of natural rubber in Japanese yen, and futures prices ($P_{ft}$) are investigated with the help of Dickey Fuller tests. With respect to world market prices, the outcome provides a basis for estimating a price equation that characterizes expectation and variance of price. Test statistics are presented in Table 7.1. From the table we conclude that the world market price and futures price are integrated of the order 1 (or I(1)), although the statistics are not convincing in all test equations.

**Table 7.1**  Testing the order of integration of world market price ($P_w$) and futures price ($P_{ft}$) (sample period: 90I-95IV)

|  |  | ADF,nct,nt | | ADF,ct | | ADF,ct,t | |
|---|---|---|---|---|---|---|---|
| lags |  | 1 | 4 | 1 | 4 | 1 | 4 |
| variable | hypothesis |  |  |  |  |  |  |
| $P_w$ | (1) | 0.31 | 0.54 | -1.13 | -1.63 | -1.56 | -1.38 |
|  | (2) | -3.80 | -2.11 | -3.79 | -2.15 | -4.11 | -2.61 |
| $P_{ft}$ | (1) | 0.24 | 0.39 | -1.20 | -1.79 | -1.30 | -1.18 |
|  | (2) | -4.02 | -1.95 | -3.94 | -1.92 | -4.56 | -2.50 |
| Mc Kinnon critical values (5%) |  | -1.96 | -1.96 | -3.00 | -3.02 | -3.62 | -3.66 |

(1) $H_0$: I(1) against $H_A$: I(0), in levels; (2) $H_0$: I(2) against $H_A$: I(1), in first differences;
where: ADF,(n)ct,(n)t = Augmented Dickey Fuller statistic, test equation with(out) a constant term (ct) and with(out) a trend variable (t).

A simple error correction specification of prices in first differences follows as an appropriate characterization of the price formation process, in particular:

$$(P_{w,t} - P_{w,t-1}) = n_0 + n_1 \cdot P_{w,t-1} + \varepsilon_{Pw,t} \tag{35}$$

where $P_{w,t}$ = world market price in Japanese yen

or, equivalently:

$$P_{w,t} = n_0 + (1+n_1).P_{w,t-1} + \varepsilon_{Pw,t} \tag{36}$$

Equation (35) is estimated and generates the following estimation result:

$$P_{w,t} = 0.023216 + 0.813645\ P_{w,t-1} \tag{37}$$
$$\phantom{P_{w,t} = }(1.3) \qquad\quad (5.2)$$

absolute t-values are presented in brackets below the coefficients

sample period:          1990I-1995IV

| | | | |
|---|---|---|---|
| sum of squared residuals | = 0.599177 e-2 | Durbin's h | = 0.301 |
| variance of residuals | = 0.272353 e-3 | F-statistic | = 27.0872 |
| adjusted R-squared | = 0.531 | log(L) | = 65.4905 |

The error term ($\varepsilon_{Pw,t}$) can be shown to be normally distributed. It should be noted that this outcome is an unexpected but fairly comfortable result, most likely due to the small sample period. Unexpected, because both theoretically and empirically it has been shown that prices in commodity market tend to depart from normality (see e.g. Deaton and Laroque (1992), Hughes Hallett and Ramanujam (1990)). Comfortable, because it would complicate the derivation of behavioral equations if prices are not normally distributed. The stochastic process of the model is partly caused by this equation.

Expectation and variance of prices, in Japanese yen, are implied by the estimated price equation, equation (37):

$$E_{t-1}(P_{w,t}) \quad = \quad 0.023216 + 0.813645\ P_{w,t-1} \tag{38}$$
$$VAR_{t-1}(P_{w,t}) \quad = \quad 0.272353\ e\text{-}3 \tag{39}$$

The above tests are applied to world market prices in Japanese yen. Price variables in the model, however, are in domestic prices (Indian rupees). To make the step from world market prices towards domestic price we have assumed perfect foresight with respect to real exchange rates and, hence, $E_{t-1}(rer_t) = rer_t$ and $VAR_{t-1}(rer_t) = 0$. This yields the following equation for expectation and variance of (domestic) price:[10]

$$E_{t-1}(p_t) \quad = \quad rer_t.E_{t-1}(P_{w,t})\ \text{and} \tag{40}$$
$$VAR_{t-1}(p_t) \quad = \quad rer_t^2.VAR_{t-1}(P_{w,t}) \tag{41}$$

---

10     Upper case and lower case letters for prices refer to nominal and real prices.

Prices of futures contracts need to be expressed in terms of expected prices, especially for the case of a dynamic simulation, or, formally: $P_{ft,t} = f(E_t(P_{w,t+1}))$. After substitution of expected world market price (the expected value of equation (36)) we get:

$$P_{ft,t} = f(n_0 + (1+n_1).P_{w,t}) \tag{42}$$

A linear specification of the function that describes the relationship between futures price and world market price is suggested. Both series are shown to be I(1), as is clear from Table 7.1, and, hence, a simple error correction formulation is specified:

$$\Delta P_{ft,t} = m_0 + m_1.\Delta P_{w,t} + m_2.P_{ft,t-1} + m_3.P_{w,t-1} + \varepsilon_{Pft,t} \tag{43}$$

The following estimation result is obtained:

$$\Delta P_{ft,t} = 0.00360 + 0.885904\ \Delta P_{w,t} - 0.410659\ P_{ft,t-1} + 0.379140\ P_{w,t-1} \tag{44}$$
$$(0.7) \qquad (18.8) \quad (2.6) \qquad\qquad (2.6)$$

absolute t-values are presented in brackets below the coefficients;

sample period:       1990I-1995IV

| | | | |
|---|---|---|---|
| sum of squared residuals | = 0.244805 e-3 | | |
| variance of residuals | = 0.122403 e-4 | F-statistic | = 131.270 |
| adjusted R-squared | = 0.944 | log(L) | = 103.863 |

The stochastic process in the model also originates partly from this price equation. This completes the determination of expectation and variance of prices as well as determination of the properties of the stochastic process underlying price formation on the world market.

## 7.4.2 Fitting behavioral equations to observations

We continue with searching for appropriate parameters of the model based on realisations for the period 1990.1 1995.4. None of the agents in the Indian natural rubber market that we distinguish in this study have been active on futures exchanges during the period under consideration. Hence, we confront the data with the 'no policy' model (equations (1) to (9) for growers and (17) to (24) for stockholders). In the Indian natural rubber market stockholding is done by manufacturers of rubber products, producers and traders. The available data distinguish two stockholding agents: stockholding of producers and traders (so-called growers and dealers) denoted with the acronym gd and stockholding by manufacturers, denoted with mf. Hence, we have four series of variables that need to be explained, namely production, stockholding by growers and dealers, stockholding by manufacturers and consumption. As mentioned before, consumption is left out of consideration as their welfare is assumed not to be affected by the hedging scheme.

In order to find the parameters of the model, behavioral equations have been estimated empirically. Both stockholders and producers are assumed to be subject to seasonal fluctuations, on top of the derived behaviour with respect to risk. This is allowed for by imposing a multiplicative seasonal pattern on all these variables. The real interest rate on a quarterly basis is fixed to 1.5%, which corresponds roughly with observed values of the real interest rate from 1990 to 1995.[11] Values of coefficients of the quadratic cost function, coefficients of absolute risk aversion and coefficients of target stockholding are selected on the basis of estimating equations with non-linear least squares (NLS). Details on the strategy to run these estimations are presented below, agent by agent. Essential feature of this strategy is the need to use proper starting values for the NLS estimations.

In case of production we first look for plausible values of the cost parameter and of the parameter of absolute risk aversion. Plausible values of the cost parameter are found by relating costs - according to our quadratic cost function - to the value of production or turnover ($z_g.q_t^2 / p_t.q_t$), and by calculating the average of this parameter over the whole sample period. The starting value of our cost parameter is chosen in such a way that the this share is 50% ($z_g$ is around 0.00015). For the coefficient of absolute risk aversion we calculate the inverse of average income, assuming, for the moment, relative risk aversion to be equal to unity. Note that eventual values of relative risk aversion and cost parameter could very well be different, which in fact they are. With these selected values of the cost parameter and for the parameter of absolute risk aversion we calculate

$$q_t^* = q_t / (E_{t-1}(p_t)/(\hat{z}_g+\hat{A}_g.VAR_{t-1}(p_t))) \tag{45}$$

and run the regression:

---

[11]     The real interest rate is calculated as the market rate of interest (commercial lending rate, ICLR) deflated by the consumer price index (consumer prices, CPIIFS) as given in International Financial Statistics, International Monetary Fund.

$$q_t^* = a_0 + a_1.sd1 + a_2.sd2 + a_3.sd3 \tag{46}$$

where sd1 to sd3 are quarterly dummies

The estimated values of $a_0$ to $a_3$ and the selected values of $z_g$ and $A_g$ are used as starting values in the NLS estimation of the equation (cf. equation (9)):

$$q_t = [\alpha_0 + \alpha_1.sd1 + \alpha_2.sd2 + \alpha_3.sd3] \, . \, [E_{t-1}p_t/(\alpha_4 + \alpha_5.VAR_{t-1}p_t)] \tag{47}$$

As estimation with these starting values does not lead to convergence, the coefficient $\alpha_0$ is given a fixed value ($a_0$, obtained from the auxiliary estimation) and the loglikelihood of the equation is maximized using a grid of values around this coefficient. In the case of production a dummy for the observation 93IV has been imposed to control for an outlier.[12] The following equation is selected:

$$q_t = [1.756 \ -0.593 \ sd1 \ -0.533 \ sd2 \ -0.442 \ sd3].$$
$$\quad (-) \qquad (7.4) \qquad (5.9) \qquad (5.0)$$
$$\qquad\qquad\qquad [E_{t-1}(p_t)/(0.213e\text{-}3 + 5.194e\text{-}6 \ VAR_{t-1}(p_t))]$$
$$\qquad\qquad\qquad\qquad (10.6) \qquad (2.1)$$

sample period: 90I-95I;        Log(L): -222.089                                                   (48)

absolute t-values are presented in brackets below the coefficients

In case of stockholding by growers and dealers we postulate that the target stockholding level is specified as a linear function of production ($\bar{s}_{gd,t} = \phi_{gd}.q_t$ with $\phi_{gd}>0$) and calculate a value for $\phi_{gd}=0.40$, which parameter has been kept fixed throughout the estimations. Next, and along the same lines as in the case of production, we look for plausible values of the cost parameter and for the parameter of absolute risk aversion. Plausible values of the cost parameter are found by relating costs to the value of stocks at the start of the period ($z_{sgd}.(s_{gd,t} - \phi_{gd}.q_t)^2/(p_t.s_{gd,t-1})$) and by calculating the average of this parameter over the whole sample period. Operational costs of stockholding as a percentage of the value of stocks at the start should be less than 5%, implying a cost parameter in case of stockholding by growers and dealers ($z_{sgd}$) close to 0.001 or lower. Also, like in the case of production, we calculate a starting value of the coefficient of

---

12      Dummies in this equation, but also in the other two behavioral equations, are added purely to improve the significance of the key parameters, the risk aversion parameter and the cost parameter. Both in the graphical presentation of the fit of the equation (Figure 3 to 5) and the simulations these dummies are omitted.

absolute risk aversion by taking the inverse of average income, assuming a unit relative risk aversion for the moment. With these selected values of the cost parameter and for the parameter of absolute risk aversion we calculate

$$s_{gd,t}^* = s_{gd,t} / [(E_t p_{t+1} - 1.015 \cdot p_t - \hat{z}_{gd} \cdot \hat{\phi}_{gd} \cdot \hat{q}_t)/(\hat{z}_{gd} + \hat{A}_{gd} \cdot VAR_t p_{t+1})] \qquad (49)$$

and run the regression

$$s_{gd,t}^* = b_0 + b_1.sd1 + b_2.sd2 + b_3.sd3 \qquad (50)$$

The estimated values of $b_0$ to $b_3$ and the selected values of $z_{gd}$ and $A_{gd}$ are used as starting values, while $\phi_{gd}$ has a fixed value, in the NLS estimation of the equation:

$$s_{gd,t} = [\beta_0 + \beta_1.sd1 + \beta_2.sd2 + \beta_3.sd3].[(E_t p_{t+1} - 1.015 \cdot p_t - 0.4.\beta_4.q_t)/(\beta_4 + \beta_5.VAR_t p_{t+1})]$$
$$(51)$$

In the case of stockholding by growers and dealers two dummies for outliers have been imposed (93III and 93IV). The following equation is selected:

$$s_{gd,t} = [1.245 - 0.107.sd1 - 0.347.sd2 - 0.208.sd3]. \qquad (52)$$
$$\quad\ (18.8)\ (2.3) \qquad\quad (7.2) \qquad\qquad (4.4)$$

$$[(E_t p_{t+1} - 1.015 \cdot p_t + 0.371e-3.(0.40.q_t))/(0.371e-3 + 7.188e-6\ VAR_t p_{t+1})]$$
$$\qquad (4.8) \qquad\qquad\qquad (4.8) \qquad\qquad (2.4)$$

sample period: 90 I-94 IV;   Log(L): -179.601

A similar procedure is applied to stockholding by manufacturers. For stockholding by manufacturers we postulate that the target stockholding level is specified as a linear function of consumption ($\bar{s}_{mf,t} = \phi_{mf}.c_t$ with $\phi_{mf}>0$ and calculate a value for $\phi_{mf}=0.27$, which parameter has been kept fixed throughout the estimations. As in the case of stockholding by growers and dealers, we find plausible values of the cost parameter by relating costs to the value of stocks at the start of the period ($z_{smf}.(s_{mf,t}-\phi_{mf}.q_t)^2/(p_t.s_{mf,t-1})$) and by calculating the average of this parameter over the whole sample period. With observed values of less than 5% the cost parameter in case of stockholding by manufacturers ($z_{smf}$) is calculated to be less than 0.0007. Again, we calculate a starting value of the coefficient of absolute risk aversion by taking the inverse of average income, assuming a unit coefficient of relative risk aversion. With these selected values of the cost parameter and the parameter of absolute risk aversion we calculate

$$s_{mf,t}^* = s_{mf,t} / [(E_t p_{t+1} - 1.015 \cdot p_t - \hat{z}_{mf} \cdot \hat{\phi}_{mf} \cdot \hat{c}_t)/(\hat{z}_{mf} + \hat{A}_{mf} \cdot VAR_t p_{t+1})] \tag{53}$$

and run the regression

$$s_{mf,t}^* = d_0 + d_1 \cdot sd1 + d_2 \cdot sd2 + d_3 \cdot sd3 \tag{54}$$

The estimated values of $d_0$ to $d_3$ and the selected values of $z_{mf}$, $A_{mf}$ and $\phi_{mf}$ are used as starting values in the NLS estimation of the equation:

$$s_{mf,t} = [\gamma_0 + \gamma_1 \cdot sd1 + \gamma_2 \cdot sd2 + \gamma_3 \cdot sd3] \cdot [(E_t p_{t+1} - 1.015 \cdot p_t - 0.27 \cdot \gamma_5 \cdot c_t)/(\gamma_5 + \gamma_6 \cdot VAR_t p_{t+1})] \tag{55}$$

In the case of stockholding by manufacturers also two dummies are used to control for outliers (92IV and 93I). The following equation is selected:

$$s_{mf,t} = [1.250 + 0.285 \cdot sd1 + 0.148 \cdot sd2 - 0.180 \cdot sd3]. \tag{56}$$
$$\phantom{s_{mf,t} = [} (8.5) \quad (2.5) \qquad (1.5) \qquad (1.8)$$

$$[(E_t p_{t+1} - 1.015 \cdot p_t + 0.530e\text{-}3 \cdot (0.27 \cdot c_t))/(0.530e\text{-}3 + 29.62e\text{-}6 \ VAR_t p_{t+1})]$$
$$\phantom{[(E_t p_{t+1}} (2.0) \qquad\qquad\qquad (2.0) \qquad (1.8)$$

sample period: 90I - 94 IV;  Log(L): -183.965

Table 7.2 summarizes selected parameters that are used in the simulation exercise. Quadratic cost functions together with the selected coefficient in the quadratic cost function imply average costs expressed as a percentage of the value of production of about 62%, and average costs expressed as a percentage of the value of beginning of period stocks 0.9% in case of stockholding by growers and dealers and 1.7% in case of stockholding by manufacturers. These estimates seem acceptable in view of empirical observations (see also Newbery and Stiglitz (1981), Table 20.7 for estimates of storage costs). Relative risk aversion, calculated on the basis of the selected parameters and profit per period, and averaged over t periods, is 3.1 for growers, 2.1 for stockholding by growers and dealers and 1.4 for stockholding by manufacturers, indicating a relatively high risk aversion of growers.

**Table 7.2**      Selected parameters

|  | growers | stockholders | stockholders |
|---|---|---|---|
|  |  | growers and dealers | manufacturers |
| coefficient in quadratic cost function* $(z_i)$ | 0.213 | 0.371 | 0.503 |
| coefficient of absolute risk aversion** $(A_i)$ | 5.194 | 7.188 | 29.62 |
| coefficient of relative risk aversion $(R_i)$*** | 3.1 | 2.1 | 1.4 |

* x$10^{-3}$; ** x$10^{-6}$; *** calculated as $A_i$*$profit_{i,t}$, averaged over all periods

Earlier estimations in this study (see Chapter 3, 4 and 5) do not allow an assessment of the selected values of the coefficients for risk aversion, cost functions and target-stockholding. These estimations are made with the assumption of risk neutrality and endogenous prices that are determined on the domestic market. However, we can compare the selected parameters with the choices made in a few simulation exercises based on a similar theoretical framework. This comparison is summarized in Table 7.3. Rolfo (1980) calculates risk parameters for a number of cocoa producing countries based on a logarithmic utility function. Evaluated at the mean values of income, these risk parameters range from 24.7 to 39.7. The comparable risk parameter in our simulation $(A_g.AVG(p_t.q_t-0.5.z_g(q_t)^2)$ is equal to 3.1. This is out of range with Rolfo's parameters. It should be noted, however, that most simulation studies take a value of R=1. No comparable values of stockholders are calculated in Rolfo's study. In Kawai's simulation exercise focusing on the long run variance of spot and futures prices (see Kawai (1983a)), cost coefficients are slightly lower for producers and stockholders compared to our study. In their attempt to shed light on the distribution of spot prices and the welfare of agents in the market after the introduction of a futures market, Turnovsky and Campbell (1985) use a parameter set that covers the values used in this study. Without information on income, the coefficient of absolute risk aversion used by Turnovsky and Campbell (with values between .001 and .1) cannot be compared. It should be noted that both Kawai and Turnovsky and Campbell do not give explicit empirical support for their selected parameters. Finally, Newbery and Stiglitz (1981, chapter 7) propose a probable value of the coefficient of relative risk aversion of between 0.5 and 2.0. Compared with choices made in simulation studies using a similar theoretical framework, we can conclude that the selected values of parameters are similar to the ones chosen in other studies. Next to using the selected values of the risk parameters in simulations (see Table 7.2), we have calculated welfare effects with values of the risk parameter one standard deviation above and below the mean estimate.

**Table 7.3**    Parameters compared with other studies

| | $1/z_g$ | $1/(\rho.z_g)$ | $1/z_s$ | $1/(\rho.z_s)$ | $R_g$ |
|---|---|---|---|---|---|
| Rolfo (1980) | | | | | 24.7-39.7 |
| Kawai (1983) | 0.4-3.0 | | 1.2-1.8 | | |
| Turnovsky and Campbell (1985) | | 0.5-10.0 | | 0.2-4.0 | |
| Newbery and Stiglitz (1981) | | | | | 0.5 - 2.0 |
| this study | 4.7 | 4.6 | 2.0; 2.7 | 2.0; 2.7 | (1.4-)3.1 |

From Figure 7.3 to 7.5 it is seen that estimated behavioral equations track the realisations reasonably well. The direction of development is correct in all cases with only a few exceptions. These exceptions mainly concern a number of observations of stockholding by manufacturers. In Figure 7.6 the size of risk of different agents and over time is presented. This variable is measured as the product of the coefficient of absolute risk aversion and variance of revenue, or in formula $A_i.VAR_{t-1}\pi_{i,t}$. Especially in the later years of the sample period prices

**Figure 7.3**    Production: fitted and actual values

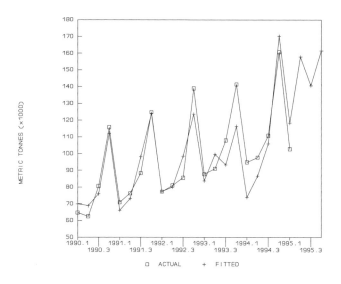

**Figure 7.4**     Stockholding at growers and dealers: fitted and actual values

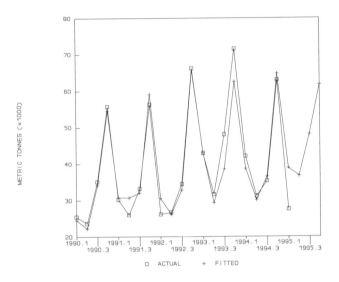

**Figure 7.5**     Stockholding at manufacturers: fitted and actual values

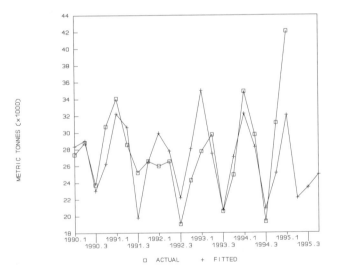

**Figure 7.6**

Risk measured as absolute risk aversion times variance $(A_i.VAR_{t-1}\pi_{i,t})$

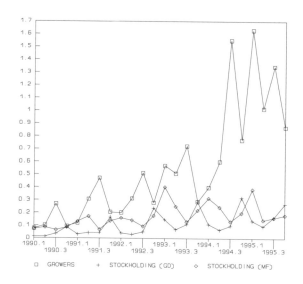

increased tremendously. These price rises also increased the variance of prices, and consequently the size of the risk of different agents. For all agents this impact on risk is clearly observed, but in the case of stockholding the impact is smaller, pointing at a risk aversion closer to risk neutrality.

## 7.5 Simulation

### 7.5.1 Calculating the costs of the commodity board: a static simulation

The selected parameters as presented in Table 7.2 are used in the model with forward contracts (equations (10) to (16) for growers, (25) to (31) for stockholders and (32) to (34) for the commodity board). Observed prices during 1990 to 1995 should be considered as one outcome out of many possible outcomes: such a random outcome is not sufficiently representative to base an evaluation on. A more reliable procedure is to evaluate the proposed hedging scheme by calculating average outcomes over a number of simulations using a random number generator that imposes a shock on the model. As a first step we run a static simulation in which all lagged endogenous variables are given their historical values. We have assumed that the futures price (equation (43)) and the world market price (equation (36)) are the source of the stochastic shock. The stochastic behaviour of the world market price follows in a straightforward way from the disturbance term ($\varepsilon_{Pw,t}$) in equation (36). In the forward price the stochastic behaviour originates from the random disturbance term in the futures price equation ($\varepsilon_{Pft,t}$), but also through dependence on stochastic world market prices (the term $m_1.\Delta P_{w,t}$ in equation (43)). In the static simulation lagged values in these two price equations are historical observations. The random futures price is converted into a random forward price by multiplication with the appropriate perfect foresight real exchange rate for one quarter ahead. The random shock in the current forward price, i.e. the price for one quarter ahead delivery, affects the decisions on current production and stocks (equation (14) and (29)) and also the amount of hedging by these agents (equation (15) and (30)), in the model with forward contracts (equation (10) to (16) and (25) to (31)). The random shock in the current world market price also affects stockholding (equation (24) and (29)). Expectation and variance of price are non-stochastic and given by equation (40) and (41). Expected profit and expected utility is subsequently calculated using equation (11) and (1) for growers, and equation (26) and (17). For the next period the same sequence of steps is made. A sample for the period 1990.1 to 1995.4 has been generated, calculating averages of 1000 iterations per quarter.

Figure 7.7 shows to what extent growers, stockholders at the production side and stockholders at the manufacturing side cover their production or stock in this particular situation. Growers cover production to a large extent ranging from 31.4% to 100%, with an average of about 74.5%. Stockholders have a lower risk aversion and consequently tend to cover a smaller share than growers. On average coverage of stockholding by growers and dealers is about 66.8%. Despite their even lower risk aversion the average coverage of stockholding by manufacturers is 85.7%. This must be attributed to their large target stockholding.

With world market price endogenized there is little reason to simulate the income of the commodity board as this income is, by implication, zero. Historically observed prices, i.e. observed world market prices and observed prices of expiring contracts on the Tokyo Commodity Exchange, however, differ from our model predictions. Therefore we have simulated the costs of the board using these prices. Figures 7.8 and 7.9 show revenue of the board evaluated at these ex post realised prices. Physical transactions in the Indian rubber market are evaluated at actual world market prices, and the paper transaction on the Tokyo International Rubber Exchange is evaluated at futures prices at the time of expiration. From the figure one can see that realised revenue becomes negative in the years 1994 and 1995 due to the increases in prices in those years. Especially during 1994 and 1995 large basis risk losses are generated. This outcome of our calculations should not come as a surprise: in general, during a time of rising prices one can expect hedging to have a negative result. Large profits made in 1990 and the start of 1991 should not be given much weight: from Figure 7.1 it is seen that domestic prices are slightly out of pace with world market prices as opening-up of the Indian economy only started at that time. In Figure 7.9 the aggregate revenue is split up in revenue from the paper transaction on the international futures exchange and revenue from the physical transaction. The figures confirm the general purpose of the hedging scheme: losses or profits of the physical transaction are (partly) offset by profits or losses of the paper transaction. The figure also shows large profits of the physical transaction in 1990 and 1991 and large losses of the paper transaction in 1994 and 1995.

In these simulations we have assumed that the forward prices offered by the board to domestic producers and local traders are equal to the futures prices in Indian rupees, or $\tau_t = 0$ for all t. Under these assumptions the board runs a small loss over the years 1991 to 1995. If the commodity board does not offer a forward price that is exactly equivalent to the futures price converted at the relevant real exchange rate, but slightly lower, it can improve its financial position. We assume that a surcharge ($\tau$) is levied which is constant for the whole sample period and calculate the level of the surcharge that equalizes costs and benefits of the board. The results of this exercise are reported in Table 7.4. It turns out that only a very moderate percentage of between 2.4 and 2.8% is required to make revenue of the board break-even. Such a procedure could also be applied to even out interest costs due to margin payments. It should be noted that these costs are not accounted for in the current study.

Additionally, and for this particular situation - a static simulation using historical world market prices and futures prices at the time expiration to evaluate the income of the board - we can calculate the welfare gains of the introduction of forward contracts, and compute the welfare cost of a break even strategy of the board. To compare expected utility in a situation with and without forward contracts, we calculate the compensating variation, i.e. the amount of additional income required to make discounted expected utility in both situations equal. The compensating variation is derived by solving:

$$\sum_{t=0}^{T} E_{t-1} \left( U_i(\pi_{i,t} + compvar_i) \right) \cdot \delta^t = \sum_{t=0}^{T} E_{t-1} \left( U_i(\pi^*_{i,t}) \right) \cdot \delta^t \tag{57}$$

where compvar = compensating variation; $\delta = 1/(1+r)$;
i denotes growers, stockholding by growers and dealers, and stockholding by manufacturers; an asterisk (*) indicates a situation with forward contracts

**Figure 7.7**     Coverage with forward contracts (static simulation)

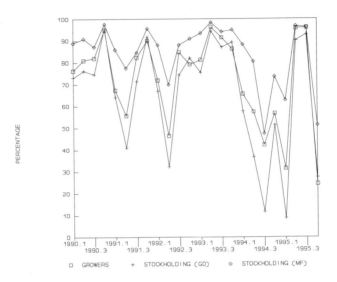

**Figure 7.8**     Total revenue of the commodity board

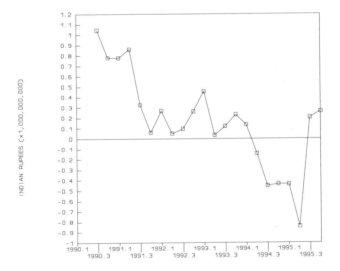

**Figure 7.9**    Revenue of the commodity board on the physical and paper transaction

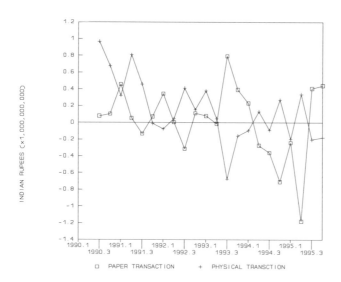

From Newbery and Stiglitz (1981, p. 75) we calculate expected utility as:

$$E_{t-1}\ [U_i(\pi_{i,t})] = -E_{t-1}\ [\exp(-A_i.\pi_{i,t})] = -\exp[-A_i.E_{t-1}(\pi_{i,t}) + 0.5\ A_i^2.VAR_{t-1}(\pi_{i,t})]\ (58)$$

In this calculation the variable compvar is assumed to have the same value each period. In order to capture a sufficiently representative range of situations we have simulated with different values of risk aversion. In particular we have simulated with the estimated mean value of the coefficient of absolute risk aversion as well as one standard deviation above and below this estimated mean value. The combination of the three low coefficients of risk aversion are denoted with 'low' in Table 7.4: 'medium' and 'high' are defined analogously.

The result of these calculations are also reported in Table 7.4. In the table the compensating variation is reported under the break even strategy of the board. Next to the figures on the welfare gain, between brackets, we report the share of this break even gain relative to the welfare gain in the case of a zero surcharge. From the table we observe that the welfare gain under the break even strategy of the board ranges from a low of 2.5% (stockholding by growers and dealers) to a high of 17.9% (stockholding by manufacturers). The welfare costs of the breakeven strategy of the board is 20 to 30% in the case of growers and stockholding by manufacturers, and 40-50% in the case of stockholding at growers and dealers, leaving a considerable welfare gain in most cases. We conclude that financial failure easily can be avoided while maintaining a substantial welfare gain.

**Table 7.4**      Surcharge of the board ($\tau$) and accompanying welfare increases

coefficient of absolute risk aversion[*]

|  | low | medium | high |
|---|---|---|---|
| break-even surcharge (in %) | 2.4 | 2.7 | 2.8 |
| welfare[**]  growers | 6.1 (69.9) | 8.8 (72.0) | 11.2 (76.4) |
| stockholding by growers and dealers | 2.5 (50.3) | 2.9 (46.9) | 2.5 (38.4) |
| stockholding by manufacturers | 3.9 (68.8) | 10.9 (81.0) | 17.9 (85.3) |

[*]      Low coefficients of absolute risk aversion: $A_g$ = 2.7; $A_{sg}$ = 4.2; $A_{sm}$ = 13.2; medium risk aversion: $A_g$ = 5.2; $A_{sg}$ = 7.2; $A_{sm}$ = 29.6; high risk aversion: $A_g$ = 7.7; $A_{sg}$ = 10.2; $A_{sm}$ = 46.1; all coefficients of absolute risk aversion: $\times 10^{-6}$; upper and lower values of $A_i$ are chosen as one standard deviation above and below the mean estimates of $A_i$. See also table 7.5.

[**]      Compensating variation expressed as a percentage of base quarter (90I) revenue of growers without forward contracts; the welfare increase with a break-even surcharge relative to the welfare increase without surcharge ($\tau=0$) is presented between brackets.

### 7.5.2   Calculating welfare effects of the use of forward contracts: a dynamic simulation

The autoregressive properties of the model justify a simulation in which the lagged endogenous variables are not historically observed values, but variables that are generated by the model. This is implemented by running a dynamic simulation. The sequence of steps is analogous to the sequence of steps in a static simulation with the notable difference - as mentioned - that the lagged endogenous variables are now generated by the model. Expected prices and variances are not stochastic by themselves, but become stochastic after some periods through this dynamic process. The calculation of expected utility in a situation with and without forward contracts enables a welfare evaluation.

Figure 7.10 shows to what extent growers, stockholders at the production side and stockholders at the manufacturing side cover their production or stocks. Again growers sell the largest part of their production forward. Their coverage always moves above 82.4%, with an average of 89.9%. Stockholders at the production side cover a smaller share than growers. Nevertheless their coverage is never lower than 70.2%. On average their coverage is about 81.5%. Stockholders at the manufacturing side have a minimum hedge ratio of 88.0%, and on average this ratio is 92.9%.

Figures 7.11 to 7.13 show production, stockholding by growers and dealers, and stockholding by manufacturers both with and without forward contracts. Compared to the situation without forward contracts it is observed that production as well as stockholding by growers and dealers increase enormously: average growth of production is about 0.9% point higher (per quarter). Note that capacity constraints might prevent such an increase in the growth rate. However, it does show the unambiguous incentive to production if uncertainty is reduced. Part of this growth automatically channels through to stockholders. Average growth of stocks with growers and dealers is about 1.0% point higher and average growth of stocks with manufacturers is about 1.9% point higher.

**Figure 7.10**   Coverage with forward contracts (dynamic simulation)

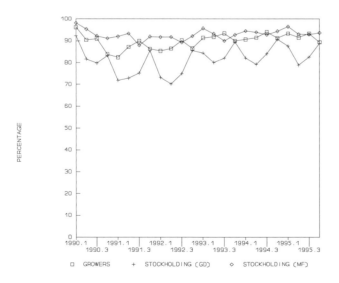

**Figure 7.11**   Production with forward contracts

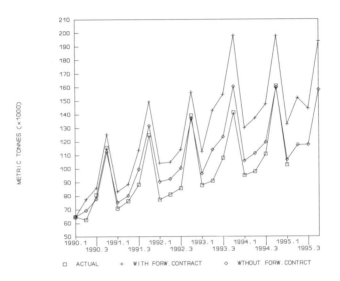

**Figure 7.12**   Stockholding by growers and dealers

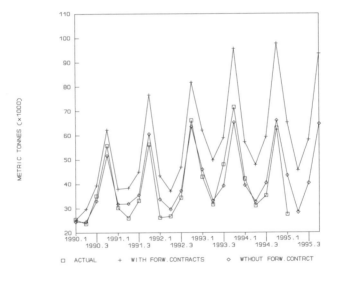

**Figure 7.13**  Stockholding by manufacturers

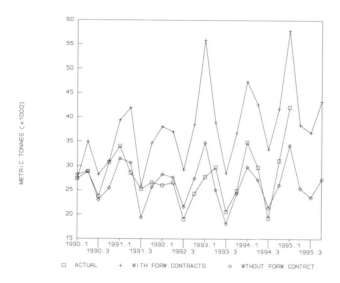

Welfare gains are calculated by determining compensating variation as set out in equation (57), and specified in equation (58). Again, in order to capture a sufficiently representative range of situations we have simulated with the estimated mean value of the coefficient of absolute risk aversion as well as one standard deviation above and below this estimated mean value. Also a grid of plausible values of the discounting factor have been used. In Table 7.5 the results of the welfare calculations based on dynamic simulation are summarized. The following observations of the simulation results are worth reporting: all welfare gains are, as expected, positive but also of substantial size; with higher real interest rates the gain decreases in the case of growers and remains more or less stable or even increases slightly in the case of stockholders: this is caused by the discounting of negative future income; a higher risk aversion for each agent implies as expected a larger welfare increase, if forward contracts are introduced; the spread of the growth in welfare is, however, particularly small in the case of growers and relatively large in the case of stockholders. More specifically we observe that for growers an increase in income is needed of between 12.3 and 14.5% to make discounted expected utility the same as in the case of forward contracts. For stockholding the change in income needed to equate discounted expected utility is less, but still substantial (between 3.2 and 19.0%).

**Table 7.5**     Welfare gains of providing forward contracts
(compensating variation: expressed as a percentage of base quarter revenue of growers without forward contracts)

| activity | production | | | stockholding by growers and dealers | | | stockholding by manufacturers | | |
|---|---|---|---|---|---|---|---|---|---|
| $r \setminus A_i^*$ | 2.7 | 5.2 | 7.7 | 4.2 | 7.2 | 10.2 | 13.2 | 29.6 | 46.1 |
| 0.01 | 13.1 | 13.9 | 14.4 | 3.2 | 8.6 | 14.2 | 7.7 | 14.6 | 18.7 |
| 0.02 | 12.6 | 13.4 | 14.1 | 3.3 | 8.6 | 14.3 | 7.6 | 13.9 | 18.5 |
| 0.03 | 12.3 | 13.0 | 14.1 | 3.6 | 8.9 | 14.0 | 7.0 | 14.2 | 18.2 |

* $\times 10^{-6}$; upper and lower values of $A_i$ are chosen as one standard deviation above and below the mean estimates of $A_i$; simulation outcomes are obtained as averages from 1000 runs.

Some qualifications of this result should be made. The calculated welfare gains will certainly be an exaggeration of the true gains. Costs of operating on the Tokyo Commodity exchange, mainly interest costs due to margin payments, are not incorporated in the model. These costs, however, will be low compared to the welfare gain and not affect the main result: the average real interest rate is around 1.5% on a quarterly basis. Additionally, commodity transactions which are hedged often can make use of credit at reduced interest rates. Nevertheless, these costs do affect the decision of growers and stockholders on how much to hedge, and, hence, the welfare gain of such a scheme will be slightly lower if these costs are incorporated. Next, relaxing the assumption of perfect foresight will entail additional costs due to the hedging of exchange rate risks. Further, in our model we have assumed that the growers and stockholders earn an income with natural rubber and have no other sources of income. In practice, however, growers and stockholders in our case, but also in general, have diversified their risk by cultivating other crops, by initiating other commercial business or by having a paid job outside agriculture (see Chapter 2). Although one can wonder if these activities are not created merely for the sake of diversifying risk as there are no better risk diversification possibilities (such as our hedging scheme), they will decrease risk, and, hence, will also decrease the welfare gain of transferring risk to a commodity exchange. The assumption of one income earning crop in production and stockholding also takes away any possible welfare gain from price volatility.

However, the welfare gains we have calculated are so large that these qualifications are unlikely to upset our main result that futures trading can offer substantial welfare gains. This raises the obvious question why hedging facilities have not been established earlier, either through private sector initiatives or through some type of government intermediation. The absence of hedging can be explained by restrictions on the implementation of such a hedging scheme. Restrictions on the foreign exchange requirements will be a serious impediment to hedging operations: the foreign reserve position in the recent years in India and, more in general, the foreign reserve position in any developing country may obstruct implementation of such schemes. Also the regulatory framework to support international financial transactions is not fit for the implementation of such schemes. A final reason is that the current domestic financial infrastructure in India is not appropriately equipped to support hedging operations (see UNCTAD / World Bank (1996), see also Chapter 6). The changes in trade policy that started in the early 1990s suggest that the conditions required for the implementation of our scheme most probably will improve in the near future.

## 7.6    Summary and conclusion

In this chapter we calculated costs and benefits of an Indian commodity board offering a forward contract to growers and local traders of natural rubber and simultaneously covering this commitment on the Tokyo Commodity Exchange. Additionally we evaluated the welfare implications of such a scheme. The empirical work covered the period 1990 to 1995. We have derived risk aversion and cost parameters from empirical observations. Our estimates suggest that relative risk aversion of growers is one and a half to two times as high as that of local traders. Expected utility is substantially affected by risk, particularly in the case of growers. The negative impact of risk on utility almost completely vanishes if forward contracts are available.

The availability of forward contracts also has a substantial impact on the behaviour of agents. Overall supply grows 1-1.5 percentage points faster. A dynamic simulation shows that for growers an increase in income is needed between 12 and 15% to make discounted expected utility the same as in the case of forward contracts. For stockholders the change in discounted expected utility is equal or less but also with a larger spread.

Implementation of the policy entails basis risk which is assumed to be on the account of the board. Over the period 1991 to 1995 revenue of the board is marginally negative. If the forward price offered by the board on the domestic market is a small fraction lower than that of the international futures exchange (e.g. a flat rate of around 2.5-3.0% for the whole period) the board would be able to break-even. This is shown to be a moderately sized welfare cost, leaving a considerable welfare gain from the introduction of forward contracts. In summary we conclude that the providing domestic primary producers and local traders access to an international futures exchange increases welfare substantially. Intermediation by a commodity board can be implemented without making basis risk losses.

A number of caveats of this study should be mentioned. First, production is assumed to be certain. Although production is relatively certain with our perennial crop, some production uncertainty remains and should be allowed for in the analysis. Secondly, we have assumed perfect foresight with respect to real exchange rates. This is a strong assumption in view of depreciations and devaluations of the yen/dollar and rupee/dollar exchange rates. Also the use of an exponential utility function might influence the outcome. Finally, the costs of trading (particularly interest costs due to margin payments) are not incorporated in the analysis. More work is needed to extend the current study to relax these assumptions.

In this thesis we study how perennial crop growers and stockholders of a storable primary commodity have dealt with income risk due to price fluctuations. In the empirical work we make use of data of the Indian natural rubber market for the period from 1965 to 1995. An important way to reduce income risk is by stockholding and, hence, it is interesting to study stockholding more closely. Is it possible to obtain evidence of the characteristics of stockholding or the behavior of stockholders in this market? Is their role of any significance in terms of price formation in this market and in terms of a risk reducing mechanism? For a number of years during the period under consideration, a price band scheme has been effective. Such schemes are popular policy reactions to overcome income risk. Are such schemes more efficient in reducing price risks relative to instruments that are (already) available in the market? Hedging price risks with financial risk management instruments is hardly possible in India. These financial risk management instrument, however, are often suggested as attractive devices to reduce income risk. To what extent can welfare gains be obtained with the introduction of futures trading in this market and at what costs? These questions constitute the centerpiece of this thesis. The contributions of this thesis are the empirical specification of the behavior of stockholders, the assessment of the effectiveness of a domestic price stabilization scheme relative to private stockholding and the calculation of welfare gains from futures trading. Chapters 3, 4, 5 and 7 represent the major empirical work of this thesis.

In Chapter 1 the literature on the welfare impact of price stabilization, futures trading and the behavior of stockholding is summarized. The major micro-economic benefit of price stabilization for primary producers is the reduction in price risk. Empirical calculations of the micro-economic benefits of price stabilization show that these benefits most likely will be very small. Price stabilization by use of buffer stocks has been shown to be a very costly and impractical way to stabilize income. Futures trading may be a more efficient alternative. The introduction of futures markets most likely stabilizes prices. Futures trading will be superior to price stabilization using a buffer stock, as it stimulates stockholding and, hence, stabilize prizes indirectly. The theory on the behavior of stockholders is dominated by two features of stockholding, notably the occurrence of positive stocks when (expected) arbitrage returns are negative and the non-negativity of stocks. The complementary inequality conditions that characterize optimal behavior of stockholders combines arbitrage behavior and the non-negativity of stocks. The models that elaborate on the complementary inequality conditions, the so-called competitive storage models, are studied with stochastic dynamic programming techniques. To some extent these models are capable of reproducing commodity market prices. However, these models are shown not to be capable of generating the high autocorrelation of prices, an important characteristic of prices in commodity markets. The failure of the competitive storage models to reproduce sufficient autocorrelation in prices may very well be caused by omitting convenience yield. Convenience yield is also the major explanation of positive stocks when (expected) arbitrage returns are negative.

The quantitative description of the Indian natural rubber market in Chapter 2 shows that production of natural rubber experienced a tremendous growth in the period from 1970 to 1995, largely due to government promotion of cultivation in general and of high yielding varieties of rubber trees in particular. The combination of extensive promotion of natural rubber growing combined with restricted imports, obviously aimed at becoming self-supporting in natural rubber. Smallholders, a large majority of which have very tiny plots, account for the largest share in aggregate production and area. Price risks of cultivating natural rubber are to some extent diversified, by cultivating other crops and by having non-agricultural sources of income. Natural rubber production is also almost exclusively consumed domestically, mainly for tire manufacturing. Substitution of natural rubber by synthetic rubber is technically possible but economically unattractive due to high prices of synthetic rubber. Price policies in the Indian natural rubber market have a mixed record: floor prices are defended fairly well, but the commitment to maintain ceiling prices seems to be influenced by the returns to importing and by the foreign exchange reserves. Until the beginning of the 1990s the establishment of the STC, import licensing, and foreign exchange shortages have effectively isolated the Indian rubber economy from the world market. From the beginning of the 1990s onwards prices are much closer linked to world market prices.

In Chapter 3 stock behavior in the Indian natural rubber market is investigated for the period from January 1980 to December 1989. During this period the Indian natural rubber market was relatively isolated from the world market so that price data can be considered as the outcome of domestic market clearing. The empirical work provides clear evidence of speculative behavior in stockholding. Short term price responsiveness of production could not be confirmed. Consumption of natural rubber is to some extent price elastic in the short run, but the price elasticity is much lower than the price elasticity of speculative stock demand. Most short run responsiveness to prices comes from arbitrage activities of stockholders (growers, dealers and manufacturers), and not by increasing or decreasing production or consumption. Substantial inter-temporal arbitrage in this market by stockholders suggests that prices can be stabilized without government intervention.

The available data of the Indian natural rubber market offer an opportunity to investigate periods with and without a centrally imposed price band policy: centrally imposed price bounds were in effect from March 1984 to March 1989, locally known as Buffer Stocking Scheme (BSS). In Chapter 4 an estimation technique is proposed that incorporates the truncation of prices and expected prices during a price band scheme. An appealing feature of the applied technique is that coefficients in the current and expected prices are estimated simultaneously and price bounds are modelled to have an impact on prices even if these price bounds are not effective. However, the results of this estimation technique turned out to be disappointing. Both price equation and behavioral stock demand equations were hardly affected. Possible reasons for the marginal changes in the estimation results are the low credibility of BSS, a short operational period of BSS and the structural breaks in the parameters of the model due to BSS. The latter is investigated in Chapter 5.

In Chapter 5 it is assessed whether the BSS is more effective in reducing price fluctuations in commodity markets than the arbitrage activities of private stockholders. The extent to which stockholders are actively arbitraging is shown to differ substantially between the periods before and after BSS, relative to during BSS: the elasticity of stock demand for arbitrage purposes, before and after the BSS, is almost twice as high as in the BSS period in the case of growers and dealers and one and a half to three times as high in the case of manufacturers. Simulated prices confirm the stabilizing impact of arbitrage stock behavior: simulations with pre- or post-BSS elasticities generate price series with lower coefficients of variation during BSS compared to simulations with BSS elasticities. We conclude that arbitrage behavior of stockholders is more effective in reducing price fluctuations than a bandwidth price policy.

The potential of achieving risk reduction by using financial risk management instruments in the Indian natural rubber market is assessed in Chapter 6. Of the available instruments (forward contracts, futures, options, swaps, commodity linked loan) the option and swap seem most attractive for hedging purposes in commodity markets; the former because it offers protection to falling prices, but leaves open the possibility to profit from rising prices; the latter because it is a long term instrument particularly suitable for perennial crops. However, the poor liquidity in the markets where these instruments are traded makes their attractiveness for hedging strategies limited. The choice of a financial risk management instruments is guided by liquidity and the size of basis risk. In practice this implies that futures are often chosen as the most attractive hedging instrument. A large number of studies show that hedging operations in commodity markets can be effective in reducing price risks. The limited use of financial risk management instruments is remarkable in view of this hedging potential and is explained by the requirements that should be met to implement hedging strategies (establishment of an appropriate framework for international financial transactions, the establishment of a firm set of operating rules of the commodity exchange and the limited government involvement in price formation in commodity markets). India is shown not to be sufficiently equipped yet to meet these preconditions: in particular it is constrained because some firms are denied access to commodity exchanges, the brokerage network is not fit to modern hedging needs and the regulatory framework is inadequate. There seems to be scope for the government to improve the conditions for using financial risk management instruments. Under these circumstances it seems most appropriate to make use of a foreign commodity exchange instead of establishing a domestic commodity exchange, in the design of a hedging strategy for the Indian natural rubber market.

In Chapter 7 a hedging scheme in a domestic commodity market is investigated. Under the proposed scheme a commodity board offers a forward contract to domestic primary producers and local traders, and simultaneously covers its commitments on an international futures exchange. The purpose of the analysis is to quantify welfare gains to agents in the market and costs and benefits of the commodity board. The empirical work covers the period 1990 to 1995 and makes use of data of the Tokyo Commodity Exchange (TOCOM). We have derived risk aversion and cost parameters from empirical observations. Relative risk aversion of growers is shown to be one and a half to two times as high compared to local traders. The negative impact of risk on utility almost completely vanishes if forward contracts are available. The availability of forward contracts also increases production and stockholding. The hedging scheme is shown to increase welfare substantially, particularly welfare of growers. The 'basis risk'-costs for the commodity board of providing such a facility are negligible. If the forward price offered on the domestic market is a small fraction below the international futures price the board will be able to prevent losses at only slightly lower welfare gains.

# References

Akiyama, T. and P.K. Trivedi, 1987, 'A Global Tea Model: Specification, Estimation, and Simulation', World Bank Staff Commodity Working Paper, no. 17;

Binswanger, H.P., 1980, 'Attitudes towards Risk: Experimental Measurement Evidence in Rural India', *American Journal of Agricultural Economics*, 62, 3, August, pp.395- 407;

Boswijk, H.P., 1994, 'Testing for an Unstable Root in Conditional and Structural Error Correction Models', *Journal of Econometrics*, 63, pp.37-60;

Boswijk, H.P., 1992, *Cointegration, Identification and Exogeneity: Inference in Structural Error Correction Models*, Thesis Publishers, Amsterdam;

Boswijk, H.P. and P.H. Franses, 1992, 'Dynamic Specification and Cointegration', *Oxford Bulletin of Economics and Statistics*, 54, pp.369-381;

Brennan, M.J., 1958, 'The Supply of Storage', *American Economic Review*, 47, pp.50-72;

Budd, N., 1993, 'Legal and Regulatory Aspects of Financing African Coffee Exporters and the Provision of Bank Hedging Line Credit', paper presented at the Workshop for Senior Government Policy makers, Nairobi, 29 November-3 December 1993, *UNCTAD*, UNCTAD / COM / MISC.55 / ADD.1 GE.94-50117;

Burger, K., V. Haridasan, H.P. Smit, R.G. Unny and W. Zant, 1995, *The Indian Rubber Economy: History, Analysis and Policy Perspectives*, Manohar Publishers and Distributors, New Delhi;

Chanda, A., and G.S. Maddala, 1983, 'Methods of Estimation for Models of Markets with Bounded Price Variation under Rational Expectations', *Economics Letters*, 13, pp. 181-184, North Holland; and 'Erratum', *Economics Letters*, 15, pp.195-196;

Charemza, W.W. and D.F. Deadman, 1992, *New Directions in Econometric Practice, General to Specific Modelling, Cointegration and Vector Autoregression*, Edward Elgar Publishing, Aldershot;

Claessens, S. and R.C. Duncan (eds.), 1993, *Managing Commodity Price Risk in Developing Countries*, Johns Hopkins University Press, Baltimore/London;

Claessens, S and P. Varangis, 1993, 'Implementing Risk Management Strategies in Costa Rica's Coffee Sector' in Claessens and Duncan (eds.);

Claessens, S and J.R. Coleman, 1993, 'Hedging Commodity Price Risks in Papua New Guinea' in Claessens and Duncan (eds.);

Claessens, S., 1993, 'Risk Management in Developing Countries', World Bank Technical Paper No. 235, The World Bank, Washington DC;

Crook, C., 1997, 'India's Economy', *The Economist*, 22nd February;

Danthine, J.P., 1978, 'Information, Futures Prices, and Stabilizing Speculation', *Journal of Economic Theory*, 17, pp.79-98;

Davidson, J.E.H., D.F. Hendry, F. Sbra and S. Yeo, 1978, 'Econometric Modelling of the Aggregate Time-Series Relationship between Consumers' Expenditure and Income in the United Kingdom', *Economic Journal*, 88, pp.661-92;

Deaton, A. and G. Laroque, 1991, 'Estimating the Commodity Price Model', document de travail no.9131, Research Program in Development Studies, Princeton University / INSEE, Paris;

Deaton, A. and G. Laroque, 1992, 'On the Behaviour of Commodity Prices', *Review of Economic Studies*, 59, pp.1-23;

Deaton, A. and G. Laroque, 1994a, 'Estimating a Nonlinear Rational Expectations Model with Unobservable State Variables', mimeo, Research Program in Development Studies, Princeton University / INSEE, Paris;

Deaton, A. and G. Laroque, 1994b, 'Competitive Storage and Commodity Price Dynamics', mimeo, Research Program in Development Studies, Princeton University / INSEE, Paris;

Deaton, A. and R. Miller, 1995, 'International Commodity Prices, Macroeconomic Performance and Politics in Sub-Saharan Africa', *Journal of African Economies*, 5, (AERC Supplement), pp.99-191;

Engle, R.F. and C.W.J. Granger, 1987, 'Co-integration and Error Correction: Representation Estimation and Testing', *Econometrica*, 55, pp.251-276;

Engle, R.F. and B.S. Yoo, 1987, 'Forecasting and Testing in Co-integrated Systems', *Journal of Econometrics*, 35, pp.143-159;

Faruquee, R. and J.R. Coleman, 1996, 'Managing Price Risk in the Pakistan Wheat Market', World Bank Discussion Paper No. 334, The World Bank;

Fertö, I., 1995, 'Methods for Stabilizing Agricultural Prices in Developing Countries', *Acta Oeconomica*, 47, pp.155-170;

Gardner, B.L., 1979, *Optimal Stockpiling of Grain*, Lexington Books, Mass., Lexington;

Gardner, B.L., 1989, 'Rollover Hedging and Missing Long-Term Futures Markets', *American Journal of Agricultural Economics*, 71, pp.311-318;

Gazanfer, S., 1995, 'Guidelines for Facilitating Access to Risk Management Markets through the Stimulation of Local and Regional Exchanges: the Case of Cotton in the Near East/CIS/Pakistan', *UNCTAD*, UNCTAD / COM / 65;

Gemmill, G., 1985, 'Forward Contracts or International Buffer Stocks? A Study of Their Relative Efficiencies in Stabilizing Commodity Export Earnings', *Economic Journal*, 95, pp.400-417;

Ghosh, S., C.L. Gilbert and A.J. Hughes Hallett, 1987, *Stabilizing Speculative Commodity Markets*, Clarendon Press, Oxford;

Gilbert, C.L., 1985, 'Futures Trading and the Welfare Evaluation of Commodity Price Stabilisation', *Economic Journal*, 95, pp.637-661;

Gilbert, C.L., 1988a, 'Buffer Stocks, Hedging and Risk Reduction', *Bulletin of Economic Research*, 40, pp.271-286;

Gilbert, C.L., 1988b, 'Optimal and Competitive Storage Rules: The Gustafson Problem Revisited' in O. Güvenen (ed.), *International Commodity Market Models and Policy Analysis*, Kluwer Academic Publishers;

Gilbert, C.L., 1989, 'Futures Trading, Storage and Price Stabilisation', *Review of Futures Markets*, 8, pp.152-76;

Gilbert, C.L., 1990, 'The Rational Expectations Hypothesis in Models of Primary Commodity Markets', The World Bank, International Economics Department, Working Paper;

Gilbert, C.L., 1993, 'Domestic Price Stabilization Schemes for Developing Countries' in S.Claessens and R.C.Duncan (eds.);

Gilbert, C.L., 1995, 'Risk Management in the Cocoa Industry', paper prepared for the 8th meeting of the Advisory Group on the World Cocoa Economy of the ICCO in Yaounde, Cameroon, 26-28 June 1995;

Gilbert, C.L., 1996, 'International Commodity Agreements - An Obituary Notice', *World Development*, 24, 1-19;

Greene, W.H., 1993, *Econometric Analysis*, Macmillan Publishing Company, New York, second edition;

Gustafson, R.L., 1958a, 'Carryover Levels for Grain: A Method for Determining Amounts that are Optimal under Specified Conditions', Technical Bulletin, Vol. 1178, US Department of Agriculture, Washington D.C.;

Gustafson, R.L., 1958b, 'Implications of Recent Research on Optimal Storage Rules', *Journal of Farm Economics*, 40, pp.290-300;

Hazell, P.B.R. and Scandizzo, P.L., 1975, 'Market Intervention Policies when Production is Risky', *American Journal of Agricultural Economics*, 57, pp. 641-49;

Herrmann, R., K. Burger, H.P Smit, 1993, *International Commodity Policy: A Quantitative Analysis*, Routledge, London;

Holt, M.T. and S.R. Johnson, 1989, 'Bounded Price Variation and Rational Expectations in an Endogenous Switching Model of the US Corn Market', *Review of Economics and Statistics*, 71, pp.605-13;

Hughes Hallett, A.J. and P. Ramanujam, 1990, 'The Role of Futures Markets as Stabilizers of Commodity Earnings' in L.A. Winters and D. Sapsford (eds.);

*Indian Rubber Statistics*, Rubber Board of India, various issues;
    *Import and Export Policy*, Government of India, Ministry of Commerce, 1985-88 and 1990- 93;

*International Financial Statistics*, International Monetary Fund, various issues;

Joshi, V. and I.M.D Little, 1994, *India: Macroeconomics and Political Economy, 1964- 1991*, The World Bank, August, Washington DC;

Kaldor, N., 1939/40, 'Speculation and Economic Stability', *Review of Economic Studies*, 7, p.6;

Kaldor, N., 1976, 'Inflation and Recession in the World Economy', *Economic Journal*, 86, pp.703-714;

Kanbur, S.M.R., 1984, 'How to Analyse Commodity Price Stabilisation? A Review Article', *Oxford Economic Papers*, 36, pp.336-358;

Kapoor, R., 1988, 'Why ....Never the twain shall meet?', *Rubber News*, August, pp.33-36;

Kawai, M., 1983a, 'Price Volatility of Storable Commodities under Rational Expectations in Spot and Futures Markets', *International Economic Review*, 24, pp.435-459;

Kawai, M., 1983b, 'Spot and Futures Prices of Nonstorable Commodities under Rational Expectations', *Quarterly Journal of Economics*, 95, pp.235-254;

Kawai, M., 1984, 'The Effect of Forward Exchange on Spot Rate Volatility under Risk and Rational Expectations', *Journal of International Economics*, 16, pp.155-72;

McKinnon, R.I., 1967, 'Futures Markets, Buffer Stocks, and Income Stability for Primary Producers', *Journal of Political Economy*, 75, pp.844-61;

Kofman, P., 1991, *Managing Primary Commodity Trade (on the Use of Futures Markets)*, Tinbergen Institute Research Series;

Krishnan Kutty, P.N., 1985, 'Rubber Market: an Analysis', *The Planters' Chronicle*, January;

Krugman, P.R., 1991, 'Target Zones and Exchange Rate Dynamics', *Quarterly Journal of Economics*, 106, pp.669-682;

Larson, D.F. and J.R Coleman, 1993, 'The Effects of Option Hedging on the Costs of Domestic Price Stabilization Schemes' in Claessens and Duncan);

Larson, D., 1993, 'Policies for Coping with Price Uncertainty for Mexican Wheat', Policy Research Working Paper 1120, The World Bank, Washington DC;

Lee, L., 1994, 'Rational Expectations in Limited Dependent Variable Models', *Economics Letters*, 46, pp. 97-104;

Maddala, G.S., 1983a, *Limited-Dependent and Qualitative Variables in Econometrics*, Econometric Society Monographs in Quantitative Economics, Cambridge University Press;

Maddala, G.S., 1983b, 'Methods for Estimation for Models of Markets with Bounded Price Variation', *International Economic Review*, 24, pp.361-387;

Maddala, G.S., 1990, 'Estimation of Dynamic Disequilibrium Models with Rational Expectations: the Case of Commodity Markets' in Winters and Sapsford (eds.);

Massell, B.F., 1969, 'Price Stabilization and Welfare', *Quarterly Journal of Economics*, 83, pp. 284-98;

Massell, B.F., 1970, 'Some Welfare Implications of International Price Stabilization', *Journal of Political Economy*, 79, pp. 405-17;

Masuoka, T., 1993, 'Asset and Liability Management: Modern Financial Techniques' in Claessens and Duncan (eds.);

Meyers, R.J., 1993, 'Strategies for Managing Coffee Price Risks in Costa Rica' in Claessens and Duncan (eds.);

Miranda, M.J. and J.W.Glauber, 1993, 'Estimation of Dynamic Nonlinear Rational Expectations Models for Primary Commodity Markets with Private and Government Stockholding', *Review of Economics and Statistics*, 75, pp.463-470;

Muth, J.F., 1961, 'Rational Expectations and the Theory of Price Movements', *Econometrica*, 29, pp.315-35;

National Council of Applied Economic Research, 1980, *Ten Year Perspective Plan for Rubber, 1980-81 to 1989-90*, Cambridge University Press, Delhi;

Newbery, D.M.G. and J.E Stiglitz, 1979, 'The Theory of Commodity Price Stabilisation Rules: Welfare Impacts and Supply Responses', *Economic Journal*, 89, pp. 799-817;

Newbery, D.M.G. and J.E Stiglitz, 1981, *The Theory of Commodity Price Stabilization: A Study in the Economics of Risk*, Clarendon Press, Oxford;

Newbery, D.M.G. and J.E Stiglitz, 1982, 'Optimal Commodity Stockpiling Rules', *Oxford Economic Papers*, 34, pp.403-427;

Newbery, D.M.G., 1987, 'When Do Futures Destabilise Spot Prices?, *International Economic Review*, 28, pp.291-97;

Newbery, D.M.G., 1988, 'On the Accuracy of the Mean Variance Approximation for Futures Markets', *Economics Letters*, 28, pp.63-68;

Newbery, D.M.G., 1990, 'Commodity Price Stabilization', in M. Scott and D. Lal (eds.), *Public Policy and Economic Development*, Clarendon Press, Oxford;

Nguyen, D.T., 1980, 'Partial Price Stabilization and Export Earning Instability', *Oxford Economic Papers*, 32, pp.340-352;

Oi, W.Y., 1961, 'The Desirability of Price Instability under Perfect Competition', *Econometrica*, 29, 1, pp.58-64;

Ouattara, K., T.C. Schroeder and L. Orlo Sorensen, 1990, 'The Potential Use of Futures Markets for International Marketing of Côte d'Ivoire Coffee', *Journal of Futures Markets*, 10, pp.113-121;

Pagan, A., 1984, 'Econometric Issues in the Analysis of Regressions with Generated Regressors', *International Economic Review*, 25, pp.221-247;

Pesaran, M.H., 1987, *The Limits to Rational Expectations*, Basil Blackwell, Oxford;

Pesaran, M.H., 1990, 'Comment on G.S. Maddala (1990)', in Winters and Sapsford (eds.);

Pesaran, M.H. and H. Samiei, 1992, 'Estimating Limited-Dependent Rational Expectations Models with an Application to Exchange Rate Determination in a Target Zone', *Journal of Econometrics*, 53, pp.141-63;

Pesaran, M.H. and H. Samiei, 1993, 'Limited-Dependent Rational Expectations models with Future Expectations', DAE discussion paper no.9321, Cambridge University, Cambridge;

Pesaran, M.H. and H. Samiei, 1995, 'Limited-Dependent Rational Expectations models with Future Expectations', *Journal of Economic Dynamics and Control*, 19, pp.1325-53;

Pesaran, M.H. and F.J. Ruge Murcia, 1996, 'Limited-Dependent Rational Expectations Models with Stochastic Thresholds', *Economics Letters*, 51, pp.267-76;

Powell, A. and C.L. Gilbert, 1988, 'The Use of Commodity Contracts for the Management of Developing Country Commodity Risks', in D.A. Currie and D.A. Vines (eds.), *Macroeconomic Interactions between North and South*, Cambridge University Press;

Rolfo J., 1980, 'Optimal Hedging under Price and Quantity Uncertainty: the Case of a Cocoa Producer, *Journal of Political Economy*, 88, pp.100-116;

*Rubber Asia*, various issues;

*Rubber Chemical Review*, various issues;

*Rubber India*, various issues;

*Rubber News*, various issues;

*Rubber Statistical Bulletin*, International Rubber Study Group, various issues;

Salant, S.W., 1983, 'The Vulnerability of Price Stabilization Schemes to Speculative Attack', *Journal of Political Economy*, 91, pp.1-38;

Satyanarayan, S., E. Thigpen and P. Varangis, 1993, 'Hedging Cotton Price Risk in Francophone African Countries', Policy Research Working Paper 1233, *The World Bank*, Washington DC;

Savosnick, K. and N. Sood, 1993, 'Government Controls and Commodity Price Risk Management Instruments (the Experience of Kenya)', paper presented at the Workshop for Senior Government Policy makers, Nairobi, 29 November-3 December 1993,*UNCTAD*, UNCTAD / COM / MISC.55 / ADD.1 GE.94-50117;

Schmitz, A., 1984, 'Commodity Price Stabilization, The Theory and Its Applications', World Bank Staff Working Papers, no. 668, The World Bank, Washington;

Shonkwiler, J.S. and G.S. Maddala, 1985, 'Modelling Expectations of Bounded Prices: An Application to the market for Corn', *Review of Economics and Statistics*, 67, pp.697-702;

Soumah, A, 1995, 'The Price Guarantee Facility', paper presented at the Eight Meeting of the Advisory Group on the World Cocoa Economy of the ICCO in Yaounde, Cameroon, 26-30 June;

Sree Kumar, B., V. Haridasan and P. Rajasekharan, 1990, 'Farm-gate Price of Natural Rubber', *Indian Journal of Natural Rubber Research*, 3, pp.111-115;

Tharian George K. and K.K. Thomas, 1997, 'Five Decades of Rubber Board and The Indian Rubber Industry: an Assessment in Retrospect', Rubber Board of India;

Thompson, S.R. and G.E. Bond, 1985, 'Basis and Exchange Rate Risk in Offshore Futures Trading', *American Journal of Agricultural Economics*, 67, pp.980-991;

Thompson, S.R. and G.E. Bond, 1987, 'Offshore Commodity Hedging under Floating Exchange Rates', *American Journal of Agricultural Economics*, 69, pp.46-55;

Thurman, W.N., 1988, 'Speculative Carryover: An Empirical Examination of the US Refined Copper market', *RAND Journal of Economics*, 19, pp.420-37;

Townsend, R.M., 1977, 'The Eventual Failure of Price-Fixing Schemes', *Journal of Economic Theory*, 14, pp.190-199;

Turnovsky, S.J., 1976, 'The Distribution of Welfare Gains from Price Stabilization: the Case of Multiplicative Disturbances', *International Economic Review*, 17, pp. 133-48;

Turnovsky, S.J., 1978, 'The Distribution of Welfare Gains from Price Stabilization: A Survey of Some Theoretical Issues' in F.G. Adams and S.A. Klein (eds.), *Stabilizing World Commodity Markets*, Lexington, Heath Lexington;

Turnovsky, S.J., 1979, 'Futures Markets, Private Storage and Price Stabilization', *Journal of Public Economics*, 12, pp.301-327;

Turnovsky, S.J., 1983, 'The Determination of Spot and Futures Prices with Storable Commodities', *Econometrica*, 51, pp.1363-87;

Turnovsky, S.J. and R.B. Campbell, 1985, 'The Stabilizing and Welfare Properties of Futures Markets: A Simulation Approach', *International Economic Review*, 26, pp.277-303;

UNCTAD, 1994a, 'Report of the Ad Hoc Group of Experts on Risk Management in Commodity Trade', TD/B/CN.1/22, TD/B/CN.1/GE.1/4;

UNCTAD, 1994b, 'A Survey of Commodity Risk Management Instruments', UNCTAD/COM/15/Rev.1;

UNCTAD, 1995, 'Feasibility Study on a Worldwide Pepper Futures Contract', report by the *UNCTAD* secretariat;

UNCTAD/World Bank, 1996, 'India, Managing Price Risks in India's Liberalized Agriculture: Can Futures Markets Help?', Report no. 15453-IN;

Vaillant, C., C.W. Morgan, A.J. Rayner and T.A. Lloyd, 1997, 'Futures Markets for Agricultural Commodities in Developing Countries', Centre for Research in Economic Development and International Trade, CREDI Research Paper 97/1, University of Nottingham, Nottingham;

Varangis, P., E. Thigpen and T. Akiyama, 1993, 'Risk Management Prospects for Egyptian Cotton', The World Bank, Policy Research Working Paper 1077, IED, ITD, Washington DC;

Varangis, P., E. Thigpen and S. Satyanarayan, 1994, 'The use of New York Cotton Futures Contracts to Hedge Cotton Price Risks in Developing

Countries', Policy Research Working Paper 1328, The World Bank, Washington DC;

Varangis, P. and D. Larson, 1996, 'Dealing with Commodity Price Uncertainty', Policy Research Working Paper 1667, The World Bank, Washington D.C.;

Varian, H.R., 1992, *Microeconomic Analysis*, third edition, W.W. Norton, New York / London;

Viaene, J.-M., 1989, 'Comment on Gilbert (1989)', *Review of Futures Markets*, 8, pp.177- 178;

Wallis, K.F., 1980, 'Econometric Implications of the Rational Expectations Hypothesis', *Econometrica*, 48, pp.49-73;

Waugh, F.W., 1944, 'Does the Consumer Benefit from Price Instability?', *Quarterly Journal of Economics*, 58, pp. 301-303;

Waugh, F.W., 1966, 'Consumer Aspects of Price Instability', *Econometrica*, 34, 2, pp. 504-508;

Weymar, F.H., 1968, *The Dynamics of the World Cocoa Market*, MIT Press, Cambridge, Massachusetts;

Williams, J.C and B.D. Wright, 1991, *Storage and Commodity Markets*, Cambridge University Press, Cambridge;

Winters, L.A. and D. Sapsford (eds.), 1990, *Primary Commodity Prices: Economic Models and Policy*, Cambridge University Press, Cambridge;

Wright, B.D. and J.C. Williams, 1989, 'A Theory of Negative Prices for Storage', *Journal of Futures Markets*, 9, pp.1-13;

Working, H., 1949, 'The Theory of Price of Storage', *American Economic Review*, 39, pp. 1254-62;

World Bank, 1995, 'India: Recent Economic Developments and Prospects', World Bank Country Study;

Zant, W., 1994a, 'Price and Stock Formation with Rational Expectations in the Indian Rubber Market', Discussion Paper TI 94-34, Tinbergen Institute Amsterdam- Rotterdam;

Zant, W., 1994b, 'Modeling Rational Expectations of Bounded Prices: An Application to Stock Behaviour in the Indian Natural Rubber Market under the Buffer Stocking Scheme', Discussion Paper TI 94-94, Tinbergen Institute, Amsterdam-Rotterdam;

Zant, W., 1997, 'Stabilizing Prices in Commodity Markets: Price Bounds versus Private Stockholding', *Journal of Policy Modeling*, 19, pp.253-77;

# VOORRAADVORMING, PRIJSSTABILISATIE EN GOEDERENTERMIJNHANDEL:
## Enkele empirische onderzoeken op basis van de Indiase natuurrubber markt
door Wouter Zant

De verbouw van primaire grondstoffen vormt voor veel ontwikkelingslanden en voor veel boeren in ontwikkelingslanden een belangrijke bron van inkomsten. De opbrengsten van deze activiteiten voor individuele boeren variëren sterk. Schommelingen in opbrengsten worden veroorzaakt door variatie in kosten, maar ook, en eigenlijk vooral, door sterke fluctuaties in prijzen, en mee- of tegenvallende oogsten. Het succes of het mislukken van oogsten wordt hoofdzakelijk veroorzaakt door weersomstandigheden, door ziektes van gewassen en door andere natuurlijke oorzaken. Onder bepaalde voorwaarden worden de opbrengsten van een mee- of tegenvallende oogst (gedeeltelijk) gecompenseerd door tegengestelde fluctuaties in prijzen, en is het uiteindelijk effect op het inkomen gering. Echter, prijsfluctuaties die hun oorzaak elders hebben, spelen wel een belangrijke rol in inkomensfluctuaties. De verbouw van de meeste primaire grondstoffen brengt met zich mee dat de aanwending van produktiemiddelen voor een bepaalde tijd vastgelegd moet worden. Dit is in het bijzonder het geval bij meerjarige gewassen, gewassen die enige jaren nodig hebben voordat er geoogst kan worden, maar dan ook voor enige tientallen jaren produktief zijn. Zodra produktiemiddelen zijn vastgelegd ten behoeve van de verbouw van zulke gewassen, beïnvloeden prijsfluctuaties direct de opbrengsten. Als die opbrengsten het inkomen of een groot deel van het inkomen bepalen - we laten diversificatie buiten beschouwing - dan betekenen prijsfluctuaties dus ook fluctuaties in het inkomen. Strikt genomen hoeft dat nog geen probleem te zijn zolang boeren in staat zijn om de fluctuaties in opbrengsten te spreiden over de jaren, door te sparen en te ontsparen, of door te lenen. Wil dat het geval zijn dan moet er sprake zijn van goed functionerende kapitaalmarkten: banken moeten bereid zijn om leningen te verstrekken aan boeren bij tegenvallende opbrengsten. Dergelijke kredietfaciliteiten bestaan in zijn algemeenheid niet, en zeker niet in ontwikkelingslanden. Door het ontbreken hiervan vormen de fluctuaties in opbrengsten een ernstig probleem voor boeren. Verder is inkomensonzekerheid van belang. De meeste boeren in ontwikkelingslanden verbouwen doorgaans maar een klein stukje grond en hebben de beschikking over weinig financiële middelen: om die reden zijn deze boeren afkerig van fluctuaties in opbrengsten en hebben potentiële fluctuaties in opbrengsten een negatieve invloed op hun welvaart.

Er zijn verschillende manieren waarop boeren inkomens-risico's kunnen verminderen. Een van die manieren is het aanhouden van voorraden. Een individuele boer kan door voorraadvorming fluctuaties in inkomen opvangen. Bij een goede oogst brengt de boer slechts een deel van de produktie naar de markt om te verkopen, en slaat een deel op om op een later tijdstip te verkopen bij minder gunstige oogst. Zo'n gedrag zal een stabiliserende werking hebben op het inkomen van de boer. Tegelijk is er ook een reactie van de markt: prijsfluctuaties in de markt verminderen doordat, gemiddeld genomen, voorraadvorming meer vraag en minder aanbod creëert in periodes met relatief lage prijzen, en het omgekeerde in periodes met relatief hoge prijzen. De activiteit van het aanhouden van voorraden kan ook 'uitbesteed' zijn aan handelaren of voorraadhouders.

In deze studie is een markt onderzocht die wordt gevormd door producenten, consumenten en voorraadhouders. Of het uitbesteden van de opslag-activiteiten per saldo gunstig is voor het inkomens-risico van boeren is moeilijk vast te stellen. Wel is aannemelijk dat met een stabiele vraag en een inelastisch aanbod, de rol van voorraadhouders in de prijsvorming groot is. Bovendien zullen, zoals eerder gememoreerd, de activiteiten van voorraadhouders de prijsfluctuaties verminderen en langs die weg het inkomensrisico van boeren verlagen.

Het empirisch werk in deze studie is gebaseerd op een specifieke grond-stoffenmarkt, te weten de Indiase natuurrubbermarkt. Deze markt is, zoals de meeste agrarische markten in India, voor een lange tijd geïsoleerd geweest van de wereldmarkt, waardoor de prijzen beschouwd kunnen worden als het resultaat van binnenlandse vraag en binnenlands aanbod. Dit maakt het mogelijk om de bijdrage aan de prijsvorming van de verschillende marktpartijen te identificeren. De empirische resultaten laten zien dat vooraadhouders zich in hun gedrag laten leiden door potentiële arbitrage-inkomsten. Bij de schattingen van de invloed van potentiële arbitrage-inkomsten is gebruik gemaakt van een specificatie van rationele verwachtingen van toekomstige prijzen. De empirische resultaten zijn minder duidelijk over het gedrag van boeren: de resultaten wijzen niet op enige reactie van boeren bij een verandering van prijzen. De vraag naar rubber, voornamelijk van producenten van rubberprodukten, is wel prijselastisch, maar de prijselasticiteit ligt veel lager dan in het geval van voorraadhouders. Op basis van de resultaten kan gesteld worden dat de sterkste reactie op prijsveranderingen toegeschreven moet worden aan de arbitrage-activiteiten van voorraadhouders, en niet aan boeren (de aanbieders op de markt) en in beperkte mate aan de consumenten. De rol die voorraadhouders bij de prijsvorming in grondstoffen-markten kunnen vervullen, duidt op mogelijkheden in zo'n markt om zonder overheid-sinterventie de prijzen te stabiliseren.

Een populaire beleidsreactie, onder andere bedoeld om inkomenrisico's van boeren te verminderen, vormt prijsstabilisatie met behulp van een buffervoorraad. Onder zo'n beleid wordt de fluctuatie in prijzen beperkt: als de prijs lager dreigt te worden dan de minimum prijs dan koopt de buffervoorraadhouder hoeveelheden op tegen de minimumprijs, totdat de markt de prijs weer boven de minimum prijs uitduwt. En, naar analogie, als de prijs hoger dreigt te worden dan de maximumprijs dan verkoopt de buffervoorraadhouder uit de buffervoorraad, totdat de markt de prijs beneden de maximumprijs duwt.

In de Indiase natuurrubbermarkt is gedurende de periode van maart 1984 tot en met maart 1989 zo'n prijsbeleid gevoerd, bekend onder de naam Buffer Stocking Scheme (BSS). De effecten van dit prijsbeleid op het gedrag van voorraadhouders zijn onderzocht. In hoofdstuk 4 is een schattingstechniek uiteengezet die rekening houdt met de afknotting van prijzen en verwachte prijzen. Een aantrekkelijke eigenschap van de toegepaste techniek is dat de coëfficiënten van huidige en toekomstige prijzen simultaan geschat worden en dat de prijsgrenzen een invloed hebben op de prijsvorming ook als die prijsgrenzen niet geraakt worden. In dit hoofdstuk is verondersteld dat het gedrag van de voorraadhouders, d.w.z. de coëfficiënten in de gedragsvergelijkingen, hetzelfde blijft tijdens en buiten de BSS: alleen de afknotting van prijzen en verwachte prijzen beïnvloedt de uitkomsten. De resultaten van deze schattingstechniek zijn teleurstellend: zowel de prijsvergelijking als de gedragsvergelijkingen van voorraadhouders blijken slechts in beperkte mate andere resultaten op te leveren. Mogelijke verklaringen voor de matige resultaten zijn de beperkte geloofwaardigheid van het gevoerde beleid en de veranderingen in het gedrag van voorraadhouders als gevolg van het gevoerde beleid.

Dit laatste is in hoofdstuk 5 onderzocht: er is gekeken of de coëfficiënten van de gedragsvergelijkingen van voorraadhouders gewijzigd zijn als gevolg van het gevoerde prijsbeleid. Hoewel de wisselwerking tussen prijsbeleid en vooraadvorming door de particuliere sector in de literatuur is besproken (zie b.v. Newbery and Stiglitz (1981)), heeft de mogelijkheid dat het gedrag van voorraadhouders tijdens periodes met interventies verandert weinig aandacht gekregen. Uit de schattingen blijkt dat de elasticiteit van de vraag van voorraadhouders op grond van arbitrage motieven voor en na de BSS anderhalf tot drie maal zo hoog is als tijdens de BSS. Verder is onderzocht of het gevoerde prijsbeleid beter in staat is om prijsfluctuaties te dempen dan de arbitrage-activiteiten van voorraadhouders in de markt. Op basis van de verschillende elasticiteiten van de vraag van voorraadhouders op grond van arbitrage-motieven zijn marktprijzen gesimuleerd. De resultaten van deze simulatie maken duidelijk dat het arbitrage-gedrag van voorraadhouders een grotere bijdrage levert aan de beperking van prijsfluctuaties dan het gevoerde prijsbeleid.

Een andere mogelijkheid om het inkomensrisico te verminderen is die risico's af te dekken op een goederentermijnmarkt. In het algemene geval is dit te verwezenlijken door parallel aan de transactie op de fysieke markt, een tegengestelde transactie uit te voeren op de goederentermijnmarkt, de papieren markt. Bij levering op de fysieke markt wordt ook de transactie op de goederentermijnmarkt beëindigd: het eventuele verlies op de transactie in de fysieke markt wordt dan gecompenseerd door de eventuele winst op de transactie in de papieren markt, of vice versa. Het prijsrisico is dan afgewenteld op speculanten die actief zijn op de goederentermijnmarkt. Verder zullen de mogelijkheden om risico's af te dekken op goederentermijnmarkten ook het aanhouden van voorraden stimuleren. En dit zal op zijn beurt de prijsfluctuatie in de markt weer verminderen. Met andere woorden, in een markt waar producenten en voorraadhouders prijsrisico's afdekken op een goederentermijnmarkt, wordt reductie van inkomensrisico zowel direct als indirect gerealiseerd.

Door wijziging in de handelspolitiek in het begin van de jaren negentig in India, is ook de waarschijnlijkheid dat Indiase boeren en voorraadhouders de mogelijkheid krijgen om van financiële instrumenten gebruik te maken om prijsrisico's af te dekken, aanzienlijk gestegen. In hoofdstuk 7 zijn de welvaartswinsten gekwantificeerd van het verminderen van prijsrisico's van risico-averse boeren en voorraadhouders door deze risico's af te dekken via de goederentermijnhandel. Een situatie is onderzocht waarin een nationaal grondstoffen-instituut aan binnenlandse boeren en lokale handelaren een contract aanbiedt voor in de toekomst te leveren hoeveelheden tegen een vastgestelde prijs. Het instituut dekt zijn contractuele verplichtingen af op een internationale goederentermijnmarkt. Met behulp van de mean-variance benadering zijn optimale hoeveelheden produktie, voorraden en termijnverkopen afgeleid. De waardes van risico- en kostenparameters die gebruikt zijn in de simulaties zijn verkregen door het model voor een situatie zonder termijncontracten te schatten op basis van data voor 1990 tot 1995. Relatieve risico-aversie van boeren is anderhalf tot twee keer zo hoog als die van voorraadhouders. De simulaties laten zien dat het negatieve effect van risico op welvaart bijna volledig verdwijnt als termijncontracten beschikbaar zijn. Zo'n faciliteit bevordert ook de produktie en voorraadvorming. De kosten voor het instituut dat bemiddelt tussen binnenlandse boeren en lokale handelaren enerzijds en de internationale goederentermijnmarkt anderzijds (basisrisico) zijn gering in omvang. Als het termijncontract tegen een iets lagere prijs dan de internationale prijs wordt aangeboden dan kan deze faciliteit zonder verlies worden verleend, terwijl nog steeds omvangrijke welvaarts-winsten worden gerealiseerd.

Het empirische werk benadrukt het belang van voorraadhouders bij prijsvorming, laat zien dat de arbitrage activiteiten van particuliere vooraadhouders prijsfluctuaties meer matigen dan interventies van de overheid en kwantificeert de mogelijke welvaartswinsten van het gebruik futures om prijsrisico's af te dekken.